The Halal Food Handbook

Edited by:

Kailash R. Malode

Delve
PUBLISHING

www.delvepublishing.com

The Halal Food Handbook

Kailash R. Malode

Delve Publishing
224 Shoreacres Road
Burlington, ON L7L 2H2
Canada
www.delvepublishing.com
Email: orders@arclereducation.com

ISBN: 978-1-77469-116-8 (Hardcover)

ABOUT THE EDITOR

Dr. Kailash Malode (1980) is presently serving as Assistant Professor, Department of Soil Science and Agriculture Chemistry, college of Agriculture, Parul University, Vadodara, Gujarat. He obtained his B. Sc.(Ag.) in 2006 from Marathwada Agriculture University, Parbhani. M. Sc. (Ag.)2009 in Dr. Panjabrao Deshmukh Krishi Vidyapeeth,Akola and Ph. D. Soil Science And Agriculture Chemistry in 2014 from Vasantrao Naik Marathwada Krishi Vidhyapeeth, Parbhani. He started his career as Assistant professor in 2014. His field of specialization is soil fertility. He has published 09 research paper in National and international journals of reputed. He has participated many National, State Seminar and symposiums. He has written 02 practical manuals for under graduate course for the benefit of students besides several Radio talk, Lectures in farmer traning programme. Dr. Kailash has also written 16 popular articles in Shati Bharti, Shati pragati and other reputed Magazines. He has Best writer award on 2015 for Krishi dooth popular Magazines of Maharashtra

TABLE OF CONTENTS

LIST OF FIGURES

Figure 3.8. A pig's body contains several parasites, germs, and viruses that can be transmitted to humans and animals. Pigs eat some of the most revolting foods known to man, and this consumption brings with it a slew of diseases that can be passed on to anyone who consumes pork. Contrary to assertions that contemporary technology can render the pork safe, disease erupts wherever swine are kept, even in the most developed countries.

Figure 3.9. Pig flesh has a lot of fat and cholesterol. This unclean flesh is difficult for our bodies to digest. There is evidence that the pork you consume can linger in your system for up to two months. Pig fat is difficult to metabolize and digest, making it unsuitable for use as a source of energy. It frequently remains in the human body, where it turns to fat. Pig fat consumption leads to obesity, cardiovascular illness, and intestine cancer.

Figure 3.10. Even when some haram components, such as gelatin or pork by-products, were used in the creation of medicine, it was still considered halal because the materials were completely converted and changed into a different substance. The principle of Istihalah, or the change of a product into something else, is known. Consider the following scenario: Although alcohol is haram, it is unquestionably halal once it has been converted to vinegar. The same criterion applies to substances that were originally considered haram but have since altered, gaining new characteristics and names.

Figure 3.11. Because Almighty Allah forbade these items in the Qur'an and Hadith, Muslims abstain from alcoholic beverages, intoxicating narcotics, swine-flesh, and other haram foods. We abstain from these forbidden substances because Almighty Allah has directed us to do so and to protect ourselves from His wrath and eternal punishments by doing so. Allah is aware of what is good for us spiritually, morally, and physically.

Figure 3.12. The admissibility of rennet is determined not by whether the slaughterer is Muslim or not, but by whether the rennet has life and absorbs the pollutants found in the stomach of a freshly slaughtered calf. The divergence amongst Imaam Abu Hanifah and his two students, the Saahibayn, has resulted in this.

Figure 3.13. Halal foie gras, spring rolls, chicken nuggets, ravioli, lasagna, pizza, and baby food are among the processed meals and goods available from several food firms. Halal ready meals are a developing consumer market for Muslims in the United Kingdom and the United States, with an increasing number of stores offering them. If there is no alcohol in vegetarian food, it is halal.

Figure 4.1. KFC restaurant. The restaurant is opened worldwide and is famous as it serves Halal meat.

Figure 4.2. Muslims in India. An area densely populated by Muslims has a restaurant serving halal foods.

Figure 4.3. Salad on a plate. Salads are served in halal restaurants but it should not include additives that are non-Halal.

Figure 4.4. The holy Quran. Most of the Muslim dietary laws are from the Holy Quran.

Figure 10.9. With Muslims accounting for over a quarter of the global population, the pharmaceuticals business has seen a rise in halal awareness. Many of us, even Muslims, rely on modern medicine to treat our illnesses. We rely significantly on the pharmaceutical sector, whether it's popping a fast painkiller to treat a headache or going to the doctor when our knee hurts. Without our knowledge, the medications we take may contain non-halal substances (or excipients) or be prepared in a way that is not consistent with Islamic beliefs.

Figure 10.10. Trade is crucial. Take a look at how much attention is devoted to global currency devaluation. The Ringgit is devaluing, the Chinese yuan is declining, and the Kazakh Tenge has become free-floating. The value of the currency in the nations where goods are produced and consumed has a considerable impact on the quest for a competitive edge in trade. Another unit of currency for halal business is the halal certification, which impacts the value of a halal product differently depending on where it was made (and certified) and where it would be eaten. The producer's certification value impacts the size of the market for their product.

Figure 10.11. The halal concept is absolutely critical to consumption in Malaysia, which has a Muslim majority. Today's Muslim customers have access to a wide range of products and services. Furthermore, each product category offers a variety of brands, both locally known and internationally recognized. Some local firms attempt to carve out niches for themselves by representing themselves as "Islamic" companies through imaginative packaging and labeling. This also serves as an indirect indication to their primary target market – Muslim consumers – that their products are halal. Similar efforts are being made in the banking and insurance sectors on the service side.

Figure 10.12. The certification procedure is a thorough one that includes an audit of the facility, a study of the stated ingredients, the size and complexity of the production location, and personnel training. Some businesses, on the other hand, try to get around these regulations in order to deceive the public and save money. In today's mass-production atmosphere, unethical behavior and profiteering are only encouraged. The blame game is one of the most significant issues that halal certification authorities face. Some companies even accuse the certifying authority of being "untrustworthy," despite the fact that the fraudulent acts are the consequence of their own mistakes.

LIST OF ABBREVIATIONS

ABIEC	Brazilian Beef Exporting Industries Association
ASPCA	American Society for Prevention of Cruelty to Animals
CCZ	Concerned Christians of Zimbabwe
DHCE	Department of Halal Certification EU
ECG	Electrocardiogram
EEG	Electro-Encephalograph
EFZ	Evangelical Fellowship of Zimbabwe
EHZ	European Halal Certification Institute
EIAC	Emirate International Accreditation Center
EMA	European Medicines Agency
FAO	Food and Agriculture Organization
GAC	GCC Accreditation Center
GHP	Good Hygienic Practice
GM	Genetically Modified
GMOs	Genetically Modified Organisms
GMP	Good Manufacturing Practices
HACCP	Hazard Analysis and Critical Control Point
HCBs	Halal Certification Bodies
HCBs	Halal Certification Organizations
HCG	Halal Certification Germany
HCPs	Halal Control Points
HFA	Halal Food Authority
HFCE	Halal Food Council of Europe
HMC	Halal Meat Certification
HQC	Halal Quality Control
IHI	International Halal Standards
INHAC	International Halal Conference

ISBEIA	IEEE Symposium on Business, Engineering and Industrial Applications
JISED	Journal of Islamic, Social, Economics, and Development
KFC	Kentucky Fried Chicken
MS	Malaysian Standard
MUI	Indonesia Ulema Council
OIC	Organization of Islamic Cooperation
SMIIC	Standards and Metrology Institute for Islamic Countries
SPUC	Single-Pulse Ultrahigh Current
WHC	World Halal Council

ABSTRACT

The halal business has encountered significant progress, particularly in the food sector. This volume seeks to investigate the challenges and prospects of the halal food sector in different counties across the globe. The volume suggests that the growth of the halal industry was set off by the expanding interest for halal accreditation and quality approval, just as the advancement of the food business. This is an extraordinary chance for entrepreneurs to fulfill the increasing need for halal food. The test is on the way to improve quality and meet halal guidelines to satisfy a worldwide demand. Some of the topics covered include; Chapter 1: Introduction to Halal Food, Chapter 2: The History of Halal Food, Chapter 3: The Difference Between Halal and Haram Foods, and Chapter 4: How Do You Assure a Restaurant Is Serving Halal Food.

The Muslim world has been experiencing quick population growth, vibrant socio-dynamic development, and income levels have equally expanded. Such conditions have supported increased halal consumption universally, particularly the utilization of halal items. The international halal market right now covers 16.7% of the worldwide food business. Driven by expanding demand, the halal industry keeps gaining momentum across the international food supply network. As per the volume, in 2014 alone, it is projected that worldwide Muslim expenditure on food and beverages expanded 4.3% to hit $1.128 billion. These statistics show that the future potential for halal foods will soon hit 16.7% of international spending in the next few years.

PREFACE

In Europe alone, the Muslim populace in 2030 is projected to reach more than 10% in most countries, for example, Georgia (11.5%), France (10.3%), Bulgaria (15.7%), and Belgium (10.2%). In view of such developments, the halal food sector in Europe and the entire globe will develop quickly. This volume makes reference that finding halal food for Muslims has gotten simpler. In many countries, there are fast food outlets, or cafés that occasionally have halal accreditations. Halal stores exist in a few urban communities, and even in standard grocery stores, many halal items can be found. Notwithstanding, some do exclude the halal logo, but this is not recommended at all since the customers are disadvantaged. But checking for halal food on standardized tags is likewise accessible. In certain nations, the market for halal items is expanding so quickly that the marketplace keeps growing. Halal methods are supported by Islamic law, while thoyyib implies quality and wellbeing.

This volume suggests that in Islamic law, a wide range of food and beverages are fundamentally halal, while a few are prohibited. On the other hand, halal can be haram whenever contamination is detected within the processing and packaging stages. This volume contains the following interesting chapters; Chapter 1: Introduction to Halal Food, Chapter 2: The History of Halal Food, Chapter 3: The Difference Between Halal and Haram Foods, Chapter 4: How Do You Assure a Restaurant Is Serving Halal Food, Chapter 5: Halal Food Certification, Chapter 6: Halal Food Laws, Chapter 7: Islamic Slaughter: Islamic Halal Meat Preparation and Supervision, Chapter 8: Halal Food Marketing Supervision, Chapter 9: Ethical, Organic, and Safety of Halal Food, and Chapter 10: Issues in Halal Food.

Individuals consume food not exclusively to satisfy their hunger, but also for social reasons. In Islam, there is an emphasis on the purity of both soul and food. Eating is seen to be a type of sacred event. Halal is Islamic dietary law is gotten from the Quran and Hadith, specifically the deeds of Prophet Mohammad, Qiyas, and Ijma. As per the volume, Halal goes past strict commitment. It is important for the Islamic lifestyle, which incorporates dietary needs as well as to conduct, language, and dress code. Besides, observing the fundamentals of halal can ensure proper food handling and create a plan of action for the food market. The advantages of halal regardless, an absence of trust in the market can risk the food's apparent validness and give credibility challenges. This particularly applies to Syrian, Pakistani, and Afghanis who emphasize on halal meat's taste, but more so on its social and religious value. New approaches are consequently being used to promote the halal food chain, subsequently making it acceptable to different consumers' needs.

This volume mentions that while any Islamic association or organization can give a halal authentication, the adequacy of the declaration relies on the nation of import or the Muslim population served through such accreditation. For instance, to give a halal authentication for the meat items sold to Malaysia and Indonesia, the responsible body of the halal declaration should be recorded on every nation where the meat is coming from. Case in point, there are in excess of 40 associations which issue halal accreditations in the U.S.; however, just five of them are recognized in Indonesia and only three in Malaysia. It is crucial that food makers know about not just the halal prerequisites for various nations and the standards of halal, but additionally the associations which address their halal requirements the best. To a Muslim, food products must not only be healthy but also meet halal recommendations.

Chapter 1

Introduction to Halal Food

CONTENTS

1.1. INTRODUCTION

Halal is a term of great importance among the Muslim community. The term is common among all Muslims as Islam is one religion. However, it is important to note that Muslim people are not of one homogeneous group. Muslims are said to come from about 70 countries, namely Africa, Asia, Europe, South and North America, and Pacific Islands. In Australia, there are about 400,000 Muslims. Muslims worship one God known as Allah. They also believe in prophets sent by Allah, including Muhammad, Moses, Abraham, and Jesus. They believe that the prophets were given laws to direct Muslims on what to do. These laws are written in the Qur'an. From the Qur'an, the term Halal is derived. The term is used to refer to actions or objects that people are permitted to engage in or use. It refers to foods, clothing, and actions permitted for the Muslim community.

Figure 1.1. The Qur'an defines what is Halal and Haram.

Source: https://madrasatelquran.com/the-holy-quran-speech-of-allah-and-miracle-of-islam/.

The opposite of the term Halal is known as Haraam meaning prohibited or illegal. The term Halal is used in drawing boundaries on the types of foods Muslims are allowed to eat. The word Halal is of Arabic origin. In the Arabic definition, the word Halal means permitted or lawful. With regards to food, Halal is used to refer to dietary standards in line with Muslim scripture. The term Haram is used to refer to foods that are prohibited or unlawful. Both terms are used universally and apply to all aspects of life. They are used with respect to food ingredients, meat products, pharmaceuticals, cosmetics, food products, food contact materials and personal care products. However, though there are foods known to be Haram or Halal there is a form of lack of clarity with some foods. This is why there other rules and information that can be used in further categorizing materials. For items surrounded with lack of clarity concerning them are referred to as Mashbooh. The term means questionable or doubtful.

Generally, all foods are considered acceptable in the Muslim community and hence are termed as Halal. However, those that are not acceptable are unlawful according to the Qur'an or Hadith. Therefore, in the Muslim community halal foods are those that do not contain elements prohibited for consumption according to their laws or those that have been manufactured, processed, produced, made or kept and stored using machinery, equipment and utensils that are considered clean according to their Islamic laws. Laws set with regards to food have been set to enable Muslims retain a healthy and strong physique to enable them make their contributions of effort and knowledge to help the society. The laws require them to make good decisions with regards to their nutrition therefore they should make all necessary efforts to live a healthy lifestyle. This is evident in the Hadith. It is said that prayers made by individuals who consume unlawful foods are rejected by Allah. Therefore, every food is considered lawful except some foods containing certain elements.

For instance, foods containing enzymes though Microbial Enzymes are acceptable. Animal fat, lard, non-Halal animal shortening, unspecified Meat Broth and Rennet are not acceptable. Fish meat derived from non-Halal sources are considered illegal. L-cysteine is considered haram if it is obtained from human hair. In the case of lipase, those obtained from animals should not be consumed. Animal shortenings that are not obtained from Halal sources are considered unlawful. All pig products such as ham, pork and bacon are all considered haram. The same case applies to all tallow and synthetic-rennet obtained from non-Halal sources. It is prohibited to consume birds of prey and carnivorous foods. All foods containing all the above products are considered Haram unless they are obtained from Halal sources (Zulfakar et al., 2012).

Ingredients such as emulsifiers, flavors, gelatin and enzymes are doubtable in the Muslim community. This is because the source of these ingredients are not well known. In the case of poultry and meat industries, meat obtained from animals such as chicken, turkey, gamebirds, ducks, goat, cows, sheep, veal, lamb and venison are considered lawful. However, they should be prepared in accordance to Islamic laws for the meat to be considered acceptable for consumption. Meats obtained from both fresh and salty waters such as seafood and fish considered Halal. However, Muslims are not allowed to eat meat from frogs, crocodiles and alligators.

While preparing seafood and fish it is prohibited to include alcohol such as wine or batter. Individuals should check whether they have allergies or a certain dietary preference. There are exceptions made for certain situations. In situations where there is a limitation in necessities foods considered Haram are considered Hal. According to the Qur'an, life is more important than death. For this reason, Haram foods can be consumed in emergency situations.

The Islam religion has many rules on meat consumed by individuals. Meat products are considered expectable however, the manner in which the animal's life end it taken into consideration. In the Muslim community, life is considered sacred. The community focuses more on the manner in which the animal is slaughtered. Animal should be slaughtered according to Islamic laws. According to the Qur'an, life is sacred and therefore God's blessing to creation. The Qur'an requires that if life is ended to ensure the survival of a human being then its slaughtering should be done in the name of God. In the slaughtering process the phrase "in the name of God" is uttered. Any animal slaughtered in the name of another deity, idol or man is considered Haram and should not be consumed by Muslims.

1.2. HALAL FOODS

Figure 1.2. Halal foods are acceptable for consumption among Muslims.

Source: https://www.dentaldevotee.com/2019/05/what-is-halal-food.html?m=1.

Halal foods are foods considered acceptable and lawful for Muslims to consume. These are foods acceptable in the Qur'an. There are foods that are not contaminated with substances said to be Haram. There foods are contain good nutritional balance. With regards to meat, there are certain meat products that are not to be consumed by Muslims. Globally, there are different companies involved in the production of processed halal foods. Some of the food products produced include chicken nuggets, baby food, halal foie grass, pizza, spring rolls and ravioli (Wan Hassan & Awang, 2009). Most of these foods are sold in Muslim restaurants are currently being integrated to normal restaurants. Currently there is the production of ready meals as more Muslims are opting to purchase ready-made foods. There are more retailers opening halal food restaurants in America and Britain. For those offering Vegetarian options, they do not include alcohol in the cooking process.The most commonly known non-haram food among Muslims is pork and pork products. This kind of meat is not consumed by Muslims as it is forbidden in the Qur'an. Muslims cannot consume it as it is considered impure. Other foods in the pork category are considered impure and hence should not be consumed. For foods to be considered as impure or Haram, certain criteria are used in categorizing foods. They include the source of food, the manner of slaughtering or cause of death and the method of processing. Foods gotten from the sea like seafood and shellfish are considered as halal. It is really important for Muslims to ensure that all foods processes and manufactured are halal. The same applies to non-food products such as pharmaceuticals and cosmetics. In most cases, non-food items contain some ingredients and animal by-products that are considered Haram to eat or use. Some foods considered to be Haram include intoxicants such alcohol and blood.

Figure 1.3. Muslims are not allowed to consume foods containing alcohol.

Source: https://www.gettyimages.com/photos/alcohol.

For those in a life or death situation and no halal food is available, the situation allows them consume Haram foods. This is because the life of an individual is considered more important therefore, they can consume anything to ensure their survival. While on flights in cases where there are no halal foods on board Muslims are allowed to order Kosher foods but need to ensure that there are no traces on pork in the dishes. However, there are mixed concerning GMO foods. This is because there are no fixed laws concerning its consumption. There are researchers who argue that these foods are halal as the help ensure the survival of the individuals and contributing to the well-being of human beings. Those against the production of these foods argue that God has created everything in existence therefore there is no need to genetically modify foods. As natural products are perfectly created, humans have no right to tamper with anything that God has created. There are different reactions about genetic modification of genes in pigs. The question being whether after genetic modification meat products can be consumed by Muslims.

1.3. HALAL DIET

For Muslims, laws concerning foods are recorded under Islamic dietary laws. These laws define foods that are acceptable and unacceptable. Acceptable foods are known as halal as they are permitted and lawful and are much emphasized on individuals who strictly observe Islam teachings. Islamic dietary laws do not permit Muslims to consume Haram beverages and foods. Halal foods produced by manufacturing industries needs to bear the halal symbol. The company also need to receive certification to show that they have been approved by a certain agency to produce halal foods (Shafii & Khadijah, 2012). Certification process show that the company produces foods that do not contain Haram ingredients or components. Labels placed on such foods should carry the name of the certification body. The label should include all nutrients include while making the food stuffs. Some of the food considered Halal are as follows: Halal cereal products such as pasta, rice and other cereal products. All cereals are considered Halal except those containing animal gays, vanilla extract and alcohol.

All fruits and vegetables are considered Halal. Every boiled, frozen, canned, vegetable, butter and oil are Halal. In the case of riots and vegetables considered Haram are those having certain elements such as bacon, alcohol, gelatin and animal fats. In the case of dairy and milk, products such as yogurts, ice cream, cheese and milk made using bacterial culture are considered Halal. If all these products are made with animal rennet, gelatin, lipase or vanilla extract are considered Haram. Some of the poultry and meat products and their alternatives certified as Halal include seafood, legumes, nuts, halal deli meats, tofu, peanut butter and eggs. Those considered Haram include pork products such as bacon ham and sausage. The same case applies to meat and poultry products that have not been certified and those prepared using animal fats and alcohol.

Figure 1.4. Pork and pork products are not to be consumed by those observing Islamic laws.

Source: https://jiji.co.ke/kisauni/meals-and-drinks/pork-and-pork-products-lgcERAwzGSOVUv74PbQQHtjU.html.

It is quite a challenge to categorize processed foods as Haram or Halal. The challenge is presented by the ingredients added in them. It is important for individuals to inspect the products whether they have halal food certification. There needs to be a label to check whether it is specified. If the certification is absent, individuals needs to look at the ingredients used in making the products and check for any illegal ingredients such as pepsin, gelatin, pure or artificial vanilla extract, animal rennet, animal fats, lipase, alcohol, animal blood, di and mono glycerides obtained from animals. The same case applies to those having L-cysteine or Sodium stearoyl lactylate. It is important for companies to ensure that all products they are producing do not contain these Haram products to enable them supply their products to customize at a wider scale. In the Muslim community there is a major concern with regards to meat products (Shaari et al., 2019).

In the case of events some of the tips given to individuals is that they need to understand the manner in which dietary habits and food traditions are influenced by the culture and religion. It is important for event organizers or participants to get information on the dietary needs of the guests. In some cases it is important for restaurants to displaying the halal certification, the store receipt and ingredients in foods. In the case where the menu is composed of meat products it is important to provide a vegetarian entrée as an alternative to meat. It is also important for catered to regularly and carefully check products while purchasing food to avoid buy products whose ingredients had changed. With regards to beverages, fruit juice, tea, coffee, carbonated drinks, cocktail and punch are acceptable. However, beverages such as liqueur, beer, alcohol and wine are Haram.

The different forms of fats and oils such as mayonnaise, salad dressings, vegetable oils, butter and margarine are considered Halal in exception of lard and animal shortening. All desserts made with carrageenan or agar are lawful while those containing or made with gelatin are considered Haram. Spices, chutneys, jam, coconut milk and pickles are halal in exception of candies or chocolate made using alcohol. Acceptable sweeteners include sugar, honey, chocolate liquor made from ground cocoa bean syrup and syrup. Chocolate liquor made using alcohol is Haram.

Some of the main entrée dishes that can be prepared for guests include pizza, rice, pasta, any Zabihah meat and other alternative dishes. These dishes cannot be consumed by Muslims if they contain a combination of Haram ingredients or Haram foods are used in the creation process. The same applies to sauces and soups, they should not be made using Haram ingredients or foods. Vanilla extract should not be used in making desserts. Neither artificial not natural vanilla extract can be used in making desserts. No form of alcohol should be added. It is very crucial to check for Haram ingredients in food.

1.4. GUIDELINES FOLLOWED FOR FOOD HALAL LABELING

The following guidelines are followed for food to be labelled as Halal. They therefore apply when the term Halal is to be used. Foods given this label should be in accordance with the general labeling standards used in labeling prepackaged foods. The term Halal has been used by traders in trade marking their products, business names and brand names. Listed guidelines are used with the aim of supplementing Codex General Guidelines on claims.

Figure 1.5. Guidelines listed in the Codex General Guidelines on Claims should be followed when handling food.

Source: https://www.slideshare.net/Adrienna/nutrition-labeling-claims-codex-update-2012.

Under the guidelines, there is the definition of the term Halal and several explanations are used to further explain it. According to the guidelines, halal foods are those considered lawful and acceptable under Islamic laws as they meet certain conditions. The conditions are that the foods do not contain or consist of any ingredient prohibited by Islamic laws, they should not be made, processed, stored or transported using any equipment, appliance or facilities containing substances or elements considered Haram under Islamic laws. Finally, during the course of preparing, processing, storing and transporting foods should come in direct contact with foods considered haram (Samori et al., 2016).

However, there are some considerations made in the handling of Halal foods. For instance, in the process of preparing, processing and storing halal foods the processes can be done in different sections of the same premises in which the production of non-Halal food is done. However, manufacturers should ensure that those foods do not come into direct contact. Halal foods can be processed, prepared, stored and transported in premises where non-Halal food were produced. For this to be done, all cleaning procedures should be done in accordance to Islamic laws.

1.4.1. Lawful or Acceptable Food

Halal is a term used in defining foods considered acceptable or lawful under Islamic laws. Islamic laws state that all food sources are considered lawful in exception of those derived from sources considered Haram under Islamic laws. Some animal foods considered unlawful include dogs, monkeys, boars, pigs and snakes. The same applies to all carnivorous animals having fangs and claws such as bears, lions and tigers. It is considered haram to consume birds of prey having claws including vultures and eagles among others. It is forbidden for one to consume pets such as scorpions, rats and centipedes. The same applies for all animals forbidden to be killed among the Muslim community. Examples of these animals include woodpecker birds, ants and bees. Islamic laws forbid one from consuming any animal generally considered as repulsive such as maggots, lice and flies. The same applies for animals residing in both water and land such as crocodiles and frogs among others. It is considered Haram to consume any hazardous and poisonous aquatic animals and any animal slaughtered outside the Islamic laws. Blood should not be consumed.

In the case of food derived from plants, they are all considered Halal except those containing intoxicants or hazardous elements. This includes hazardous and intoxicating plants. However, it the intoxicating and hazardous element can be removed during processing. In the sector of drinks, all beverages are considered Halal except for those containing intoxicants or hazardous substances. All alcoholic drinks and hazardous drinks are considered (Rejeb et al., 2021). With regards to food additives, all are acceptable except for those containing Haram elements. The manner in which an animal is slaughtered will determine whether it is Haram or Halal. The case of slaughtering applies to all animals considered Halal. Islamic laws dictate the manner in which the animal is to be slaughtered.

Usually, meat is slaughtered according to laws laid out in the Codex Recommended Code of Hygiene Practice for Fresh Meat. The requirements are as follows: the person slaughtering the animal should be a Muslim of sound mind and aware of Islamic slaughtering procedures. The animal to be slaughtered should be considered Halal according to Islamic laws. The animal in question should be deemed alive or alive for it to be slaughtered. Dead animals should not be slaughtered. The phrase " In the name of Allah" is to be involved by the individual slaughtering the animal. The phrase is invoked before the animal is slaughtered. The phrase is to be invoked for the slaughter of each animal. Devices used during the slaughtering process should be very sharp and therefore it should not be lifted off from the animal during the slaughtering process. While slaughtering the animal, parts such as the main arteries, trachea and esophagus should be severed.

1.4.2. Handling Halal Foods

When handling halal foods, the preparation, processing, packaging, transportation and strong processes should be done in accordance to all requirements listed in the Codex General Principles on Food Hygiene. Other relevant Codex standards apply. Manufactured need to ensure that Halal foods do not come in contact with non-Halal foods. They should ensure all ingredients used are considered Halal. If a company is said to produce halal foods, all equivalent terms as well as the term Halal should be present in the labeling of the product. In line with the Codex General Guidelines on Claims, all claims on food should not be done in an in appropriate manner that could cause doubt to rise with regards to the safety of such foods. One should not claim that halal foods are healthier or much better nutritionally compared to other foods.

The Shariah Supervisory Board is known to take care of all matters health and ethical issues with regards to production of food products acceptable for human consumption. For companies producing halal foods, they need to have all the needed certification. This is to show that their products do not contain any form of Haram ingredients. There are numerous categorizes of Certificate given to companies producing halal foods. The Halal Research Council is involved in giving of these certificates. The council gives services globally (Rezaee, 2019). Their role is to scrutinize, analyze and test some products. In some instance standards are compared beyond Islamic laws with Halal laws. The council is in charge of overseeing slaughter houses for meat production, cosmetics and chemicals and production of both processed and raw foods. They offer sub-services for the production of the following products: fat products, dairy and aquatic products, ingredients, slaughtering process for halal, confections, recipes, poultry and livestock products, energy supplements, flour, fruits, corn products, drinks and snacks and dietetic Foods. For Muslims who strictly observe Islamic laws, it is very crucial that they consume Halal foods. The Holy Qur'an places more emphasis on consuming foods that qualify or meet Halal criteria. There are some verses that talk about eating of Halal foods. The following are some of the verses:

Al-Mumenoon 23:51 says, "I messenger, eat from the pure foods and work righteousness." There is also Al-Anaam 6:121 says, "And do not eat that upon which the name of Allah has not been mentioned, for indeed it is a grave disobedience." Finally, Al-Anaam 6:118 says, "So eat of that meat upon which Allah's name has been mentioned, if you are believers in His verses."

Figure 1.6. Hadiths contain guidelines concerning food consumption.

Source: http://www.quranreading.com/blog/halal-and-haram-food-in-the-quran-and-hadith/.

From Hadiths, there are numerous laws on Halal foods proven by scripture. In the Tirmidhi it is recorded that Ka'b lbn Ujrah says that Allah's Prophets once said that a body sustained by Haram foods will not enter Hannah. From Tabarani, S'ad RA recollects that Allah's messenger PBUH voiced that individuals should purify themselves so that their prayers or supplication may be. For those who consume foods considered Haram, their deed will not be acceptable. According to Baihaqi, it is said that Allah's messenger PBUH once voiced that bodies that will not enter Paradise are those sustained by Haram foods. Verses obtained from Baihaqi, Darimi and Ahmed reported that PBUH, the messenger of Allah, once said that flesh grown from Haram will not enter Paradise. He also further states that the same flesh is worthy of the hell fire.

Those who have a certificate are able to improve their branding image to meet the consumer demands. Certification enables companies and organizations enter a global Halal food market allowing them access over

1.5 billion consumers. It also gives them a sound edge giving them better ground over their competitors. Certification is given to individuals who follow rules given by the Council. The companies need to be maintained by relating with private sanitation facilities. These facilities help companies maintain the needed sanitation. This is an added advantage to the normal obligatory Hygiene practice observed by the company. Certification allows companies get a distinct logo on all their products. The Halal recognition makes it easy for companies to market and promote their products. Certification helps companies improve their food quality. This is achieved by stringent quality assurance policy according to international standards. For most companies having a Halal insignia is considered dependable, trustworthy and autonomous acknowledgment with regards to Halal food Claims. Having a certificate enables companies improve their advertisement and it also makes it easy for Muslims and Global markets to accept these products (Rahim & Abd Rahim, 2020).

Figure 1.7. There are numerous steps followed by companies to acquire a halal certificate.

Source: https://cehalal.com/steps-to-get-halal-certification/.

The producer, supplier, distributer or manufacturer downloads a Halal Application Form. The form is then carefully filled with accurate information. The application form is then submitted by the company alongside some credentials. Some the credentials include the Company name, information on the processing plants and a list of all products produced by the company. With regards to products being produced, companies seeking to get halal certification need to specify the nature of the products produced. This means the company shows whether is a non-food or food product. They should also include the name of the brand as well as the sources of all ingredients used in making products. The process flow chart used by the company should be submitted. The viability and market plan used by the company is also needed.

Once the application is submitted it is taken to the HRC. Once obtained by the HRC, the concerned body takes the application to the concerned office. The office will then screen the submitted documents. The screening process involves checking whether all documents have been properly filled. When properly filled, the application can then proceed to the next level. The next level involves auditing and scrutiny. If the documents have not been properly filled then the application is rejected. In the case where the application proceeds to the next level, a processing fee is charged by HRC Haram (Park & Lee, 2021).

Once the fee is paid, there are stages followed to complete the application process. In the initial stage involves documents being reviewed by Audit Team and Inspection Committee. The Committee is made up of a food scientist, Islamic academician and an industrial manufacturing specialist. Once the initial audit and inspection clearance is done, the documents are sent to the Shariah Supervisory Board. The board will then evaluate the documents. Once the documents have been evaluated and approved by the board, the case is sent to the Research wing. In these stage, the company sends its products to the Research wing. The wing then extracts samples of the products, raw materials and processes. Once the samples are obtained, they are sent to the Inspection Team. They are then sent to the laboratory for further evaluation and analysis resulting in the production of a detailed report. The report is written by the research wing. There are required to take into consideration all details submitted during the application process as well as laboratory results. The report is then submitted to the Audit and Inspection Committee. The Committee then controls the clearing of the report. The final report is then taken to the Shariah Supervisory Boards for Halal Fatwa. The Halal status of the products is decided upon by the board. For products that qualify, they are awarded a certificate. Those that don't qualify don't get a certificate. The issued certificate runs for a period of a year. However, during the course of the year the process can still remain subject to a review and observation. The Audit and Inspection Committee call the shots with regards to the review.

For a company to be awarded a certificate it means that they have met all qualifications. In different countries, there are different boards that give the certificate. Generally, the certificate is issued under a Halal Certificate and Halal Label Order established in 2005. For establishments having these certificates with regards to food it means that their products do not contain any element of animal components considered Haram under Islamic laws. This applies to meat that has not been slaughtered with regards to Islamic laws. Their products do not contain any element considered impure according to Islamic laws. It also means that they have not been prepared using equipment or instruments having impure elements and there was no contact with non-Halal foods or Haram elements during the preparation or storage process.

1.5. HALAL FOOD LABELING

For a company to acquire a halal label, they need to be in possession of a halal certificate. For the company to acquire the label, they need to ensure that their products do not contain and animal matter or elements considered Haram under Islamic laws. Much energy is focused on slaughtering of meat. Companies should ensure that animals are slaughtered according to Islamic laws (Omar & Jaafar, 2011). The food products should not contain any ingredients or other elements considered Haram. The products are not prepared using any instruments containing substances considered impure according to Islamic laws. Also there was no form of contact between halal food products and non-Halal food products or Haram ingredients.

1.6. APPLICATION PROCEDURES FOR HALAL LABEL

Figure 1.8. Companies have their own labels showing their food products are halal.

Source: https://www.vectorstock.com/royalty-free-vector/halal-food-labels-set-vector-15000418.

For a company to have a halal label, it needs to apply to get a label. The application process is as follows:

The company or the individual applying for the Halal Label should fill an application form. In the case of the labeling, the application process requires the applicant fill a form for each product. Applicants can get application forms from the Ministry of Religious Affairs, Halal Food Control Division and the Department of Syariah Affairs. Applicants should ensure that all fields are properly filled with accurate and relevant information. Once filled, the form is to be submitted alongside relevant documents and certificates. Some of the needed documents are as follows: the company profile, a copy of the applicant's passport or identity card, a copy of the business license as well as the registration certificate, a copy of Miscellaneous License if company if present, the name and information of the business and the products, a list of ingredients used, the name and address of the ingredient supplier and producer. In some instances, the company may be required to further specify ingredients used. The Halal status if ingredients as well as their specifications is taken into consideration (Nurrachmi, 2018).

Other information required from the company is information on processing and production procedures, the process flow of the product, International Standards Organizations, Good Hygiene Practices, Control Point Plan, Total Quality Management, Good Manufacturing Practices, Veterinary Inspection Logo and health mark. If possible, the company may be required to submit a map of the business area. It is important for applicants to ensure that they have properly filled all fields. Once the form has been submitted to one of the boards, the applicant proceeds to open a special file. The special file contains all information in the report obtained during the certification process. The completed form is then taken to the Inspection Committee who given auditors the go ahead to audit the area of business and all ingredients used in creating products. The auditing process includes auditors getting samples of products. In the case of food, the food samples are obtained and submitted to a food analyst who conducts extensive analysis.

There are fees incurred by the applicant. The fees are used to cater for the analysis, audit and traveling expenses. Payment is given to the Majilis. Once the auditing is done a report is generated and is submitted to the Inspection Committee along with a certificate of laboratory analysis. The full report is then taken to the Majilis within a period of 14 days after the Committee has completely studied it. The Majilis also reads and studies the report after which they are able to use the information from the report to determine whether the company or applicant has met all Halal requirements and procedures. If the requirements are met and all fees have been paid, the company is given a permit which allows them use the Halal Label.

1.7. HALAL FRIENDLY FOOD

For Muslims, Islamic laws require strict observers to consume Halal foods. However, there has been a challenge in providing foods for Muslims. This led to the production of halal-friendly foods. There are still controversies regarding the production of halal-friendly foods. Halal-friendly in some instances is referred to as Muslim-friendly (Nusran et al., 2018). This refers to production of foods that can be consumed by Muslims. Several establishments have been put in place to ensure that there is an option of Muslim-friendly foods. However, those establishment needs to revive

friendly foods cannot be identified or recognized by the Trust as it is not under Islamic laws.

The Sheik also explained that there is a grey area. The grey area explains the fact that a majority of the International Muslim Community is known to offer non-Halal food options such as alcohol in areas where socializing and food are offered. The Trust has the power to limit the adoption of halal-friendly foods. In South Africa, provision of Haram foods in Muslim homes and restaurants is not acceptable. The term halal-friendly can also be used to refer to modifications made to food stuffs to that they fit the category of Halal. However, the concept of halal-friendly I'd not legally identified in Shariah. There is much un-familiarity with the term as it is either halal compliant, non-halal or halal. Sedick also stated the Trust understands that the term halal-friendly is used in referring to facilities or situations where a company Licensed to offer halal foods starts offering non-Halal foods to allow interactions between Muslims and non-Muslims.

In the case of restaurant offering halal-friendly foods but use halal certificates are not complying with the regulations. However, the trust does not have legal mandate to handle such issues. The trust believes that the term halal-friendly should instead be replaced with the term Halal compliant. The trust would like Muslims to strictly observe Islamic laws with regards to food. Provision of halal and Haram foods in the same premises could result in Muslims consuming Haram foods.

1.8. MASHBOOH

Under Islamic laws there are three main terms with regards to food. As established earlier, the term Halal refers to all food stuffs and ingredients acceptable by Islamic laws. There is also the term Haram which refers to all foods and ingredients considered unlawful. While there is usually a clear line between halal and Haram foods there is a sense of lack of clarity concerning some foods. In Islamic laws, there is an Arabic word Mashbooh or Mushbooh which is a general name for a certain category of foods. The word is used to refer to foods that are considered suspected or doubtful. Foods under this category are usually labelled as Mashbooh.

Figure 1.10. There is a lack of clarity dealing with Mashbooh foods.

Source: https://icons8.com/icon/57939/mushbooh-food.

With Mashbooh foods, there is lack of clarity in whether the food should be termed as Haram prohibit Muslims from consuming or halal allowing Muslims consume them. For the Muslim communities, the term Mashbooh is used to mean suspect or doubtful. There are many instances where foods fall under the category of Mashbooh. For instance, if the Individuals involved in the slaughtering process are not sure about the slaughtering process or lack knowledge on the type of ingredients used in preparing the foods then the meat products will be termed as Mashbooh. Most cases of Mashbooh revolve around ingredients. Numerous ingredients are used by Muslims in preparing foods. Ingredients used by Muslims can be obtained from plants or animals (Mostafa, 2020). Depending on the types of ingredients used, it is difficult to know or understand whether the food in question is Haram or Halal. However, Islamic laws limit individuals from eating any Mushbooh food to avoid them eating any ingredients considered Haram.

Though there are uncertainties regarding Mashbooh foods, some foods have already been short listed. For most of these foods there under this category there is inadequate information concerning it. Some of them are still indistinguishable.

1.8.1. Examples of Mashbooh Food Items

There are numerous food stuffs that fall under the Mashbooh category. These food items fall under different categories. Among the common food items in this regard is good additives. Most of the food additives are prohibited for consumption are there are many uncertainties with regards to their source. This has resulted in some of them being termed as Haram. Some food additives considered as Mashbooh include emulsifiers, gelatin, fats and enzymes. In the case of fats, those obtained from pure sources are considered Halal. The same case applies for ghee obtained from Halal animal. If these elements are obtained from plant or animal source they can be considered as halal. There are many questions regarding meat food products. There is an issue is that though the meat was derived from an animal was it slaughtered with regards to Islamic laws. Foods contain additives termed as Mashbooh are generally considered to be Haram.

1.9. ZABIHAH

There is a great variation between halal and Zabihah. As halal is term generally used to refer to all food products while Zabihah is a term used to specially refer to meat products. There are numerous animal said to be halal. They include goats, game birds, cows, ducks, sheep, chicken, moose and deer. In as much as these animals are considered Halal m, they should also fit the category of Zabihah. This means that all Islamic Rites were followed the animal is slaughtered. Meat products should follow all procedures for Muslims to consume such products. A brief outline of the procedure of the Zabihah includes the animal being slaughtered by a Muslim. The animal is to be placed on the ground and if possible be held if it's smaller in size. A sharp device is used in cutting the animal's throat ensuring that all main veins are severed. While cutting it, the person involved is required to pronounce a certain phrase containing the name of Allah.

Figure 1.11. Muslims are allowed to consume Zabihah products as they are considered Halal.

Source: https://www.caribbeanmuslims.com/zabihah.

There are numerous questions following the slaughtering of animals following Islamic laws. Among the main questions is why the animal should only be slaughtered by a Muslim. There are those who question why they cannot eat products slaughtered by people of the book. Most questions regarding Zabihah are answered by scriptures. One of the Islamic Sheiks notes that in the Quran there are foods given to Muslims considers as Halal (Mostafa, 2018). The individual slaughtering the animal should be a Muslim as the individual possess better understanding of Islamic laws. They will conduct the slaughtering process according to the Quran. Verses used by the Quran are inter-related. One verse is used in explaining another. From the Quran 6: 121, the holy book says that if the name of Allah has not had not been taken then the meat should not be consumed. In the case where the name has not been taken then the process is taken as a form of transgressions.

The Quran states that Zabihah is allowed for Muslims however verse 6:121 of the Quran requires the name of Allah to be invoked. This means that Zabihah is permitted if the phrase "in the name of Allah" is mentioned during the slaughtering process. The entire phrase may not be mentioned but the name of Allah must be mentioned. Taking Allah's name during the slaughtering was mostly common among the Ahlul-kitaab. Invoking the name of Allah during the slaughtering process made Zabihah Halal for Muslims. Those involved in slaughtering animals are known as Ahlul-kitaab. Currently these individuals are identified by their Muslim names and less by their faith. No one can guarantee whether they invoke the name of Allah during the slaughtering. Currently the Ahlul-kitaab are no longer trusted with regards to issues regarding to Haram or Halal products.

Currently there are numerous uncertainties with regards to the manner in which animals are slaughtered. As no one can guarantee whether the Ahlul-kitaab invoke the name of Allah during the slaughtering process there are concerns as to whether Muslims are consuming meat that is Haram. The Quran warns Muslims against eating meat which is doubtful. They are allowed to eat meat if they are sure that the Ahlul-kitaab took the name of Allah when slaughtering the animal. There are Halal Councils who encourage their Muslim communities to slaughter their own animals. In the U.K and USA, there are Committees that have been established their main role being to ensure that halal slaughter houses hire Muslims to slaughter animals. This means that these committed are independent of Jewish and Christian sources. In some countries the meat is sold in the market though they are packed, sealed and stamped with a label used by Muslim organizations. In most cases, the Muslim Organizations are made up of reliable scholars and individuals who have adequate knowledge on Islamic laws concerning foods.

1.9.1. Prerequisites of Zabihah

There are particular prerequisites with regards to product of meat products. Some of the prerequisites are as follows: the animal in question should be considered Halal according to Islamic laws namely the Sunnah and Quran. It is crucial that the person slaughtering the animal be a mentally stable adult Muslim. There are numerous verses in the Quran that indicate that only the name of Allah should be mentioned during the slaughtering process. This means that any name of another deity should not be mentioned and if mentioned the neat should not be considered as Haram. Muslims scholars have placed much emphasis on those slaughtering animals to mention the name of (Mannaa, 2020). Though there are different understanding with regards to slaughtering of food, if the individual slaughtering the animal forgets to invoke the name of Allah or decides not to invoke the name then the act of slaughtering the animal is in vain as the meat cannot be consumed. This makes invoking of Allah's name an obligation. Scholars with this ideologies view animal slaughter a supreme law according to the Quran.

There are numerous laws that support this ideology. They include the Quran 5:3, al-Ma'idah 5:3 and al-An'am 6:121. The three verses place emphasis on the need for the name of Allah to be invoked during the slaughtering process. Also names of other deities should not be mentioned. Islamic laws prohibit Muslims from eating meat gotten from animals who have been strangled, slaughtered using blunt weapons, one killed by another animal, died by falling or those eaten by other animals. Muslims scholars further Islamic laws prohibiting consumption of meat from animals slaughtered under certain circumstances. Muslims are not allowed to consume meat of an animal slaughtered by a Christian. In the United States, there are certain regulations placed by the government to control slaughtering of animals while taking different traditions into consideration. Slaughtering of animals is covered under the Humane Slaughter Act. The act lists a number of prerequisites to be done before any form of religious slaughter Is done. These regulations require the animal be taken to consideration by ensuring that they are insensitive to pain before they are killed. Most slaughter houses used techniques such as electronacrosis.

1.10. TAYYIB FOOD

Figure 1.12. TAYYIB is a Muslim word used to mean good.

Source: https://mytayyib.business.site/.

The word tayyib strongly related to the term Halal. As halal is used to mean permissible or acceptable. The word can be used to refer to foods, actions or behavior as per the Traditional Muslim Juristic interpretations of Islamic laws. The interpretation of the term tayyib means good. The word has been derived from the Quran as believers are instructed to consume from tayyib foods availed for them. Islamic traditions have different understandings and interpretation of the word tayyib. For some, the word translates to tasty, pleasant or fragrant. With regards to food, the term is interpreted as good or wholesome. The term bears certain connotation for Muslims today. The term is used to refer to halal foods that are clean, nutritious, healthy or ethically obtained. It is used to refer to organically or naturally sourced foods Allah (Mathew, 2014).

For food products such as vegetables and fruits, they are naturally sourced. They do not contain any pesticides or experienced any form of genetic modification. This means that plants or animals are eaten in their organic form. For Muslims who are focused on eating tayyib foods need to avoid any form of genetically modified maize, beans or other products. The word tayyib can be used with regards to different food products. With regards to meat, the term tayyib-halal is generated. For Muslims, they need to ensure that they are consuming meat products produced according to Islamic laws. However, there are those concerned about the type of meat they consume. This trend has been noted throughout the world. More individuals are becoming sensitive to what they ingesting with most opting to choose completely organic foods. More Muslims are becoming more sensitive and want to get more information on the source of meat. Information on whether that animal was tested in a factory farm, the type of treatment given to then type of feeds and whether or not antibodies and hormones were given to the animal is crucial information. To a great extent, tayyib focused on food safety. It brings to light all products used in producing food products. Numerous studies have been done to establish different kinds of foods that can be categorized as tayyib.

For the Muslims, these foods need to be lawful hence halal. For instance if it is meat, it should be from a halal animal and all slaughtering activities are done according to Islamic laws. If the source is considered Halal, further investigation is done to know more about the food source. One establishes whether the Halal animal was raised on organic or inorganic feeds. Healthy conscious Muslims can go for the more organic food products. Tayyib foods are halal foods obtained from naturally organic sources. The Quran contains numerous verses on tayyib foods and con be used in expounding information on tayyib concepts. There is certification given to companies and organizations offering tayyib food products. In the Quran 10:37, the verse sheds light on the general concept of tayyib. Verse 2:168 of the same book describes the concept of tayyib with regards to food. From the verse, halal is translated as things that are lawful while the term tayyib is translated as things that are good.

For the verse (2:168), there are two conditions for food to be consumed. The food to be consumed must be considered Halal and also tayyib. Verse 7:157 of the Quran highlights the meaning of tayyib as good things while its opposite is Al-Khaba'ith meaning evil. The term evil is generally used to refer to things considered harmful, disgusting or impure. The verse has been used in creation an Islamic law on food requiring all harmful, impure and abominable foods be avoided. All what is considered the opposite of Tayyib is unlawful (Lubis et al., 2016). The verse alongside other has been used in generating other definitions of Tayyib. The term Tayyib is used to refer a substance or thing that is not abominable. In other words it is attractive and an individual of sound mind can consider it a good food. It is also used to refer to wholesome, tasty and delicious foods that are free from any elements or substances that pose a threat to human health. It can also there to any substance considered to be medically stable and can be consumed by humans.

From a brief overview of the Quran, one learns that these laws champion for food safety. Some may refer to it as an intrinsic element of the Halal. One verse supporting this argument is verse 2:195 which requires every individual to abstain from any form of destruction including danger from food. Laws requiring people to stay away from anything hazardous in the food sector is listed in verse 2:195. The verse states that individuals should stay away from hazardous substances meaning that they should be careful not to consume any agents that could result in injury or illnesses if there is no control. The agents in this case refer to chemical, physical or biological substances harmful to human health. With regards to food, these agents are presented in the form of pathogenic bacteria know to cause harm to consumers' health. This means that those handling production of food need to have a better understanding of these agents and adopt all necessary measures to ensure that these substances do not contaminate food. Some scholars say that the verse requires food handlers be given a good working environment that is safe for their health.

Some may say that tayyib is inter-related to the Halal sector as the major goal is to ensure food safety. Numerous Islamic bodies have been involved in the food sector and have been useful in expounding information on tayyib. This has allowed the production of organic halal foods. Companies producing such kinds of food need to bear a certificate showing indicating that their foods are organic.

1.11. HALAL MEAT

Figure 1.13. Halal meat are those which can be consumed by Muslims.

Source: https://seattleglobalist.com/2016/07/14/halal-eat-halal-even-not-muslim/53928.

It has already been established that the term Halal is used to refer to food considered lawful or acceptable according to Muslim laws. Therefore, the term Halal meat is used to refer to meat or meat products acceptable for consumption by Muslims. However, with Halal meat, the source, method of preparation and processing will be useful in determining whether the meat is permitted for individuals. There are certain animals that are considered lawful for human consumption. Some of these animals include domestic birds such as chicken, goat, fish, cattle, locust, buck, camels and rabbits. There are some Muslims who consider consumption of certain sea animals such as shellfish to be Halal though there are those who do not have the same views. Among all Halal food products, meat is the most regulated. Most of these animals go through slaughter houses in exception of fish, locust and shellfish (Khan et al., 2018).

As most of these animals have to go through slaughter houses, there are certain processes followed during these processes. The slaughter process in the Muslim community is referred to as dhabiha. The slaughter process includes three main body organs namely the windpipe, carotid artery and jugular vein are severed. For the Muslim community, it is important to ensure that devices used in the slaughtering process are sharp so that the cutting process is done once. This is to ensure that the animal does not feel much pain. Muslim laws require all animals to be slaughtered are healthy and alive during the slaughtering time. After the slaughter process, the blood is drained from the animal's body to ensure that people are not served foods containing blood. Blood consumption is said to be Haram according Islamic laws.

The person who conducts the slaughtering process should be a Muslim. During the slaughtering process there is a phrase to be recited. There are those who refer to the phrase as a dedication as the animal is dedicated to Allah. The recited phrase is referred to as a Shahada or tasmiya. With the slaughtering of animals following the halal process, there are some controversies that have sparked up debates. Among the controversies is stunning method of slaughtering animals whether or not it should be considered Halal. There are those who feel that stunning should not be used in killing animals. This ideology is upheld by the Halal Good Authority. The organization's main goal is to ensure Halal principles are monitored and adhered to. The organization allows stunning to be used when the animal survives. Once it is done, halal methods are used in killing the animal. There are organizations which feel that slaughtering of animals with the elimination of pre-stunning results unnecessary suffering in animals. Reports form food standard agencies show that a large percentage of animals used in generating halal meat products were stunned before the slaughtering process.

It is believed that meat and meat products produced by stunned animals are blessed. For countries who are members of the European Union, they have to follow laws that require slaughter houses stun all animals before they are slaughtered. There exemptions are made for religious slaughter houses. Countries like Denmark have banned slaughter houses that do not stun animals. There are countries that want to ban religious slaughter houses (Krishnan et al., 2017).

Different countries have different methods of preparing Halal meat. For instance, in Australia, there is a body known as the Australian Federation of Islamic Council. The peak body is in charge of giving slaughter houses certificates. It is also involved in training Islamic slaughter men who work in both the poultry and meat industry. The body has been involved in supervising production of halal products. The body charges individuals with the duty of going to farms, organizations and companies producing meat and non-meat, cosmetics and drugs. The individual inspects all the organizations according to Islamic laws. They check whether all the Halal products have been obtained from sources that are acceptable and after extraction, they are prepared according to Islamic laws. This involves reciting the phrase, "In the name of Allah." It is crucial to ensure that all processes and products are well produced and are not in contact with non-Halal products.

Figure 1.14. Islamic laws should be followed during the slaughtering process.

Source: https://www.google.com/amp/s/www.pri.org/stories/2015–12–02/inside-halal-slaughterhouse-where-knives-are-sharp-and-tradition-endures%3famp.

It is forbidden for Muslims to consume meat or meat products that have not been produced with regards to Islamic laws. There are numerous controversies with regards to Islamic slaughter with animal tights activists challenging methods used by Muslims. They argue that these methods cause unnecessary suffering incurred by animals. Halal councils disagree with animal activists by championing the ideology that Islamic methods of slaughter have been catered in a manner that ensures the animal does not suffer due to distress or pain. Islamic bodies in charge of slaughter houses have different laws controlling the slaughter process. In the case of Australia, the AFIC has integrated strict laws on slaughtering of halal animal. The rules require the individual slaughtering the animal be a Muslim. This is to ensure that the individual is knowledgeable on Islamic laws. The slaughterer should be of sound mind. The rules require the slaughterer invoke the name of Allah before slaughtering the animal. The name of Allah is invoked so as to place much focus on the sanctity of life. The Quran places a great value on life, animals included therefore invoking the name of Allah is like acquiring Allah's consent.

The laws require the animals be killed by having a sharp device cut the throat of the animal through a continuous notion. They also require the slaughterer ensure that at least the blood vessels, esophagus and the trachea are cut. In as much as these vessels should be severed, the slaughterer should ensure the spinal cord is not cut. The rules require the animal be treated well before slaughter. It requires animals be slaughtered one at a time ensuring that other animals to not witness another animal being killed. Devices used during the slaughter process should not be sharpened while the animal watches. Devices used should not contain any form of blemishes that could result in wounds being teared. The animal should not be placed in an uncomfortable situation during the slaughter process. After the slaughter, the slaughterer should allow the animal's body bleed out and ensure the animal has actually died for them to proceed with other activities (Karahalil, 2020).

There are those who believe that Islamic methods of slaughtering animals is much better as it is assumed that animals will not suffer. This is the case when the slaughter is done cleanly and fast. By doing the animal would have lost consciousness before the brain perceives pain. Some Islamic scholars who say that the Islamic way of slaughtering animals is the most humane method. There are those who argue that slaughter methods used in Western countries cause pain to the animal. One of the methods is captive bolt stunning. Ritual cutting is perceived to be more humane. There are those who opt to use ritual slaughter methods in slaughtering calves and sheep. However, there are those feel that animals being allowed to bleed out till they die is inhumane. There is no scientific knowledge to back this ideology. Once devices through swift motion cut the animal's throat the animal becomes unconscious within a few hours. However, the loss of consciousness is not brought about by blood loss. Instead, it is as a result of cerebral hypoxia.

1.12. CONDITIONS FOR FOODS AND DRINKS TO BE CONSIDERED HALAL

Generally, all drinks and foods are considered Halal in exception of those that have been listed as Haram by Islamic laws. Foods that forbidden for consumption include blood, pork, alcohol, meat from dead animals that were not slaughtered, domesticated donkeys, frogs, mice, scorpions, snakes, carnivorous animals like tigers and lions, meat slaughtered for idols and meat obtained from birds of prey know for their claws such as falcons, hawks and vultures among others. This also includes all ingredients considered Halal. It is forbidden for Muslims to eat meat sourced from animals that have not been slaughtered according to Islamic laws. This is in exception of sea creatures and fish. For foods and drinks to be considered as Halal, they have to meet the following prerequisites:

They should not have any ingredients or elements considered Haram according to Islamic laws. Some of the components include alcohol and animal fat among others. The foods should not be processed, prepared or made impure by being contaminated by Haram elements. The processing, preparation, storage and transportation of these foods should not be done in facilitates contaminated by Haram elements. The foods should not entail materials considered unclean according to Islamic laws. In the case of Halal meat, it should be slaughtered according to Islamic laws. Equipment used in preparing, processing or manufacturing foods should not be contaminated with Haram materials. These foods should be completely for human consumption meaning that it should not contain poisonous, hazardous or intoxicating elements.

Chapter

2 The History of Halal Food

CONTENTS

2.1. INTRODUCTION

The terms halal and haram are distinguished in the Quran (forbidden). This dichotomy evolved into a more complicated grouping known as "the five decisions": obligatory, suggested, neutral, repugnant, and prohibited. Formalized paraphrase Islamic scholars are divided about whether the word halal refers to the first two or the first four of these groups. In recent years, Islamic groups aiming to unite the masses, as well as writers writing for a general audience, have stressed the simpler distinction between halal and haram.

The word halal is particularly synonymous with Islamic dietary laws and, in particular, meat that has been processed and cooked in compliance with those specifications.

The word halal means lawful or legitimate in Arabic. It applies to any event or object that is legal under Islamic law. As a result, halal foods are those that are permissible to consume as per Islamic dietary guidelines. Foods that are prohibited are alluded to as haram, which implies "forbidden" in Arabic.

The term kosher is Hebrew for "proper" or "fit," and it is equivalent to the Arabic term halal. Unlike Jews, who do not say the name of God every occasion they kill an animal, Muslims say a prayer over the first and last animal in each specified slaughter (Kamarulzaman et al., 2016).

The terms halal and haram are often used in the Quran to distinguish between what is permissible or permitted and what is unlawful or prohibited. The root word halal in the Quran signifies lawfulness and can also mean leaving the ceremonial state of a pilgrim and entering a puerile state. It has the opposite meaning to that expressed by the root haram in both of these senses (cf. haram and ihram). In a literal sense, the term can refer to dissolution (for example, violating an oath) or alighting (for example, of God's wrath). In the Quran, lawfulness is normally represented by the verb ahalla (to render lawful), with God as the specified or inferred subject.

Muslims view the topic of halal and haram as the foundation of studying Islam and applying religion. In order to determine the status according to Islamic law, a Muslim should escape matters of doubt (syubuhat). The object of the precaution in work, consuming, and use of products is to make sure that people become truly devoted Muslims (abid) and wish for Allah the Almighty to approve all of their actions.

These points are distinct for the general population and those who do not understand Islam's teachings. Sometimes, halal simply refers to consuming and drinking foods or beverages that are permissible in Islam. Halal, according to Islam, encompasses a wider range of behaviors, acts, voice, emotions, clothes, cosmetics, drugs, and so on.

According to the Fuqaha, halal and haram are what Allah and His Messenger have written. In this way, Allah represents the judgement for the people by His Messenger (al-Saadi on Tayseer Al-Kareem Al-Rahman fee Tafseer Kalaam Il-Mannan).

It is a matter of assigning servants, including religious arrangements. Allah and His Messenger have the authority to prove whether a ruling is halal or haram. According to Yusuf al-Qaradawi, God put decisions on his subordinates, but who has proved the judgement is outside God's limits. According to Qala'ji and Quneibi's Mu'jam Lugaah al-Fuqahaa,' the term halal is extracted from permissibility in the context of what is allowed in Shariah. According to al-Jurjani on Ta'rifaat, halal is conquest. The definition refers to what does not punish the act or cause Sharia to be implemented. On Qawathi' al-Adillah fi Ushul al-Fiqh, Al-Samani said that haram is what is punishable, halal is what he can do, and jaiz is not punishable nor honored for what he does. As a result, the concept of halal based on the Quran and Hadith is very plain and straightforward. Halal is all that is healthy for the body, mind, and spirit. In the opposite, everything is haram (harmful) to one's health: the body, mind, and spirit (Junaidi, 2020). According to the Ministry of Religious Affairs' Technical Guidelines for Halal Processing, food is a material to be eaten or consumed by people, as well as products used in the production of food and beverages. According to Islamic principles, halal is permissible. In conclusion, halal is something that Sharia allows to be applied, used, or attempted when it has overcome the barriers that hinder it or the elements that it presents by acquiring it well and negotiating with the parties, rather than by the effects of forbidden approaches.

For Muslims, the foundation of all conduct must be worship, specifically worship of God Almighty. God said, "I did not build the jinn and mankind for the sake of worship" (adz-Dzariat: 56). The eating practice is also a form of worship, with Sharia-compliant processes and regulations. According to the Holy Quran, eating is not only essential for halal, but it should also be healthy. This is evidenced by many expressions of halal terms in several verses of the Qur'an, which are often accompanied by good words. As previously said, "O people, eat of the good things of the world, and do not follow in the footsteps of the devil, for he is a clear enemy to you." "Eat all that you have done right, and fear Allah, for Allah is Forgiving and Merciful" (al- Anfal: 69). "Eat all that Allah has blessed you with for comfort, and praise God for His mercy if you love Him" (an-Nahl: 114). "And eat what Allah has blessed you with for comfort, and fear Allah, in whom you have faith."Since not all Halal foods are healthy, the term "Halal" becomes the justification for the instruction to eat halal and good food and drink in these verses. Tayseer Al-Kareem Al-Rahman pay Tafseer according to Al-Saadi According to Kalaam Il-Mannan, the letter from Surat al-Baqarah 168 is a call to all human beings, believers and non-believers. On Shafwat al-Tafseer, Muhammad Ali al-Sabouni affirmed the verse with the same interpretation that the verse is general, implying that all human beings ingest God's excuse for them.

2.2. THE EARLY DAYS

It's difficult to think about the 1960s as the "early days," but it was around this period that the Western world saw a wave of Muslim migrants. Many wanted to live in the United Kingdom, while some settled in countries such as France and Spain.

Figure 2.1. New far-right anti-immigrant sentiment hits German streets – The Washington Post.

Source: https://www.washingtonpost.com/world/europe/new-far-right-anti-immigrant-sentiment-hits-german-streets/2015/01/23/dd23ec5c-a282–11e4–9f89–561284a573f8_.story.html.

This influx of people resulted in an increase in demand for halal food, which was historically unavailable in western markets. The concept of a halal mark was foreign to everyone concerned. Because of where they had come from, newly arriving Muslims were used to their food being halal, while existing western industries had not historically needed to satisfy a demand for halal food. This means the halal label on food is a phenomena that is specific to western countries, rather than Muslim ones.

First generation Muslim immigrants were especially keen to maintain halal for their food products. Worries about the potential contamination of permitted meats with forbidden ones, such as pork, led to many buying their meats from Jewish butchers. The parallels between halal and kosher meats came to the fore here.

This suggests that the halal mark on food is a phenomenon exclusive to Western countries, than just Muslim countries (Jia & Chaozhi, 2021).

First-generation Muslim immigrants were particularly eager to keep their food items halal. Concerns over the possible contamination of permissible foods with banned meats, such as pork, prompted many people to purchase their meat from Jewish butchers. The similarities between halal and kosher meats are highlighted here.

Figure 2.2. The Halal Guys—A Taste of New York City.

Source: https://sites.psu.edu/coolpt3/2016/04/06/the-halal-guys/.

Meat, which had formerly been saved for important events, became a standard of the Muslim diet during this time period, and demand for halal items increased. Islamic butcher shops began to open in the 1970s, particularly in France.These stores, which were mostly run by families, were not common, but they gave Muslims greater power over the food they ate. The fact that such butcher shops were operated by Muslims was always enough of an assurance of halal that a label was not needed.

2.3. THE MOVE TOWARDS ACCEPTANCE OF HALAL FOOD

As the 1990s progressed, the overall shape of smaller halal butcher shops with no labeling persisted. However, the 1990s saw the emergence of many food crises, the two most serious of which were the spread of foot-and-mouth disease and mad cow disease.

This resulted in increased public demand to boost the standard of western meat from both Muslims and western customers. For the first time, western slaughterhouses began to outfit themselves with the required equipment to provide halal meat (Ismail et al., 2018).There were missteps and this brought a degree of industrialisation to what had formerly been a ceremonial butchering method. However, the growing popularity of the halal approach resulted in the adoption of halal certification, which gave Muslims the confidence to buy meat from conventional suppliers as well as the small butcher shops that had previously served them.

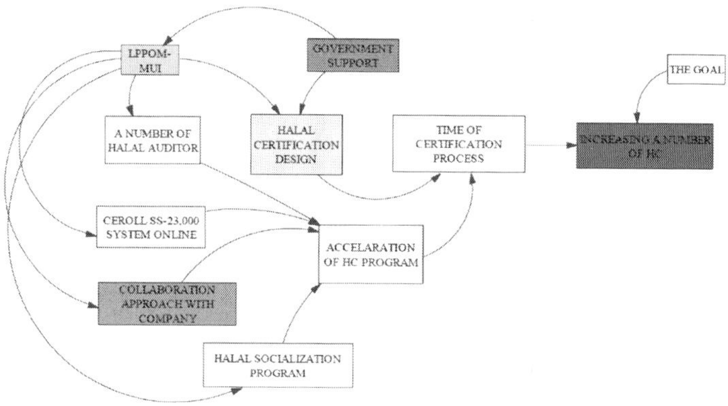

Figure 2.3. Thinking Model of Halal Certification Design.

Source: https://www.researchgate.net/figure/Thinking-Model-of-Halal-Certification-Design-Adopt-from-Nusran-2013_fig1_320010503.

2.4. THE CURRENT DAY

Today, the popularity of halal in the food industry has resulted in increased legislation to ensure that goods bearing the halal certification actually follow the regulations. Malaysia recently obtained a commitment from the Food and Agriculture Organization of the United Nations (FAO) to develop more strict halal guidance.

Figure 2.4. Food and Agriculture Organization.

Source: https://en.wikipedia.org/wiki/Food_and_Agriculture_Organization.

As a result, the halal mark is now almost as likely to appear on jewelry, cosmetics, and anything that interacts with your body as it is on meat.

All foods and drinks originating from seeds, herbs, fruits, and animals are halal, with the exception of a few that contain toxin that is harmful to humans.

The general theory is that there is no ban on eating halal food regardless of its verdict; everything is originally halal. Any prohibited objects are explained in the Quran. "He has only prohibited to you dead creatures, hair, swine meat, and that which has been devoted to other than Allah," the Almighty said. But there is no sin on him who is forced, neither desiring nor transgressing. Indeed, "Allah is Merciful and Forgiving" (al-Baqarah 173). They were bodies, blood, pork, and slaughtered animals for those who did not have the name God, strangled, beaten, fell, and ordained, and attacked by wild animals, for animals slaughtered, and slaughtered animals offered to idols.

Haram drink includes all intoxicating beverages, whether made from halal or non-kosher ingredients (Abdul Malik Kamal on Fiqhu al-Sunnah li an-Nisaa'). There is halal food by itself, but it is sometimes haram due to external care conditions (for others). Materially, all halal ingredients are halal foods. Haram foods are any foods that are legally prohibited according to islam. As for the halal and how to get it, it is true in searching and getting it, not in a haram or incorrect fashion. Food is haram because it is obtained illegally, such as by usury, burglary, robbery, bribery, corruption, and other criminal activities, despite the fact that it is often permitted.

There is one certainty in the development of the laws governing what is halal (permitted) food and drink for the Islamic faithful, as per the writers of Halal Food: A History (Oxford University Press, 2018), and that is that there are no constants. Islamic jurists have discussed, modified, and revised Halal standards to adapt to the changing needs of the Islamic faithful around the world.

Figure 2.5. Febe Armanios and Boaç Ergene.

Source: https://thecchp.com/2019/01/27/interview-with-dr-armanios/.

Febe Armanios and Boaç Ergene (both history professors at Middlebury College and the University of Vermont) referred to this theme in their lecture, demonstrating how halal laws have been recognized, perceived, and debated throughout history. The Quran, Islam's holy text, is the basis of what is halal, which means lawful or acceptable, and what is haram, which means prohibited. The controversy about dietary permissibility emerges because the Quran verses dealing with halal and haram are often ambiguous and sparse in detail. Muslim leaders needing guidance looked to the Prophet Muhammad's hadiths to help explain and establish the food laws (Ab Talib et al., 2016).

Intoxicants are a perfect example of how Islamic leaders revisited and reinterpreted halal laws to meet the needs of the moment. Although alcohol is seen as a harmful influence on the mind, body, and spirit, it is not expressly forbidden in the Quran; in fact, alcohol is presented as a blessing from Allah in verses 16:65–67 of the Quran. Nonetheless, the psychologically corrosive effects of intoxicants have led many to believe that all alcohol is haram. A current issue concerns goods containing low amounts – mostly naturally occurring – of alcohol, which has resulted in different views of whether they are permitted. Some people claim that anything that intoxicates is illegal.

This would include pure vanilla extract and, probably, nabidh, a drink made from mashed dates fermented for three days and claimed to have been consumed by the Prophet. Jurists on the other side of the argument just object to fermented grapes (i.e., wine) and drugs that produce intoxicating properties over time (such as nabidh). Current debates center on ingredients with small quantities of alcohol, such as kombucha and soy sauce.

The study of halal dietary and slaughter laws naturally brings to mind Jewish customs, and there are also parallels and variations. Both forbid the use of blood and swine, but beef and other bovines are permitted. Jewish rules, on the other hand, are more stringent in terms of food slaughter, planning, and intake. Unlike many orthodox Jews, who do not allow halal meat to be kosher, Muslims generally support all kosher meat items.

Furthermore, although all approaches to slaughter have the primary purpose of showing benevolence for the victim, kosher rules are very strict on who should perform the killing (i.e., an educated, observant male Jew), while Islam is far more tolerant on this issue, which is the key reason halal meat is refused by orthodox Jews (Indrasari et al., 2020).

The event's title reflected the fact that halal food has unquestionably become big business. In their travels around the world, both authors have seen a rise in the popularity of halal goods, as well as the proliferation of halal eateries, most noticeably in New York, where the Halal Guys food trucks have become a common fixture in the area, often creating long lines of hungry munchers down the street.

Although paying close attention to the engaging conversation, the audience was free to enjoy the vintage wine on offer at the function, as well as aylan, a drink made with Turkish yogurt mixed with water, salt, and mint, without taking sides in the intoxicant dispute.

Marinated lamb morsels from New Harlem Halal Meat legs were served with smooth hummus, pita, and smoky baba ganoush, both of which can be found at some of the city's halal food trucks. Sticky soft baklava and crumbly pistachio cookies completed the menu. The baklava came from Kalustyan's, a Middle Eastern specialty shop built in the 1940s on Lexington Avenue in what is now known as "Curry Hill."

Figure 2.6. New Harlem Halal Meat – Butcher.

Source: https://www.yelp.ca/biz/new-harlem-halal-meat-new-york.

Armanios and Ergene showed that many halal laws are a living, functioning code rather than a rigid doctrine, and that they evolve over time in response to new challenges as well as technical and social advances. More telling is their assumption that the word halal has come to be associated with a cuisine and has developed into a western food shining example.

Figure 2.7. A halal sign in Chinese (清真 qīng zhēn) at a restaurant in Taipei, Taiwan.

Source: https://en.wikipedia.org/wiki/Halal.

Halal packaged foods and beverages are available from a variety of food companies, including halal foie gras, spring rolls, chicken nuggets, ravioli, lasagna, pizza, and baby food. Formal paraphrase Halal ready meals are a rising target market for Muslims in the United Kingdom and the United States, and they are being sold by an increasing number of retailers. If it does not consume alcohol, vegetarian food is halal.

Pork is the most popular example of haram (non-halal) food. Though pork is the only meat that Muslims are prohibited from eating (the Quran prohibits it), other foods that are not pure are often called haram. The requirements for non-pork products include their origin, the cause of death, and how the animal was handled. The majority of Islamic scholars consider shellfish and other seafood halal (Henderson, 2016).

Shellfish and other seafood are considered halal by the vast majority of Islamic scholars.

Muslims must also guarantee that all foods (especially packaged foods) and non-food products such as cosmetics and pharmaceuticals are halal. Regularly, these items contain animal by-products or other additives that Muslims are not permitted to use or apply to their bodies. Blood and intoxicants such as alcoholic drinks are not deemed halal for Muslims to drink. If there is no halal food accessible, a Muslim who would otherwise starve to death is permitted to consume non-halal food. On airplanes, Muslims typically order kosher food (if halal food is not available).

Opinions on GMO ingredients vary, although there is no universally agreed ban against eating them. Some clerics and academics have voiced approval, claiming that certain food processing practices are halal because they benefit human well-being. Opponents of GMOs contend that there is no need for genetically modified food crops because God made it completely and man has no right to control anything that God has created. Others also expressed concerns about the possible intake of particular GMO foods made from pig genetics.

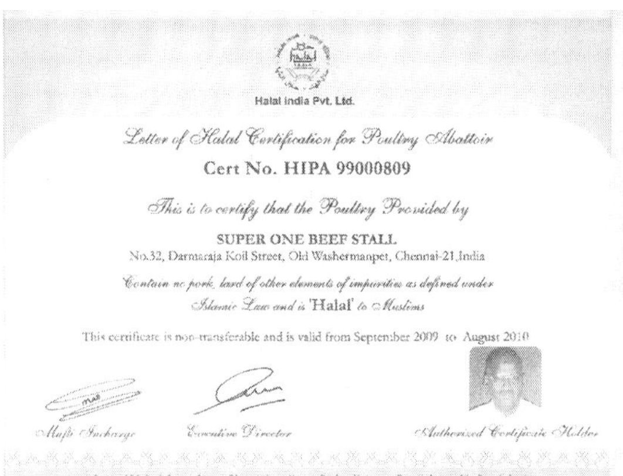
Halal India Pvt. Ltd.

Letter of Halal Certification for Poultry Abattoir

Cert No. HIPA 99000809

This is to certify that the Poultry Provided by

SUPER ONE BEEF STALL

No.32, Darmaraja Koil Street, Old Washermanpet, Chennai-21,India

Contain no pork, lard of other elements of impurities as defined under Islamic Law and is 'Halal' to Muslims

This certificate is non-transferable and is valid from September 2009 to August 2010

Mufti Incharge Executive Director Authorized Certificate Holder

Figure 2.8. An example of a halal certificate from India.

Source: https://en.wikipedia.org/wiki/Halal.

Anti-halal advocacy organizations and individuals on social media have opposed halal food certification, claiming that it amounts to customers subsidizing a specific religious ideology. In July 2014, Keysar Trad, spokesperson for the Australian Federation of Islamic Councils, told a reporter that this was an effort to capitalize on anti-Muslim feelings.

2.5. HALAL FOOD AS A BUSINESS

According to the Dubai Chamber of Commerce, the total business volume of halal food products sales was $1.1 trillion in 2013, accounting for 16.6% of the global food and beverage market and rising at a 6.9% annual rate. [20] Formalized paraphrase Indonesia ($197 million in market valuation in 2012) and Turkey ($100 million) are two emerging markets. The European Union market for halal food is expected to be worth $30 billion and to expand at a rate of about 15% per year. About $8 billion of this total is paid for in France.

The halal food and drink business has also greatly influenced supermarkets and other food businesses including restaurants. In 2011, French supermarkets sold $210 million in halal food, a 10.5% increase over the previous year. The demand for halal foods in France is much higher than the market for other varieties of common foods. In France, for example, the demand for halal foods and drinks was almost double that of organic foods in 2010 (Hanzaee & Ramezani, 2011). Auchan, a major French supermarket chain, now carries 80 licensed halal meat brands, as well as 30 pre-cooked halal meals and 40 frozen halal products. Halal ingredients have now been added to the menus of high end restaurants and food service. Many soda firms like Evian have even tried to apply a halal label to their merchandise, showing that their water and other drinks are clean, not harmful or prohibited under Islamic law.

Figure 2.9. Halal meat section at a grocery store in Canada.

Source: https://en.wikipedia.org/wiki/Halal.

2.6. HISTORY OF HALAL FOOD IN THE WEST

The halal food market is a relatively new phenomenon. From the 1960s onwards, as immigrant Muslim communities began to settle in the West, particularly in France, demand for halal meat increased. In the 1990s, a new breed of 'Muslim shoppers' emerged, who were conscious of what they put on their plates. Specialist butchers began to develop locally, then the product range diversified and globalized within the agri-food business. As previously said, halal has evolved into a commercial quality mark.

Figure 2.10. Martin Bureau – Halal sweets in a supermarket in Paris, 2013.

Source: https://www.alimentarium.org/en/knowledge/history-halal-market-west.

2.6.1. History of Halal in America

According to Dinar Standard, the American Muslim population in 2010 was between 5.8 million and 6.7 million, including 1.7 million to 2 million families, and gross Muslim discretionary cash was between USD107 billion and USD124 billion. The profiles of American Muslim buyers are also more appealing, as they are younger than the state median and have similar levels of education and income as the average American household. The threat and potential presented by the vast regional heterogeneity of the American Muslim market is a significant dynamic.

With their current national outlets and networks, mainstream national chains, stores, and brands that have not yet interacted with this demographic are well placed to meet the regional challenge. According to Dinar Standard, fifteen states in the United States account for roughly 85% of the total

Muslim population in the country. California, New York, Texas, Illinois, New Jersey, Michigan, Pennsylvania, Maryland, Virginia, Georgia, Ohio, Massachusetts, Florida, Connecticut, and North Carolina are the fifteen states mentioned in highest to lower order of Muslim population size (Han et al., 2021).

Another important feature of the American Muslim market is the significant presence of ethnic and indigenous sub-clusters, as well as the effect of immigration cycles on customer behavior, networks, and tastes. Marketers should be aware that within major ethnic groups of American Muslims, there is a large network of media coverage, organizations, gatherings, clustered mosques, Islamic centers, and commodity factors (e.g., ethnic food) that affects their purchasing decisions. Each sub-cluster also successfully communicates with national and native Muslim outlets in the United States.

Arab, South Asian (Pakistani, Indian, and Bangladeshi ancestry), African American, and Caucasian Americans are the most numerous ethnic groups in the United States, with significant Turkic, Latino, European, Sub-Saharan African, Afghan, Iranian, and East Asian minorities. The USA Halal Chamber of Commerce, Corporation was established and licensed in 1997 by Habib D. Ghanim, Sr., the co-founder and CEO. He was in control of all paperwork relating to deliveries going to the Middle East that required authorization from the Arab Embassies while serving as a licensing officer at the US Arab Chamber of Commerce in the 1990s.

Around this time, he started to receive several inquiries regarding the veracity of arguments that certain items were Halal (mostly meat and poultry). It was also during this point, around 1995, when he started to promote awareness so that people knew more about Halal goods and where to buy them. Over the next few years, envoys from Malaysia and Singapore visited the United States, and interest in halal grew, which is when Mr. Ghanim made the decision to officially begin accreditation and founded the USA Halal Chamber of Commerce, Inc.

As the industry grew, a group of Halal certification bodies agreed to join an alliance to support halal certification policies and guidelines. This resulted in the establishment of the World Halal Council in Jakarta, Indonesia, in 1999. Certification authorities from North America, Europe, Africa, the Middle East, and Asia comprised this community.

As the industry expanded in the early 2000s, so did the rules governing halal standards. What started as a raw meat and poultry industry soon expanded into other fields like frozen foods, cosmetics, and pharmaceuticals fields (Debney, 2016).

This resulted in international associations and governments recognizing and accrediting halal recognition agencies, increasing transparency. We were accredited by the GCC Accreditation Center (GAC) in 2017 and the Emirate International Accreditation Center (EIAC) in 2019. (EIAC).

The Islamic Society of the Washington Area, a local mosque, supported the USA Halal Chamber of Commerce, Inc. in 2005, and it started doing business as the ISWA Halal Certification Department. Both the mosque and the chamber are and have always been independent legal bodies, and they remain so to this day.

In our ongoing mission to help and encourage halal goods and services, we actually engage in several activities each year, including World Halal Day on Ramadan 17th, as well as many exhibitions and industry events both in the US and globally.

As the halal industry grows and expands, so do the legislation, which is why we stay up to date on and engage in coaching on all related requirements from ISO, UAE, GSO, Malaysia, SMIIC, Egypt, and Singapore, among others. Porcine and other testing is now required by all businesses pursuing halal certification.

The department is expected to be at the frontline to follow the highest standards on all halal products, ensuring that everyone who uses a product approved by us will have complete assurance that they are using products with no doubt about their halal certification.

2.6.2. Halal Food Brands in the US

The United States, though still behind Europe in terms of the size of its halal food market, has many good examples in the halal food arena. Saffron Road, a quality organic packaged food company, is one such popular halal brand. During Ramadan 2011, Saffron Road effectively unveiled its line of halal frozen meals at Whole Foods Market. Whole Foods Market and Saffron Road collaborated on a large-scale social media initiative to increase awareness to Muslim customers about the event. The web campaign featured guest posts on the Whole Foods Market blog by the Muslim blog of Saffron Road's marketing affiliate "My Halal Kitchen," as well as competitions on My Halal Kitchen blog.

Figure 2.11. New Line of Halal Bread and Buns For The American Market.

Source: https://www.worldbakers.com/product/new-line-of-halal-bread-and-buns-for-the-american-market/.

A small group of outspoken anti-Muslim bloggers chastised Whole Foods for bringing a halal brand and "celebrating" Ramadan, which was to be anticipated. Instead of drawing attention away from its affiliation with Saffron Road, Whole Foods remained strong in its willingness to support Saffron Road's brand, and both Whole Foods and Saffron Road were awarded for their steadfastness with improved brand recognition and profits at Whole Foods Market (Damit et al., 2018).

2.7. HISTORY OF HALAL IN EUROPE

Demographics of European Muslims In 2009, Europe had a population of about 735 million people (not including Turkey). While Muslims are expected to make up 5% to 8% of Europe's population, they have a very high relative population increase as compared to the broader (non-Muslim) population. According to accredited sources, there were nearly 38 million (5%) Muslims in Europe in 2009. 3 This calculation is obtained by using census statistics (usually older) as a benchmark and then making the cautious presumption that the Muslim population increased at the same rate as the rest of the population. Regrettably, this hypothesis is inaccurate.

Multiple polls, national studies, and academic sources indicate that the Muslim population is increasing at a much faster pace than the general population, especially in Europe. According to a 2004–08 census by The Office of National Statistics, the Muslim community in the United Kingdom rose ten times faster (6.68%) than the rest of the population. This rise has been due to globalization, a higher birth rate of Muslims, and Muslim conversions. According to Euromonitor's 2008 report, Europe's Muslim population grew at a rate of 140% between 1995 and 2005.

DinarStandard estimates Europe's Muslim population in 2009 to be about 54 million, or 7.4% of the total population. The ten countries with the most Muslims in Europe account for 90% of all Muslims in Europe. Russia has the largest Muslim community, with 26 million people (19% of total population.) Following Russia, France (6 million) and Germany (4.1 million) have the largest projected Muslim populations. France has the greatest population of Muslims among the five Western European countries, accounting for 10.1% of the country. A main difference between Western and Eastern European Muslims is that the Western European Muslim community is predominantly made up of new immigrants from South Asia, North Africa, and Turkey, while the Eastern Muslim population is almost exclusively made up of people of indigenous descent.

Halal meat markets in Europe are currently witnessing learning and expansion, though the intensity varies by region. Year on year growth has been occurring in the United Kingdom and France for well over a decade, while the demand in Germany is only getting started (Cuesta-Valiño et al., 2020).

The expansion of these markets is related to the number of Muslim migrants in Europe, as well as the rising intake of meat, which is a sign of vertical migration among second and third generation Muslims. Halal meat and halal animal products are becoming more widely available in non-ethnic stores, especially grocery chains and fast food restaurants, and, just as Jewish restaurants in the United States attract a significant number of non-Jewish customers, so halal meat product intake by non-Muslims is growing across Europe.

2.7.1. United Kingdom

The Muslim community in the United Kingdom is diverse, with the vast majority having origin in South Asia, specifically Pakistan, Bangladesh, and India. The population has expanded exponentially over the past decade, rising by more than 500,000 to about 2.4 million between 2004 and 2008, a rate ten times higher than the rest of population. The demand for halal meat is also expanding rapidly, with the Halal Food Authority (HFA), the only halal credentialing agency in the UK, forecasting a 30% increase in 2006.

Nevertheless, there is still considerable skepticism about purchasing fresh halal meat in supermarkets, and it is reported that 70–80% of all halal meat in the UK is false. While things are changing as grocery sales rise, many Muslims continue to tend to purchase fresh meat from independent retailers, who are seen as providing confidence in the wake of increasing questions about the validity of commercial types of halal meat that have arisen alongside consumer expansion.

The HFA, as the UK's largest and most influential certification body, has been at the center of much of the recent discussion and uncertainty sparked by business growth. The Halal Food Authority (HFA) was established in 1994 to govern halal meat by slaughterhouse licensing, at a time when halal was becoming a significant part of Islamic heritage in the United Kingdom. Previously, many Muslims believed that meat sold in western retail stores was processed by people of the Book and thus fit for ingestion.

2.7.2. France

France has Europe's biggest Muslim community. Official sources estimated that there were four million French Muslims in 2000, but a total of seven million has lately been proposed. The majority of French Muslims have links to the Maghreb region of North Africa, but there are also large concentrations from West Africa and Turkey. The French industry for halal meat has been slowly developing since the 1970s, but it has expanded exponentially in the last decade, just like the UK market, as halal has become fundamental to the religious and cultural perceptions of many young Muslims.

Figure 2.12. French supermarkets tap rising demand for halal food.

Source: https://www.dw.com/en/french-supermarkets-tap-rising-demand-for-halal-food/a-5469090.

Unlike in the UK, where the large proportion of halal slaughter is done with pre-stunning, most halal slaughter in France is conducted without stunning. Despite these distinctions, the issues that have arisen as the halal sector has grown are quite similar; market growth is currently expected to be about 15% a year, with a market size of between 3 and 5 billion euros. According to study subjects, calls for improved qualification have also increased over this time span, and this pattern is mirrored in the marketing campaigns of French supermarkets and fast food outlets, as it is in the UK.

The French industry is vast and difficult to describe, and there is common belief that it is in disarray. Consumers are constantly being cautioned against unlabeled halal meat, with reports claiming that up to 90% of commercial halal meat is false. Certification is often offered as a solution to these issues, but it is claimed that there are up to 50 different halal marks and certification systems in use across France (Bergeaud-Blackler, 2015).

2.7.3. Germany

Germany has a population of over 82 million people, with over 4% of them being Muslims of mostly Turkish descent. The German halal meat industry is still in its youth relative to the UK and French markets, despite the fact that things are beginning to improve. Public worries over animal rights have prompted supermarket chains Aldi and Lidl to consider the ramifications of selling halal meat, reigniting debate over the validity of commercial types of halal meat. As a result, as an official from Germany's major certification body, the Halal Quality Control (HQC) www.hqc.eu and European Halal Certification Institute (EHZ) found out, because German consumers are not too anxious about the development of the halal market at the moment, debate about the merits of pre-stunned and non-stunned meat has not emerged to the same extent as it has done in the United States.

Although the German industry is still stunted in comparison to the UK and French markets, foreign manufacturers and certification organizations are beginning to pay more attention to it.

German businesses will be well served to accept the halal industry, according to the German Federation of Turkish Wholesalers and Retailers, although the Malaysian National News Agency Bernama has also highlighted the opportunities the German market offers Malaysian manufacturers. The length of time it takes for the industry to develop as it has elsewhere continues to be determined by the number of halal investors who take advantage of these resources and the continuing effort to promote halal quality control.

2.7.4. Norway

The majority of Norway's 72,000 Muslims live in Oslo; the bulk are of Pakistani descent, though Somalia influx has dramatically upped. Norwegian animal care laws are generally considered as the best in the world; unlike the EU, where a violation of EU regulations for the safety of livestock at the time of slaughter requires ethnic communities to conduct stunning without slaughter in accordance with their own traditional processes all animals must be stunned pre-slaughter under Norwegian law.

While the Jewish community continues to import kosher meat to avoid the strict regulations, cooperation between the Muslim community and the Norwegian food authority has encouraged a continuing halal benchmarking initiative that has benefited all parties involved. In contrast to the EU countries mentioned above, Norway's grocery industry is horizontally rather than vertically oriented with producers and farmer's cooperatives dominant rather than supermarkets. Nortura, a farmer's association, is Norway's largest producer of halal meat.

Nortura sells halal meat butchered animals and cuts in the supermarket, but they also distribute packaged halal goods under their own-label halal brand Alfathi, which they bought outright from a Somali entrepreneur in 2006. Leading up to this, Alfathi's operator collaborated with the Norwegian Islamic Council to develop a butchering system that was acceptable to all Muslim communities and approved by the Norwegian Food Safety Authority (Battour & Ismail, 2016). This was a daunting challenge since the latter was not involved in conversation, and it took more than two years to persuade Norway's Imams that Alfathi halal was reliable.

After a small group of Imams visited Nortura's slaughterhouse to examine processing processes, both parties decided on a method of slaughter. With Imams acting as halal meat certifiers in their own communities, faith grew, and a limited selection of packaged halal goods started showing up in Norwegian supermarkets. While there are concerns that the invasion of the European market and the advent of a more diverse Muslim community—adhering to various schools of thinking—will disrupt the country's high animal welfare requirements and threaten the halal norm, discussion has occurred in recent years, especially over the inclusion of halal chicken into the Norwegian market.

2.8. HALAL FOOD BRANDS IN EUROPE

The total value of the European halal food industry is expected to be between USD55 and USD65 billion (including Russia). Western Europe's Muslim community is mostly made up of refugees, making it a more appealing demographic in terms of halal consumer needs. Major European brands are growing their halal offers after realizing the financial benefits of reaching Muslim customers. Tesco, a British supermarket chain, has halal meat branches in 27 of its locations.

It offers halal chicken, mutton, lamb, and beef, as well as National Halal Center sausages, burgers, and roast beef. In its Turkish plant, Haribo, a German multinational confectionery firm that makes gummy bears and other sweets, manufactures licensed halal gummy bears and soft candy. Dr. Oetker, Muller, Pfanni, Storck, and Maggi are among the other German labels that sell halal product lines. For years, international food giants such as Nestle and Unilever have sold halal-certified products

Their goods are approved by the Halal Control Authority, which also accredits commodities from Nestle, Langnese, Elbmilch, and Pfanni, among other major European food producers. Nestle makes more money from its halal brands than it does from its organic line.

Figure 2.13. Listing of Halal Certification Agencies & Organization.

Source: https://myhalalkitchen.com/listing-of-halal-certification-agencies-organizations/.

2.8.1. Segmentations of the Halal Market

Halal refers not only to food but also to other finished items such as toiletries, pharmaceuticals and nutraceuticals, cosmetics, and utilities such as tourism and finance. Originally, the idea of halal was overlooked since most countries were food self-sufficient. Non-Muslim countries are leading the trade in processed food and traditionally halal goods as a result of world trade and shifting lifestyles. Presently, halal certification of halal goods provides a level of verification, and can be granted by any of over 100 halal certification bodies around the world (The Halal Journal, 2008).

Each organization has its own collection of halal rules and standards. When crossing national borders, the fragmentation is exacerbated since there is currently no working mechanism for mutual recognition between countries. Due to a lack of adequate certification regulations, non-halal produce has found its way into the plates of Muslim families (IslamOnline.net, 2006).

2.8.2. Emergence of the Muslim Consumer in the West

Items with the halal stamp were once only seen in non-Muslim countries as a socioeconomic anomaly. Common practice continued to take precedence over Islamic orthodoxy among refugees from North Africa who settled in France, for example. First-generation immigrants were particularly concerned with preserving their homeland's cultures and culinary practices. While the Quran does not prohibit consuming meat cooked by 'People of the Book' (Jews and Christians), Christians' food was regarded as suspect and possibly 'contaminated' by interaction or mixing with illegal items such as pork. As a result, the first Muslim refugees purchased their meat from Jewish butchers. Meat intake grew as their quality of life in the host nation changed. Meat, which had formerly been intended for special events (such as the Eid al-Adha festival), became a symbol of social and financial prosperity and was eaten on a regular basis. As a consequence of these new eating practices, Muslim butcher shops rose in popularity. In the 1970s, they were often owned by individuals, and the mainstream culture branded them as racial and exotic markets.

The butcher's personal integrity as a religious member was enough to ensure that the meat was halal. 'Muslim customers' were gradually seen as being able to influence their bodies and sense of belongingness through what they placed on their plates (Bashir et al., 2019).

2.8.3. Industrialization of Standards

Health crises like mad cow disease and foot-and-mouth disease pushed the beef production industry to concentrate more on ceremonial slaughter in the 1990s, under public pressure for more assurances. Meat prices dropped, quality rose, and abattoirs were outfitted to produce halal meat. The introduction of halal into the industrial chain had ramifications, as what had formerly been a mere religious slaughtering method was transformed into a regulated procedure subject to sanitation and quality requirements. The number of halal certifying agents has grown to several hundred in recent years.The market for an international halal standard has increased, partly as a result of the inflexible food product assurances between non-Muslim and Muslim countries in international trade.

2.8.4. Halal Certificate and the FAO

Given that Islamic law is inconsistent with liberal commercial law, Malaysia, which hosts the World Halal Forum, a gathering of halal food industry stakeholders, obtained a commitment from the United Nations' Food and Agriculture Organization (FAO) to provide recommendations for the use of the word halal in the Codex Alimentarius to prevent it from being misused. Halal has also expanded beyond meat products to include water, candy, cosmetics, and pharmaceuticals, among other things, as an international practice. It mostly affects everything that comes into contact with the body, since power of the body is an important aspect of the expression of faith.

2.8.5. Halal Product Guarantee (Halal History in Indonesia, Malaysia and Other Parts of Asia)

"Consumers anywhere, in all countries, have universal social rights," are according to the UN Consumer Protection Guidelines of 1985. These fundamental rights include the right to direct, accurate, and equal facts, as well as the right to compensation and basic human needs. As a result, the global community's universal right to know and receive food, drinks, and products in compliance with their values becomes a fundamental right granted by the state. The Republic of Indonesia's Constitution of 1945 mandates that every person be able to practice his or her own faith and worship in accordance with his or her own beliefs (Al-Ansi & Han, 2019).

As a result, guaranteeing Halal goods to Indonesian Muslims is part of the people's human rights, which the state must encourage because halal intake and use is a part of Muslim worship. Given the rapid advancements in science and technology in the areas of health, medicine, and cosmetics, the assurance of halal goods is critical. The change in the production and use of fundamental materials from what was once plain and normal to the processing and use of raw materials generated by science has had a significant impact.

It is indeed worth noting that, prior to the advent of modern fast food processing technologies, the general perception of haram was already a very simplistic term. Just the appearance or absence of substances containing pork or alcohol determines if food or drink is halal or haram. Halal food and beverages are those that are free of all posts. But, from this viewpoint, food processing technology has advanced and improved since the manufacture of consumer products needed not only main ingredients, but also supplementary ingredients.

Producers must guarantee that Halal and good processing practices are used in the manufacturing process, which ensures the raw materials must be valid and good for customer use. Manufactured goods must be free of biological, chemical, physical, and haram degradation in order to do this. Clean equipment and locations must be used in the manufacturing process to prevent contamination. The use of supplementary components in the manufacturing process must also be in compliance with the requirements. The Indonesia Ulema Council (MUI) was the first to receive Halal certification in order to protect Muslim food from haram pollution from essential ingredients.

This conclusion was reached in a study revealed the presence of pig products in a variety of food and beverage products. This observation was first recorded in the Canopy Bulletin in January 1988, and it quickly became well-known. In this situation, prices of food and beverage goods dropped by 80%, resulting in a drop in national economic development and Muslim outrage in Indonesia. After the government accepted a Halal accredited by the MUI, the condition changed.

The MUI was only concerned about whether the substance included the basic elements of haram content, not with the question of haram external influences, implying that this practice is illegal under Islamic law. This assumes that the unified knowledge unit only looks at the fundamental components of food, alcohol, consumer products, and other applications, not how they are obtained. Halal goods, according to the MUI standard, are those that comply with Islamic law's Halal requirements:

1) No pigs or pig-derived components;
2) No haram products, such as ingredients derived from human organs, blood, or dirt;
3) All products extracted from halal animals slaughtered in compliance with Islamic Shariah protocols;
4) All substances derived from halal animals should be used and butchered in accordance with Islamic law, all storage places, and treatment organizations. Whether a pig or other hemp is used to facilitate the move, it must be washed in accordance with Islamic law.
5) Any of all foods and drinks that isn't alcoholic. MUI issues declarations (fatwas) to ensure the product's authenticity. Fatwas should be issued such that Halal certificates can be issued following review and scrutiny. Auditors perform studies and audits of Halal-certified factories (companies).

The following tests were carried out: (I) a detailed study of the product's products, including raw materials or prevailing materials; (II) a review of the textbook on the procurement of the product materials.

To achieve the test, these samples are analysed in the laboratory, specifically for compounds suspected of being impure or having impurity. The findings of the Institute of Food, Drug, and Cosmetic Evaluation's inspection and audit were then documented in a recording and news case. The case was then submitted to the Ulema Council's Fatwa Committee for a decision (MUI 2008). To guarantee the halal of a commodity that has received a halal certificate, MUI says that if it is discovered in the future that the product includes raw or impure products, the Halal certificate granted by the Council of Ulema will be revoked.

MUI aims to combine the two principles into "healthy halal" in the context of theory and experience in order to maintain commodity halal. The way of demonstrating that the sentence is correct, whether in the form of drugs, cosmetics, meats, or beverages, by sending specialists to visit the place of manufacturing of items ranging from raw materials to systems and practices, so that they know precisely what is filled in the components of the product from the cooking process of raw ingredients to the procurement of goods. In Indonesia, it has taken a couple of decades to grant Halal certificates.

However, relative to Malaysia and Thailand, the trend was less serious over time. Indonesia's competitiveness in the growth of Southeast Asia's Halal agricultural industry is sixth, higher than that of the Philippines alone. Just demand growth considerations, Halal inspection schemes, certification bodies, and raw material supply distinguish Indonesia. Indonesia is positioned under other countries in terms of logistical networks, government commitments and strategies, and diplomatic and domestic lobbying capacities. Despite the existence of Act No. 33 of 2014 on Halal Products Assurance, policy enforcement efficacy remains limited (Adekunle & Filson, 2020).

Since government rules were not official, the Halal Products Assurance Agency was not yet functional. The introduction of the Halal food policy has not been widely distributed in society, primarily among the food industry, which is the primary producer.

The application of Islamic teachings is linked to staying true to halal and away from haram. Halal refers to something that is permissible, while Haram refers to something that is prohibited by God Almighty. As a result, the life of obligatory conformity is accompanied by Allah Almighty's orders to stay away from all prohibited objects.

In Islam, food, drink, and products include components of worship that are closely linked to the halal and haram issues. While the Quran mentions a number of items that are practically forbidden for use, Halal certification is used in Indonesia and other countries because it is based on the precautionary principle. This is the percentage of consumer products that are expected to use raw products or a combination of undesirable or impure products. Indonesia has taken part in international treaties, the 1945 Constitution, and state attorney laws. MUI has earned a Halal stamp, ensuring that the country has access to halal foods, drinks, and materials. MUI has also developed halal guidelines based on Islamic law. After that, a review and analysis was performed in order to grant a fatwa and then a Halal certificate. In Indonesia, halal certification was not fully used due to a lack of political integration and insufficient facilities and resources.

Halal goes beyond conventional industry-sector borders, as well as regional, ethnic, and religious ones. From a commercial standpoint, the halal market unquestionably presents a variety of appealing possibilities. When many existing markets hit saturation, a new competition focused on halal ideals and ideals emerges, effectively establishing a modern economic model.

This is led by the food and beverage industry, but it has increasingly spread into the pharmaceutical, cosmetic, and personal-care industries, thanks to rising customer recognition and a keen eye for new business opportunities. As Malaysia is a key mover in the halal market, this industry is battling and striving to grab the specific customer segment with morals, ethics, and confidence. Since Halal is a 'farm-to-fork' mechanism that extends all the way into the supply chain, storage of goods, distribution, and logistics both play a role in ensuring and illustrating Halal compliance.

Consumers are becoming more worried about halal issues, and they want the finished product to be healthy to eat. The Halal market is a complicated and fractured Rubik's cube of flexible and changing distinguishing criteria. Variables based on cultural assumptions, behaviors, and tastes, differing legal views, and the multinational structure of food commodity supply chains all contribute to the challenge. The Halal industry is constantly shaped and pushed to new developmental stages, from consumer knowledge to technical advances.

In response to this trend, the Malaysian government is concentrating on growing halal goods in order to establish Malaysia as a global halal center. One of the biggest victories was when the United Nations designated Malaysian Halal Certification, which is intended to appeal to the halal products industries, as the world's best example for halal food standardization in 1997. Malaysia is well poised to make a significant contribution in the growth of the halal food industry as a respectable Islamic country that is tolerant and inclusive, with more than 3500 food companies and average productivity of more than USD 9 billion (Abderahman et al., 2021).

Malaysia has created special zones to attract more international and domestic investments in the cultivation and processing of food products, with the aim of being a global hub for halal food production. Malaysia, which is known for fighting for the protection of Muslims' interests, has successfully implemented a series of halal systems that have received international attention. Many parties, including non-Muslim countries, have introduced Malaysia's Islamic banking and financial structure, as well as other financial goods dependent on Islamic law.

The nation's progress in accelerating the development of the halal system in the food industry should be fully exploited by the business and production community, especially small enterprises who are primarily engaged in the agricultural and food sectors. Entrepreneurs who own small businesses are the backbone of the country's economic base. The government actively supports the advancement of small businesses by offering a variety of plans, services, processes, and aid.

The creation of government institutions such as the Development Corporation for Small and Medium Enterprises and the Ministry of Entrepreneur Development, as well as policy plans such as the industrial master plan, initiative execution such as the supplier training program, and the formation of numerous entrepreneurship funds and venture capital, are only a few examples. Without a question, industry and entrepreneurship are difficult fields to enter.

To be successful in business, a variety of factors are required, including managerial skills, skilled staff, strong financial capital, goods and services, and, most importantly, a large and stable customer base. We will continue to explain the obstacles and solutions for market players in order to have a high sensitivity to their climate through researching the past of halal. Given the government's efforts to make Malaysia a Halal center, they can take advantage of this opportunity to determine the types of goods that draw a large demand.

2.9. HISTORY OF HALAL IN AFRICA

In view of the numerous conflicts, particularly between Muslims and Christians, anti-halal food protests have been led by Christian leaders in Africa, such as in Zimbabwe, where Muslims accounted for just 3% of the population in 1996 and only 2% in Swaziland in 2010. Deriving from these and other cases, it is clear that Christian resistance to halal food in African cultures is rooted in a variety of religious, economic, and political conditions correlated with halal food in Africa.

The fact that al-Shari'ah engagement on food is a determining factor aspect of their culture has never been different in Africa – in the past or present – from other Islamic societies.

The emphasis on this particular Africa, on the other hand, seems to be the most and most obvious phenomena. As a result, it has to be investigated further.

The theory of Totemism, which is commonly practiced in African culture and asserts the existence of a sacred divine bond between a tribe and a species of animal or plant, is the most possible reason for this occurrence.

Maybe what distinguishes Islam in Africa and its approach to traditional faiths is the widespread unity and equality among Muslims and others (Nehemia Levtzion, 1987), regardless of whether Muslims are the majority or minority, in reverence for religious freedom; rather, the maintenance and defense of religious rights was the prevailing basis in African tradition cultures (Oba, 2002).

This section depicts a picture of a harmonious partnership in the African world, based on what has been identified as a relationship commitment between African Islamic heritage and Islamic food devotion.

To put it another way, extrapolating the social experience of Africa reveals that Muslims' devotion to halal food has earned them acceptance from others, owing to their resolve not to violate this Muslim "sacred" religiousness.

A analysis of the Manza culture in central Africa, which is still dominated by tribal practices, provides current evidence of this matter.

In Ghana, investigator Akinbola reported the presence of peaceful, peaceful balance between Muslims and Christians in Tamale, in the north of the region, as well as social etiquette such as religious holidays. As per the researcher, holidays in this community should be defined as "traditional Christians and Muslims sharing meals and drinks during Christmas, Easter, Eid-EL Fitr, and Eid EL Adha." There is also well-known tradition in Africa, in which non-Muslims allocate the slaughter of their livestock to Muslim neighbors so that they can share the meal (Zulfakar et al., 2012).

It should also be remembered that such social contextual unity, as well as non-Muslims' concern for Muslims' rights and feelings about halal food, has led modern African communities to endow cattle butchering to Muslims in national and public slaughterhouses in most African countries, to the point where this practice has been solely confined to Muslims. In neither of the circumstances does this imply an infringement of the interests of the minority or the majority. Rather, it is the fact of social interaction that has emerged in Africa as a result of the sharing of works and social events, with the approval of non-Muslims, whether majority or minority.

Also in countries with significant Muslim minorities, such as Malawi (16%), Mozambique (13%), Uganda (12%), Swaziland (2%), and Botswana (1%), the situation remains stable (1%). It's possible that the Ethiopian social background is an exception to this law, where "Christians and Muslims do not eat together at all," as researcher Fekete puts it. This is plausible, though, given the traumatic past history that the Ethiopian Muslim people endured as a result of forced conversion to Christianity, as well as mandatory pork and alcohol intake.

When it is understood that pig is still a taboo for Ethiopian Christians since they are orthodox, the seriousness of the situation is underscored.

The halal meat crisis in Zimbabwe in 1996 was perhaps one of the most well-known political conflicts in which halal food became a source of contention between Christians and Muslims. This dispute was sparked by the anti-halal food movement of the Evangelical Fellowship of Zimbabwe (EFZ), a missionary organization, which requested that the government stop recruiting Muslim butchers to national slaughterhouses and urged Christians to reject halal meat. According to the editors of a dissent document, following Islamic rituals in the slaughter met the demands of just 2.3% of Zimbabwe's population, and to do so without the consent of the whole population was a blatant breach of human rights.

Moreover, halal meat is an Islamic religious commodity that, if funded and promoted, would likely contribute to the spread of Islam among Christian Zimbabweans, as well as Muslim domination of national and state bodies in the future.

Following that, Christian groups organized the Concerned Christians of Zimbabwe (CCZ), which was headed by some church leaders, to stage protests. Faced with such media campaigns and street marches, some Muslims attempted to clear the reality of the matter, claiming that the sharia slaughter system ensures food safety and health standards.

Church leaders said that their opposition was to the "prayer recited" on the animal as it was killed, which they described as basmalah (by the name of Allah). In response to this criticism, the Muslim Scholars Council pointed out that the rule of invoking Basmalah at slaughter was simply a reminder to those doing the slaughter to be kind to animals during slaughter, and that the employment of National Muslim butchers in abattoirs was in response to a request from the frozen meat industry.

Closely related to the Zimbabwean crisis is the Halal meat crisis in Swaziland (2010), which erupted after KFC and Nando's proclaimed their food to be halal; Christian churches protested, and several of their supporters called for a boycott of those restaurants' food. In Swaziland, the halal food boycott movement was led by Adventists and Protestants. The KFC Company responded by saying that if the Swaziland government had approved Islam as one of the states recognised religions, why shouldn't the company do the same?

Furthermore, this practice was almost ubiquitous across the entire company's restaurants. The situation progressed until it entered a poultry firm that sells meat to restaurants and hires Muslim butchers to handle the slaughter. Christians urged the government to stop the shariah slaughter because it violated their moral conscience and feelings; however, the government's quality assurance authority stated that it would not intervene as long as sanitation and health regulations, as well as proper consumption, were accessible in KFC foods and other restaurants (Wan Hassan & Awang, 2009).

Chapter 3

The Difference Between Halal and Haram Foods

CONTENTS

3.1. INTRODUCTION

The foods that are halal and those that are haram, are specified according to Islamic law. This is based on precepts found in the Quran, Islam's sacred book, as well as Hadith and Sunnah collections, which document what the Islamic prophet Muhammad is supposed to have said and done. Mujtahids produce fatwas, which are extensions of these decisions with varied degrees of strictness, though they are not necessarily universally regarded as authoritative. The only things explicitly forbidden by the Quran are blood, flesh from animals that die of natural causes, and animals that consume or feed on skin or meat, such as pigs (pork), snakes, and others. Only cud chewing animals such as goat, sheep, deer, cattle, and antelope are halal (lawful) if slaughtered in the name of Allah (Shafii & Khadijah, 2012).

Nevertheless, a person would not have been guilty of sin if he or she is forced to ingest something that is normally illegal due to a lack of alternatives. This is known as the "rule of necessity," or "that which is essential makes the forbidden permissible" in Islamic jurisprudence. Halal foods are defined under Islamic dietary regulations. Halal foods are legal and permissible for individuals who follow Islamic principles. Haram, or forbidden foods and beverages, are not allowed to be consumed by Muslims. Foods with the halal mark on their package have been approved by an organization and are guaranteed to be free of any prohibited ingredients or components. The name of the certification body must be on the packaging or nutrition label for halal claims.

Figure 3.1. Haram is an Arabic word that literally means "forbidden." In the religious writings of the Quran and the Sunnah, haram acts are forbidden. No matter how excellent the intention or how honorable the aim, if anything is considered haram, it remains prohibited. Dietary restrictions are said to aid in the comprehension of divine will in Islamic law.

Source: https://www.learnaboutislam.in/2009/07/islamic-food.html.

There are certain principles set in considering if a food is haram or not. These are described below:

- Animals that have been plainly and expressly prohibited in the Qur'an or Sunnah, such as swine, donkeys, and so on, are without a doubt Haram.
- Apart from fish, all animals that are born and live-in water are considered Haram. Except for fish that perish naturally in the sea without any external cause, all forms of fish are Halal. It would be Halal, however, if a fish died due to an external reason such as heat, cold, colliding with a stone, being thrown to the shore by the water, and so on.
- The third premise is that among terrestrial animals, those without blood, such as hornets, flies, spiders, beetles, scorpions, and ants, are considered Haram.
- The fourth principle states that land-animals with blood but no flowing blood, i.e., animals with no flowing blood, are likewise deemed Haram, such as snakes, lizards, chameleons, and so on.
- The fifth premise is that all pests (hasharat al-Ardh), such as mice, hedgehogs, and jerboas, are also declared Haram.
- The sixth principle states that land-animals with flowing blood that survive on grass and vegetation and do not prey on other animals (i.e., non-predatory terrestrial animals) are all deemed Halal, including camels, cows, goats, buffaloes, sheep, deer, and so on, but there is a minor legitimate debate within the Hanafi School associated with consumption of horsemeat, which will be discussed later. A donkey, on the other hand, is excluded from this general rule because its meat is considered Haram for food.
- The seventh principle states that all terrestrial predatory creatures and beasts, including as lions, cheetahs, tigers, leopards, wolves, foxes, dogs, and cats, are considered Haram.
- The eighth principle states that all birds of prey, including as falcons, eagles, kites, hawks, bats, and other animals that hunt with their claws or talons, are deemed Haram (Ab Talib et al., 2016).

- The ninth principle states that birds that do not hunt with their claws or prey on other animals, but instead eat grains and crops, such as chickens, ducks, pigeons, doves, sparrows, and crows, are all deemed Halal.
- The tenth principle states that if a Halal animal only eats impure foods to the point where its meat and milk emit foul odors, it is Makruh to eat its flesh and drink its milk. However, if it consumes other foods in addition to the impure, or if its milk and meat do not produce a foul odor, the meat and milk will be completely Halal.
- The final concept is that if one parent of an animal is Halal and the other is Haram, the mother is considered. If the mother is a Halal animal, the children will be Halal as well, such as a mule with a cow for a mother. If the mother is a Haram animal, such as a mule whose mother is a donkey, the child will also be Haram.

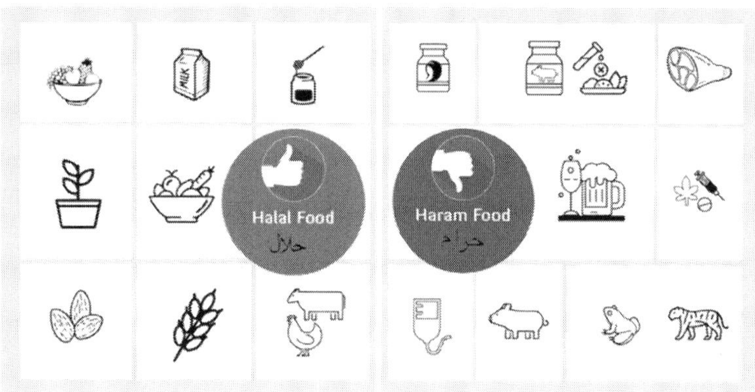

Figure 3.2. Consumption of flowing blood is forbidden for Muslims. Meats that are regarded haram, such as monkey, cat, dog, pork, or any other haram animal, can only be regarded legal in cases when a person is starving and needs to eat this meat to save his life. However, if his community has an abundance of food, these meats are not deemed necessary or permitted.

Source: https://blog.halal-navi.com/en/what-is-halal-and-haram/amp/.

Haram foods include:

- Pork by-products such as gelatin, lipase, and pepsin Meat from animals that have not been slaughtered in accordance with Islamic dietary regulations.

- Alcohol and foods containing alcohol, such as candies and cakes containing alcohol, such as rum cake Pure or artificial vanilla extract (vanilla is manufactured with alcohol) is used in foods.
- Blood pudding, for example, contains blood and blood by-products.
- Foods containing non-microbial enzyme-treated whey, L-cysteine, animal shortening, rennet, diglycerides and monoglycerides from animal sources, and sodium stearoyl-lactylate.

These Haram foods are discussed below.

3.2. ALCOHOL

It is common knowledge that Muslims do not consume alcohol. It is haram or prohibited. They avoid all intoxicating substances and avoid foods containing ethanol. They also avoid wearing perfumes that contain alcoholic ingredients. Alcohol is considered "haram" (forbidden) by most Muslims. Muslims refrain from alcohol because the Prophet Muhammad forbade it in the Qur'an, which Muslims consider to be the word of God revealed to him. Though Muhammad stated in the Qur'an that alcohol may have some medical use, he considered its propensity for sin was "far higher" than its benefits. Other intoxicants, including as hashish, were also forbidden by Muhammad, who believed that they would obscure judgment and lead to unlawful action in the same manner that alcohol did.

At first, Muslims were not allowed to attend prayers if they were inebriated. Furthermore, most devout Muslims avoid ingesting food products containing pure soy sauce or vanilla extract because these goods may contain alcohol. There is also disagreement over whether the prohibition applies to dishes in which the alcohol is boiled out or if it is virtually impossible to ingest enough of the meal to become intoxicated. Intoxicants are not forbidden in and of themselves, but their intake is. Alcohol, for instance, cannot be used as a beverage, but can be used to clean or disinfect. Unlike many other Islamic denominations, the Alevi Muslims of Turkey allow alcohol consumption. The Zaidi and Mutazili sects believe that alcohol consumption has always been prohibited, citing the Qur'an Ayah (4:43) as a sensation of tiredness and inability to stay awake. A fatwa issued in November 2015 allowed the consumption of non-alcoholic and low-alcohol beverages if the beverage contains an amount of alcohol of 0.5% or less. This does not make its consumption illegal if the alcohol has no effect on the beverage's consumption and does not intoxicate in large quantities.

Six main reasons why alcohol is haram include:

- Prayer and alcohol are incompatible – Salat is an essential part of Muslim lifestyle because it is a fivefold compulsory call to God. To make spiritual connections with the environment, health, and creation it is necessary to use the ritual "wudhu" eco before praying. The presence of alcohol in the same room does not affect prayer. According to Muslim scholars, anyone drinking alcohol will never be able to pray for a month except she or he repents.
- Alcohol is addictive – Even though early Muslims understood alcohol's medical value, Prophet Muhammad compared it to a "disease," claiming that there is no treatment for what God forbids. It is up to individual willpower to stop or continue drinking, just as it is with the first puff of a cigarette.
- Alcohol clouds the intellect – Khamr also discusses how drinking alcohol makes it impossible to distinguish between good and wrong. The intellect, reasonable thought, and sound judgment are the cornerstones of the Muslim faith. Anything that could jeopardize this behavior is prohibited, which is another reason why Muslims do not consume alcohol.

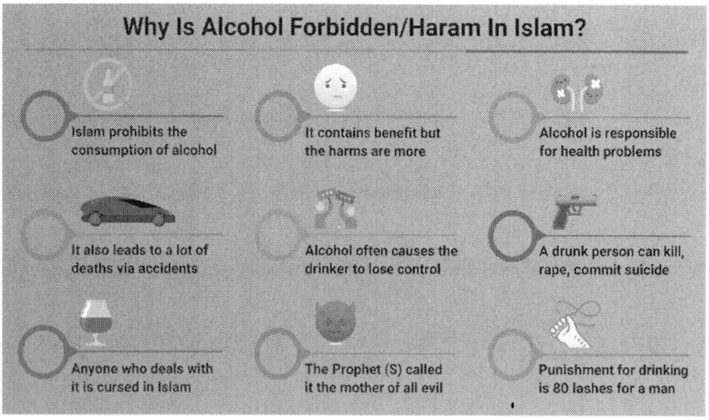

Figure 3.3. Alcohol intake brings with it a lot of evil and damage, which Islam absolutely eliminates. Even a modest amount of alcohol is forbidden in Islam. This reduces the risk of this intoxicant causing harm to society. While Islam recognizes that alcohol has some benefits, it also recognizes that its hazards exceed its benefits. This is a fact that cannot be denied, as countries where alcohol causes chaos to provide enough evidence.

Source: https://quranforkids.com/why-alcohol-forbidden-haram-islam/.

- Children get the wrong message – It is not the same to sit in a restaurant where alcohol is provided as it is to drink it. Therefore, Islamic law allows for the flexibility of saying that if someone needs to sit at such a restaurant for a business dinner or because there are no other diners available, he or she may do so, but not at a table wherein alcohol is consumed. On that topic, one may use the Zabiha globe halal guide to find local halal eateries. Bars and other places where alcohol is offered may encourage people to drink, and if there are children around, it may instruct them to experiment with alcohol (Abderahman et al., 2021). Mature Muslim individuals serve as role models, demonstrating that drinking is not required to have a good time, work, or socialize. "The distinction between [prohibitions in the environment] and [prohibitions connected to the ultimate aims] is that while both are forbidden, the former is deemed smaller in weight because it is tied to causes, whereas the latter is tied to an actual forbidden act," according to classical and modern Islamic scholars. Thus, though sitting at the table is not the same as drinking, it can lead to it, whereas drinking is strictly prohibited." – Abdullah bin Bayyah, M.D.
- Alcohol causes forgetfulness – Alcohol causes people to forget things. Any intoxicating substance, such as drugs, whiskey, gin, beer, or wine, influences one's faculties and behavior. The result is the same, and the Quran specifies that it is the intoxication that is detrimental, as it causes one to forget about God and prayer.
- It can cause criminality – Although a debatable assertion, alcohol is regarded in Islam as the "key to every evil" (hadith) due to its high intimate association with the creation or facilitation of criminal behavior. That isn't to suggest that alcohol's medicinal purposes aren't important, but it is to suggest that prevention is preferable to cure. "(In alcohol) there is a tremendous sin, and (some) benefits," the Quran says, "but the sin surpasses the benefit." (at 2:219)

While many Muslims refrain from alcohol, others feel that drinking is a personal choice that they must make in consultation with Allah. According to The Economist, some wealthy Muslims in countries like Pakistan drink to demonstrate their riches and culture, and some Islamic scholars even feel it is okay to drink alcohol derived from sources other than grapes and dates. Despite this, a Pew Forum poll found that most Muslims feel drinking is "morally reprehensible," and it is prohibited in several Islamic nations, including Saudi Arabia. As per Islamic historian Siraj Islam Mufti, drinking was ubiquitous throughout Arabia before Islam emerged, however its popularity declined as the religion spread. Alcohol causes more harm than benefit, according to an early verse in the Qur'an, which condemns praying while inebriated. "Truly, gambling, intoxicants, and divination by arrows are an abomination of Satan's doing," according to a subsequent passage of the Qur'an. Muhammad also said that individuals who bring, serve, or sell alcohol to others, even though they do not drink it themselves, are disdained by Allah.

Intoxication in Arabic is Khamr; the plural form, Khumur, is described as alcoholic beverages and liquor. It refers to some prohibited drugs in Islamic jurisprudence, and its precise definition varies depending on the legal school. Most jurists, including those from the Maliki, Shafi'i, Hanbali, and Ahl-i Hadith legal schools, have generally regarded it as a blanket phrase for any intoxicating beverage derived from grapes, dates, or other similar things. The phrase was limited by Hanafi jurists to a narrower range of beverages. According to Islamic prophet Muhammad's traditions, khamr can be prepared from two plants: date palm and grapevine.

Some Muslim jurists (especially those of the Hanafi school) interpret the idea of khamr literally, prohibiting only grape-based (or date-based) alcoholic beverages while allowing those made with honey, grains, or other fruits. However, this is a minority viewpoint. Alcohol usage is minimal in Islamic countries. Despite religious prohibitions, a small percentage of Muslims consume alcohol. A variety of regional distilled beverages, such as ram and arrack, are produced in Muslim-majority nations. In the Middle East, viticulture has a long history, particularly in Iran (where it is banned) and Egypt (where it is allowed).

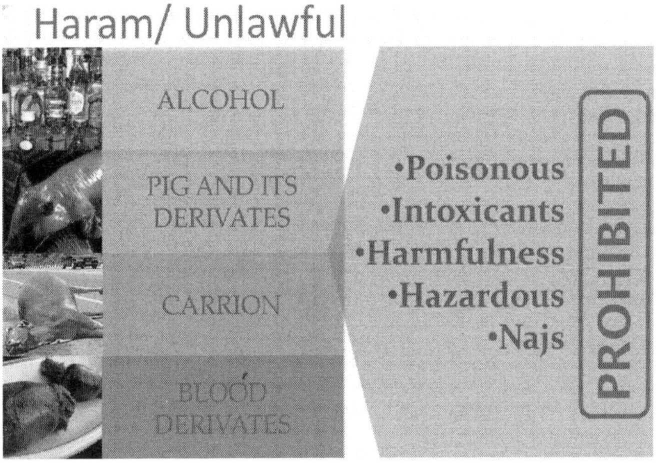

Figure 3.4. In Islam, intoxicants, or Khamr, are forbidden. Even with non-Muslims, the Prophet outlawed the dealing, export, import, and gifting of intoxicants. It is forbidden for a Muslim to work in or own a business that sells alcoholic beverages. This includes intoxicants including tobacco, paan, dokha, and khat, as well as alcohol. It is forbidden for a Muslim to sit at a table where alcohol is served. Heroin, cocaine, marijuana, and any other intoxicating substances are likewise prohibited.

Source: https://www.slideserve.com/masako/the-halal-and-haram-principle-in-islam.

3.3. CARRION

Carrion is any animal that dies without following the right religious rite, and eating it is forbidden. If it has warm blood, it is Najis (religiously impure), but if it is slain appropriately, it is clean and pure (except pig and dog which will be always Najis and never considered pure and clean). Islamic Jurisprudence has described and discussed at length and prescribed the animals whose flesh is permitted, according to a collection of Anjuman al-Tablight Islami. Only a life science professional could fully comprehend the justifications for these laws. Because carnivorous animals' stomachs contain dirt, Islam forbids the consumption of their meat. The flesh is filthy and stinky, and eating it causes illness. Herbivorous creatures, on the other hand, are generally regarded acceptable (Shaari et al., 2019).

Clawed animals are regarded Haram, but hoofed animals are typically deemed Halal, though some, like horses and asses, are regarded Makruh (unpleasant). Halal birds flap their wings more and glide less while flying, whereas Haram birds glide more and flap their wings less. Hunting is likewise governed by Islamic law. Hunters who hunt to feed their families or for sustenance can hunt. For the sake of joy and amusement, hunting is not permitted. A person who goes hunting for the sole purpose of having fun and playing must do complete prayers (this is not called Qasr) and fast because his travel is unIslamic. There are three categories of animals: flying, aquatic, and terrestrial. Domestic and wild animals are the two types of terrestrial animals.

3.3.1. Terrestrial Animals

Only camels, cows, sheep, and goats, are Halal among domestic animals, whereas horse, donkey, and mule flesh are detestable (Makruh). All other domestic animals, such as cats, are Haram. Except for deer and related species such as mule, wild donkey, wild cow, and mountain goats (12 horns), none of the wild animals are Halal. All carnivorous animals' flesh is Haram, whether they are strong and powerful like jackals, leopards, and lions, or weak like the fox; and the meat of a rabbit that is not from a wild animal is equally Haram. Rats, snakes, and other reptiles, whether wild or tamed worms and Insects, as well as lice and porcupines, are all considered Haram.

3.3.2. Birds

Pigeons and other similar birds are Halal. Ringdoves, ducks, wild ducks, and partridges, to name a few. Also, birds and their varieties, such as the Bulbul (nightingale), Chandol, and others (name of a bird), Surad (bird with broad head with a peak half-black and half-white who hunts other birds), a swan (Grayish with long head, which mostly lives on a date tree), Shagrq (lovely greenish bird that looks like a pigeon and has a black, green, and red, line on its black feather).

Bats, peacocks with webbed feet, or hunting birds like Shahin, Bashiq (also known as Bahasa), Charkh (one type of bird), Eagle, or a weak bird like crow or vulture and its kind should be avoided, as well as Baga whose color is black and white, Zagh (crow that lives in cultivated soil), and those fat and black crows who eat Carrion; all should be avoided. Traditions provide clear terminology for everything that has been mentioned. When it comes to birds, if there is no clear command, they can be declared Halal if they meet the criteria listed at the beginning of the essay: Halal birds flapping their wings more and gliding less during flight. They should also have three additional features: an extra finger below the thigh, a crop (craw), and a gizzard (Samori et al., 2016).

The ordering of a bird's egg and meat is the same. A Halal bird's egg is Halal, while a Haram bird's egg is Haram. We must examine the morphology of an unknown origin egg to identify whether it belongs to a Halal or Haram bird. It is Halal if one end is pointy and the other is rounded, as in a hen or pigeon egg. It is deemed Haram if it is perfectly round or oval with the same shape on both ends. We must also keep in mind that a permitted animal can become Haram for two reasons:

- Through ingesting Najasat.
- Once it has been sexually assaulted by a man.

Figure 3.5. Halal foods are legal and permissible for individuals who follow Islamic principles. Haram, or forbidden foods and beverages, are not allowed to be consumed by Muslims. Foods with the halal mark on their packaging have been approved by an organization and are guaranteed to be free of any prohibited ingredients or components. The name of the certification body must be included on the nutrition label or packaging for halal claims.

Source: https://blog.halal-navi.com/en/what-is-halal-and-haram/amp/.

3.3.3. Aquatic Animals

Only those fishes with scales, even if they have fallen off, are Halal in the case of aquatic creatures, such as the scales of Kan-at (a type of fish) (Qoba fish). This is a mischievous fish that smashes its head against everything and loses all its scales, leaving only the scales on its tail. Warm-blooded animals may be consumed by using the two methods for killing them, slaughter, or hunting, prescribed by Muslim law. There are two hunting methods, one by hunting an experienced dog who is obedient; he must move and stop when ordered. They should not be accustomed to eating their prey. Even the person releasing the dog on the head of a prey must be a Muslim and at the time of release the dog he must speak the name of Allah, and the dog must not be taken out by the hunter during the hunt.

Secondly, erect weapons such as sword, lance, or bullet, etc., are used for hunting. The body of the animal should be penetrated. Whether this weapon is made from ferrous metal or some other mineral, Halal's presence is provided that the archer is a Muslim; he must say 'Bismillah' when his arrow is released. If all these conditions are met and the animal is killed, the hunted animal's flesh is ready for use (Halal). If the animal is found alive, however, the hunter must massacre the animal according to the rules of slaughter prescribed. In addition, only if they can flee or fly, can all Halal flesh animals be ingested. When you shoot the young one, or a youth who cannot yet fly, of a deer who cannot run, or a young man, you do not have Halal in your flesh. First, they should be caught and then killed by a knife, etc. (Rejeb et al., 2021).

In the books Al-Kafi and Amali, Mufaddal Ibn Omar quoted Imam Sadiq asking why Allah had banned Carrion, blood, and pig? Imam answered: "Nothing has Allah prevented men from taking it Himself (we seek refuge in Allah). and he didn't allow stuff he didn't like himself. (Allah, in other words, did not frame Halal and Haram rules based on His fancies and personal whims. The truth is that Allah Alone knows what is good and necessary for the human body, when He alone creates everything. Therefore, because of his grace, he made it permissible. He is the only one who knows what is detrimental to the human body, thus he forbade it and declared it Haram. However, if you are helpless and have no other option for survival, you can eat the same (prohibited) foods. He must, however, eat only as much as is required to save his life." "Eating carrion makes one's physique week and thin," he continued. "It obliterates a person's physical prowess and cuts off his descendants. Whoever eats carrion dies suddenly."

As a result, it looks that the blood gushes out during the slaughtering process, leaving the meat free of the unclean blood and harmful elements that run through the veins. When an animal dies naturally or through any technique that leaves the blood in the body, the meat is tainted with toxic compounds that are harmful to one's health. Imam Sadiq was asked by a heretic why Allah had forbidden carrion. "Carrion is deemed Haram so that there is a distinction between it and an animal upon which Allah's name is recited," the Imam explained. "A dead animal's blood is also not evacuated from its body. It returns to its organs, making the meat heavy and unappealing. Its blood is consumed with its meat." "Then fish flesh must likewise be carrion and Haram," the heretic said, "because blood is not ejected from it." "The cleansing of fish is just to remove it from the water and leave it outside to die on its own," the Imam explained. It doesn't need to be slaughtered because it doesn't have (warm) blood. The same is true of locust. The Imam further added that because fish has little blood, it is not required to butcher it, according to the fourth volume of Bihar al-Anwar. and the blood that stays in its body is harmless and Halal, much like the blood that stays in an animal's body after it has been slaughtered.

Figure 3.6. Many foods have a strong likelihood to be combined with blood. For example, when making sausage, animal blood is boiled with a filler (meat, fat wheat) until it thickens sufficiently to coagulate when cold. Pig and cattle blood are commonly used in this scenario. Due to its potential to offer flavor or color in meat, blood is often employed as a thickening in sauces and puddings. Blood has also been used in soups and stews as part of the broth.

Source: https://www.delightedcooking.com/what-are-the-differences-between-halal-and-haram-foods.htm.

3.4. BLOOD

There are two kinds of blood, Tahir (Pure) and Najis (unclean). Najis is man's blood and every warm-blooded animal. It is a feature of the warm-blooded creatures that blood blows out with force when the main vein is separated. It is Najis, and it also causes Najis if blood is found while a cow or buffalo is milking, however small, it may be, haram is to drink this milk. By precaution (Ehtiyat) it is also necessary that the minute blood particles in an egg are absent from consumption.

Of the two types of blood, however, are tahir (pure). The blood of all cold-blooded creatures, such as fish and mosquitoes, is one example. Second, the blood that remains after a killed animal has been slaughtered. As a result, if an animal is slaughtered in accordance with Islamic law and some blood comes out, the blood that remains in its body is tahir. However, if the blood that has flowed out returns to the body owing to breathing or because its head is placed on an elevated point, the remaining blood will not be tahir. Apart from that, consuming blood, whether tahir or Najis, is strictly prohibited (Adekunle & Filson, 2020). Tahir blood, on the other hand, can be swallowed if it is a part of a fish or a slain animal and can be regarded a part of its flesh. Consumption of it, however, is considered Haram if it is deemed blood.

During the twentieth century, the rationale underlying Allah's prohibition of blood was revealed. Blood allows life to exist by transporting oxygen, hormones, vitamins, and compounds such as fat, sugar, and protein, taken through digestion to the cells. It does, however, carry a variety of poisons and waste products that must be eliminated from the body. One of the most significant functions of blood is to transport chemicals that must be eliminated from the body, such as carbon dioxide, keratin, uric acid, and urea.

As a result, if a large amount of blood is consumed, the number of products in the body that must be evacuated increases dramatically. This will raise urea levels, which are toxic compounds delivered to the kidneys for excretion. This can cause cognitive impairment and possibly unconsciousness. That is why, by definition, dangerous chemicals will always be present in blood, even if it is drawn from healthy animals. Various parasites and germs will be conveyed if it is taken from a sick animal. The bacteria may grow and spread throughout the body if this happens. and that, my friends, is the actual threat. When someone drinks blood, all the pathogens and waste particles in it can travel throughout the body, causing conditions like renal failure or liver coma. Furthermore, most bacteria carried in the blood might cause various disorders by harming the stomach and intestine lining.

Furthermore, blood is not a sterile environment; to look at it another way, germs thrive in it. Microbes have a lot of opportunities to eat in blood, thus it's a perfect environment for them. Blood does not sustain microorganisms or disease when it is in balance with the functioning of the other fluids in the body and the immune system. These microorganisms exist inside the body of a healthy person by relying on one another. When that ecosystem is significantly harmed, when the internal equilibrium is disrupted, they may transform into disease-causing microorganisms when they find the right conditions.

When the blood pH level (acid-alkali balance) is disrupted, for example, due to inadequate diet or hazardous substances, innocuous microorganisms might transform into disease-causing bacteria. The pH level of the blood should be approximately 7.3 if the body is to be healthy. Even minor changes in that level might throw the balance off, causing microbes to grow more dangerous to adapt to their new environment. When blood is sterile, it's like leaving milk outside to go bad. By adapting to their new habitat, microbes already present in the blood have negative effects.

Aside from that, blood is not suited for use as a food product. The number of digestible proteins such as fibrinogen, globulin, and albumin, in the blood is low; only 8 grams per 100 ml. Fats are the same way. Furthermore, blood contains a high concentration of hemoglobin, a complex protein that is difficult to digest and unpalatable to the stomach. When blood clots, the protein fibrinogen converts to fibrin, which forms a plate containing erythrocytes (red blood corpuscles). Because fibrin is one of the most difficult proteins to digest, blood is made even more tough to digest. Finally, health professionals concur that blood, in any form, is inappropriate for human ingestion.

3.5. PORK

The pig and the dog are two Najis animals that have Najis in every part of their bodies. Even non-bloody parts such as hooves, claws, and hair, are Najis. Slaughtering a pig or a dog is a waste of time. These animals, in other words, cannot be cleansed in any way. It is Harmful and a worse sin to eat their meat.

Figure 3.7. Muslims are prohibited from eating pork, as is well recognized across the world. Pork is forbidden in Christianity and Judaism, which may come as a surprise to some. Many people may question why, and recent research has revealed some of the logic behind the prohibition.

Source: https://muslims4peace.org/why-is-pork-haram/.

"The Almighty Allah has prohibited (declared Haram) Pork," Imam Ria says about the prohibition of pork. "Because it is a cruel and horrific creature created by Allah for humankind to learn from. People should also avoid sensuality and shameless acts that give off such a bad impression. and they are afraid of Almighty Allah turning them into pigs. (It is mentioned in the account of former nations that those who commit sexual promiscuity are turned into pigs in Barzakh and bred as pigs in Qiyma). Pigs were also allowed to live to serve as a reminder of former countries' conversion (Maskh) to pigs. Pork is also prohibited because pigs' principal diet consists of highly Najis and unclean substances, and their blood carries several hazardous pathogens." (Rezaee, 2019).

"The Almighty Allah reduced many nations into animals," stated Imam Ja'far as-Sadiq. Pigs, monkeys, and bears, for example, are among them. These creatures were then forbidden to be eaten, so that humans could learn from them and not regard the offense as minor." Pig is an animal classed by specialists among the thick-skinned animals, according to Anjuman

Tablighat Islami's book Islam wa Ilme Imroz. This family includes the rhinoceros, wild pig, and hippopotamus. Pork is extremely detrimental to the body, yet we've only included a few of its negative consequences here.

3.5.1. Moral and Spiritual Harms

In accordance with many cultures that consider pork haram, the Imans state that pigs are known for their shameless and hedonistic behavior, as well as their sexual depravity. It does not respect its own females and invites and enjoys sexual relations with other human beings. It is also filthy, as it lives on excreta and has no qualms about eating its own. As a result, eating pork degrades one's moral character and leads to spiritual bankruptcy. It is incredible that such a disgusting creature can wind up on a dinner table, where its meat is enjoyed and devoured with gusto, even though those who eat it are aware of its dirty and nasty traits. In fact, many of these people refer to someone as a pig when they want to be disgusting and offensive, but it is the pig that they seem to appreciate and enjoy the most.

It's incredible that such a disgusting creature can wind up on a dinner table, where its meat is enjoyed and devoured with gusto, even though those who eat it are aware of its dirty and nasty traits. In fact, many of these people refer to someone as a pig when they want to be disgusting and offensive, but it is the pig that they seem to appreciate and enjoy the most. Christians have the same perplexing mentality. When Christians represent Satan in religious stories, they usually represent him as a pig. Pig is Satan represented, according to Barnabas' Gospel, and the pig's body contains Satan's spirit. The Christian Bible tells how Jesus threw Satan's soul into a herd of swine and drove them to the river. Even though their own faith attributes the pig with a devilish character, Christians continue to eat it.

3.5.2. Physical Harms

Pork is damaging to the body in many ways, but Trichinosis and Dysentery are two significant disorders caused by its eating.

Figure 3.8. A pig's body contains several parasites, germs, and viruses that can be transmitted to humans and animals. Pigs eat some of the most revolting foods known to man, and this consumption brings with it a slew of diseases that can be passed on to anyone who consumes pork. Contrary to assertions that contemporary technology can render the pork safe, disease erupts wherever swine are kept, even in the most developed countries.

Source: https://www.facebook.com/135982549910340/photos/islam-main-suwer-pig-porkkhana-kiun-haram-hai-why-pig-meat-is-haraamit-is-very-i/202412483267346/.

Trichinosis – The Trichina worm, which breeds in pig flesh, causes this sickness. The female lays 10,000 to 15,000 eggs over the course of a month. Only pork eating allows the worms to enter the human system. If the person becomes infected, the worms assault the stomach's walls, causing the walls to weaken. They enter the bloodstream three weeks after entering the stomach and spread throughout the body. In the host body, they multiply at breakneck speed. The initial signs are giddiness and an unusual fever. This fever is linked to the digestive tract, and the person quickly develops Diarrhea. There is a low fever at first, but it becomes more severe as time goes on. Other symptoms include weakness, exhaustion, body itch, limb stiffness, and pain in various regions of the body. It is most noticeable in the patient's abnormal chewing, swallowing, and breathing patterns. The moderate illness grows to gigantic dimensions and kills the sufferer within seven weeks. 400 million Trichina worms can be found in a kilogram of pork (Rahim & Abd Rahim, 2020).

Dysentery – Dysentery is one of the terrible diseases of pork-eating people. The organism 'Karam Kadoo' is only responsible for such dysentery. This worm has a head that is connected to the stomach walls with two chains round its head and four branches. The outside of the worm producing eggs is separated from the principal body and expelled along with stool. Eggs expelled by stools are eaten by swine and so the eggs enter the pig's stomach. Again, the breeding cycle begins with these eggs. If man eats the flesh of this pig, it is possible that germs entering the human stomach will become infected. It has been proven beyond a shadow of a doubt that these specific worms are only related with pork intake, and that the only method to avoid them is to avoid pork.

In regions where pork is consumed in considerable numbers, this infection is widespread. Pork, in addition to being a source of illness, is difficult to digest and puts a lot of strain on the digestive system.

Before anyone knew about the dangers of pork, Islam outlawed it 1400 years ago. It's a shame that people continue to eat it 1400 years later, when the wisdom of the prohibition has been clearly demonstrated. Similarly, Islam considers dogs to be absolutely Najis and forbids them from being kept in the house. Since then, scientific advancements have proven that dogs can transmit a variety of diseases to humans. Baldness, rashes, and other skin diseases caused by germs, as well as diseases caused by lice that breed in a dog's fur. The most dreadful of all diseases that a human can contract is rabies, which is transmitted to humans by dogs.

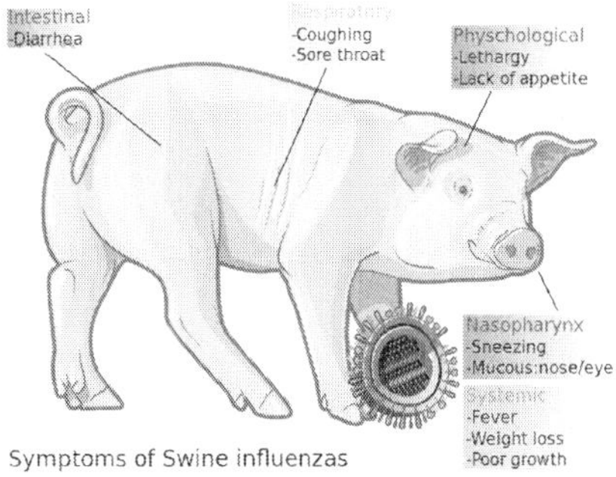

Figure 3.9. Pig flesh has a lot of fat and cholesterol. This unclean flesh is difficult for our bodies to digest. There is evidence that the pork you consume can linger in your system for up to two months. Pig fat is difficult to metabolize and digest, making it unsuitable for use as a source of energy. It frequently remains in the human body, where it turns to fat. Pig fat consumption leads to obesity, cardiovascular illness, and intestine cancer.

Source: https://insidesaudi.com/5-special-reasons-why-muslims-dont-eat-pigs-in-ksa/.

If a faithful man eats pork unwittingly or by mistake, he or she has no sin. For lack of knowledge, or for unintentional errors or forgetfulness, God does not punish anyone. If a believer is certain, however, or think any of its food, drinks or medicines might contain pork or pork products, then it is not allowed for him or her to eat it. If he has doubts, then he must try to investigate or ask for details about the ingredients. Knowledge of ingredients and the process of manufacture is currently readily available, and the ban applies whether there are a small or a large amount of pork or pork products (Park & Lee, 2021).

Whether or not altering the nature of the impurity (in this case pig products) removes the restriction is a point of contention among Islamic scholars. According to the Islamic Organization for Medical Sciences, changing the form of something (for example, food or medicine additives) to make it something else lifts the prohibition. However, there is no debate or disagreement that eating pig meat, such as ham and bacon, is prohibited. Although there is considerable empirical evidence that pigs have parasites that are hazardous to humans, and the pig has long been regarded the perfect breeding ground for influenza, the latest outbreak of swine flu in Mexico and North America has caused several countries to butcher pigs en masse.

3.6. NON-ZABIHA BEEF

Only meat products are referred known as Zabiha. The word indicates that the meat comes from animals who were slaughtered in a legal manner. The laws governing the slaughtering of animals are, once again, straightforward. Aside from reciting God's name at the start of the slaughter, special care must be taken to ensure that the animal suffers as little as possible. The animal must be slain by an adult Muslim for the meat to be declared zabiha. A sane Muslim is one who is aware of his or her surroundings. They must, as previously stated, invoke the name of God before killing the animal. They then slashed the throat in half, cutting the windpipe, esophagus, and jugular veins, in one fast action. Before the meat is further prepared for consumption or distribution, the animal must be allowed to bleed out successfully. To emphasize the humanism of the zabiha slaughter, it is necessary to note that the animal must not be slaughtered while another animal is being slaughtered. Furthermore, the knife cannot be sharpened in the presence of the animal. It is critical to allow the animal to enjoy a happy life before it is killed. It must also be in a relaxed stance while having its neck slit. Also, the knife must be thoroughly inspected for any damage that could affect the slaughter or cause the animal suffering.

3.7. GELATIN

Gelatin is available in a variety of forms, including flakes, shreds and sheets, and coarse powder. It's white or yellowish in color, has a faint but distinct odor and taste, and is stable in dry air but susceptible to microbial degradation when wet or in solution. It is insoluble in cold water, but when immersed, it progressively swells and softens, absorbing 5 to 10 times its own mass of water. It dissolves in hot water to form a thick colloidal mucilage, which cools to create a jelly.

Edible gelatin is used in a variety of food products, including meat, milk products, desserts, pastries, jams, candies, chocolate, jelly, ice cream, and confectionery. In meals, it works as a stabilizing and smoothing ingredient. Rubber substitutes, textiles, sizing papers, matches, photographic films and plates, cement, adhesives, lithographic and printing inks, are all made with gelatin. Plants, fish, animals, and synthetically produced gelatin are the four main sources of gelatin. Gelatin that is derived from plants, fish, or is synthesized is Halal.

However, we generally assume that the majority of gelatin come from pork (pig are lower in price and more tasteful) and beef, except if clearly stated (in non-Muslim countries). In all circumstance's pork gelatin is haram. If gelatin from beef is from a halal slaughtered animal or any other halal animal, then it is halal. The question of non-halal slaughtered beef gelatin remains (or other halal animals).

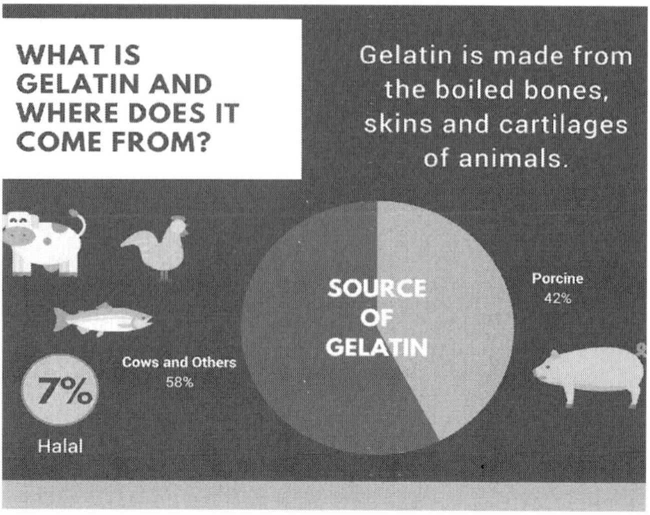

Figure 3.10. Even when some haram components, such as gelatin or pork by-products, were used in the creation of medicine, it was still considered halal because the materials were completely converted and changed into a different substance. The principle of Istihalah, or the change of a product into something else, is known. Consider the following scenario: Although alcohol is haram, it is unquestionably halal once it has been converted to vinegar. The same criterion applies to substances that were originally considered haram but have since altered, gaining new characteristics and names.

Source: https://www.quora.com/Is-gelatin-haram-or-halal.

Non-halal animals slaughtered are haram for consumption, meat and its components are regarded to be as impure as bones. The problem is, if an unclean thing changes or becomes pure, it will be unclean. This is known as Istihaala in Arabic.

3.8. DRUGS (MARIJUANA, KHAT, AND OTHER NARCOTICS)

We cannot find any direct proof in the Sirah on this topic throughout history because drugs were not known at the time of Islam; thus, the only way is to appeal to broad laws and principles of philosophy. In general, it has been stated that, because drug consumption causes significant losses, it is prohibited (Haram) unless medical crises and necessities need it. Second, buying and selling it is prohibited unless it provides sensible, legal benefits, such as in the creation of medicine. This type of usage must be strictly supervised and controlled by the authorities. Based on these facts, Muslim thinkers devised four cogent and unmistakable justifications for drug prohibition (Al-Ansi & Han, 2019).

Because of their inebriant effects as well as their physical-mental negative impacts on persons and society, all intoxicants are considered illegal. Furthermore, drug abuse leads to moral decay, body and mind degradation, catastrophic cultural, social, and economic losses, and ultimately, societal catastrophe. Someone who is addicted to drugs loses control of his actions, loses his zeal, motivation, and common sense, and as a result is willing to do everything to obtain drugs without hesitation. Drug addicts are also unable to properly stick to their Islamic beliefs, as narcotics convert them into irresponsible and ineffective humans.

Wise men all through history have consistently avoided taking drugs, which is completely consistent with Islamic law (Shari'a). Following in the footsteps of famous people and considering their way of life is an authoritative and rational technique to argue against drug use.

One of the most basic and fundamental jurisprudential rules that is applied to a wide spectrum of Islamic teachings is the "no harming nor reciprocating harm" rule. People should not engage in acts that cause disproportionate losses on this basis. We can now claim from personal experience that drug use causes enormous social and individual harm, as well as generational irresponsibility. As a result, the rule of "neither harming nor reciprocating harm" might offer us with the most rational basis for opposing drug use; its negative consequences affect not only the drug-addicted person, but also his or her family, relations, and even the entire society. Drug addiction is also one of the most common causes of self-destructive and life-ruining actions. We have a clear reinforcement of this reality from Allah Almighty, who says, "and do not plunge yourselves into destruction with your own hands" (2:195).

Every bad thing that causes enormous losses is forbidden (Haram) in Islam; clearly, the substance is categorized as highly hazardous due to its numerous bad impacts on a wide range of people. The Holy Quran expresses this claim clearly: "He makes lawful to them all good things and forbids them from all evil things" (7:157). One of the most significant disadvantages of drug use is a loss of knowledge and perceptual power; as a result, Islam considers "common sense preservation" to be the most crucial requirement for a Muslim. It is now clear why Islamic law (Shari'a) prohibits all forms of intoxication, including alcohol, drugs, and other substances.

Figure 3.11. Because Almighty Allah forbade these items in the Qur'an and Hadith, Muslims abstain from alcoholic beverages, intoxicating narcotics, swine-flesh, and other haram foods. We abstain from these forbidden substances because Almighty Allah has directed us to do so and to protect ourselves from His wrath and eternal punishments by doing so. Allah is aware of what is good for us spiritually, morally, and physically.

Source: https://www.pinclipart.com/pindetail/hmooRh_drugs-clipart-prohibited-drug-quotes-of-anti-drugs/.

Drug addiction has reached epidemic levels around the globe, according to the first-ever report on worldwide addiction statistics produced by researchers, which uses data from sources such as the World Health Organization and the United Nations Office on Drugs and Crime, and there were 230 million drug users worldwide in 2015. According to the report, drugs cause more "productive years of life lost" than any other intoxicant. That means drug addicts not only die younger, but also suffer bad health for a longer length of time. Drugs have an impact on their career, relationships, and overall quality of life. These findings demonstrate how far Islam foresees the negative consequences of drug use and why it is prohibited (Haram) in practically all Islamic laws (Omar & Jaafar, 2011).

3.9. VANILLA EXTRACT

There are two varieties of vanilla extract on the market: natural vanilla extract and synthetic/imitative vanilla extract. According to the US Electronic Code of Federal Regulations, natural vanilla extract is made by soaking vanilla beans in ethyl alcohol (the intoxicating alcohol found in wine and alcoholic beverages) at a concentration of at least 35%. Vegetable glycerin can sometimes be substituted with ethyl alcohol. The method of using natural vanilla, however, is quite expensive because vanilla is not easily available due to the law of supply and demand, which states that demand for it exceeds supply. As a result, the usage of the second type – synthetic vanilla extract – is the most viable option because it is more plentiful, less expensive, and free of forbidden substances. This second form, as far as we know, is what is most utilized in various vanilla-containing items such as ice cream, chocolate, and so on. In fact, some vanilla extract bottles on the market have the words "Alcohol-free" inscribed on them.

This is although some of the biggest and well reputable brands in chocolate and ice cream use natural ingredients in their food items, such as natural vanilla extract dipped into ethyl alcohol, rather than alcoholic vanilla imitation. Second, there is disagreement among Muslim scholars regarding the use of natural vanilla extract. Some maintain that it is forbidden to eat because the alcohol is dipped and mixed with 35% ethyl and the legal cause for the ban is which poisoning still exists and it has not been determined to be gone.

Others maintain that natural vanilla extracts can be consumed based on the following reasons: – They consider that alcohol is not smear and impure (najis) from the Shari'ah standpoint as a default in pure things (unless otherwise proven), whether the alcohol has been pure or diluted with water. Because the alcohol has no effect on the vanilla, the person who consumes it does not become inebriated. – umum al-balwa (universal plight, which is an unpleasant widespread condition impacting many people that is hard to avoid); as a result, it can eat foods that use a tiny fraction of alcohol in their manufacture to breakdown some components that are water insoluble, like dyes, preservatives, and most of the additional alcohol is evaporated during the manufacture of food (Nurrachmi, 2018).

Third, deciding about something necessitates having a correct perception and understanding of it. So, to have a proper understanding of this issue, it must be studied, researched, and kept up to date on what is going on in the manufacturing and production of food and medication, whether in traditional or modern techniques that are prone to change, as well as consulting experts and specialists in the field. What we've brought to you is based on what we've discovered so far on this subject, which is entirely speculative.

3.10. RENNET

Rennet is an enzyme that is utilized in the food industry to curdle milk and make cheese. Rennet is derived from a calf's or an animal's stomach. The animal must be slain to remove the rennet. Scholars believe that if the slaughter was halal, the Rennet will be halal as well. However, some Hanafi's (students of Imam Muhammad and Imam Abu Hanifa-Abu Yusuf) believe that rennet is Halal as a material, but its ingestion is Haram if the animal was not slaughtered according to Islamic law. This is due to contamination from the animal's stomach with other polluted fluids. According to them, rennet is fluid or viscous [flowing], and it would be impossible to purify it due to the penetration and saturation of unclean fluids, therefore such rennet would remain Haram.

Imam Abu Hanifah, on the other hand, did not consider the dampness found in the stomachs of the animals to be unclean, even if murdered in a haram manner, making the rennet Halal. The permissibility of rennet is thus determined not by whether the slaughterer is Muslim or non-Muslim, but rather by whether rennet has life and absorbs the pollutants found in the stomach of a freshly slaughtered calf. Because of this distinction, it is still legal to drink, though abstinence is preferred.

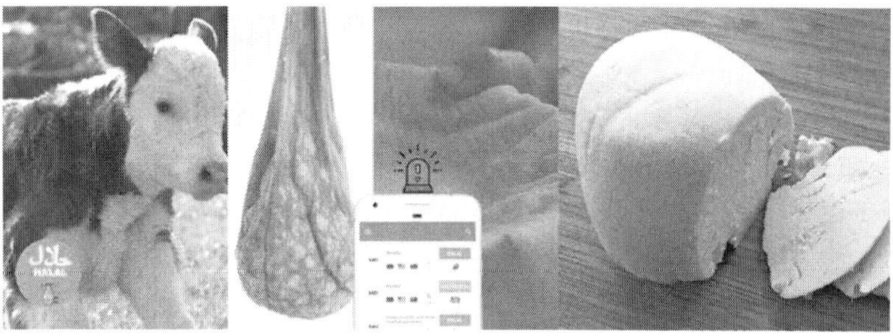

Figure 3.12. The admissibility of rennet is determined not by whether the slaughterer is Muslim or not, but by whether the rennet has life and absorbs the pollutants found in the stomach of a freshly slaughtered calf. The divergence amongst Imaam Abu Hanifah and his two students, the Saahibayn, has resulted in this.

Source: https://m.facebook.com/HalalHaramMusbooh/photos/a.490074658088609/714958008933605/?type=3&source=57.

This, according to Hanafi scholar Ali Qaari, is confirmation of the purity of rennet, because if it were polluted, the cheese would be polluted as well. Rennet is also required to produce cheese. Our Rasul was questioned about, Simn [clarified butter], Jubn [cheese], and Faraae [leather] in the hadith of Salmaan, as well as the fact that it was taken from the Majus' territories. It was mentioned to Umar about Jubn [cheese], and he was told that it was made with the rennet of deceased animals. He said that he would pray for the tasmiyyah and eat it. This, according to Imam Ahmad, is the most reliable hadith on Majus' cheese. According to Mufti Taqi Uthmaani, rennet generated from a pig's stomach is Haraam and impure if its original chemical composition makeup is not drastically altered. "Imam Malik detested cheese because it was manufactured with rennet of animals that were not slaughtered according to Islamic Law (maitah)," according to the Maliki reference, Manh al-Jaleel.

In conclusion, Halal refers to what Allah and the Prophet Muhammad (peace and blessings be upon him) have permitted to be done lawfully, whilst Haram refers to what Allah and the Prophet have expressly forbidden. Engaging in a Haram act (eating pork, drinking alcohol, having sex outside of marriage, etc.) will result in punishment in the Next Life, and possibly even this Life. For both humans and animals, life is the greatest gift of God. It should be required to sacrifice an animal's life in the name of Allah if its existence is to be ended for the sake of human survival. As a result, if an animal is slain in the name of someone other than Allah, Muslims do not believe such meat to be permitted to consume.

In Islam, it is likewise forbidden to eat an animal that has died by itself during a conflict or by any other circumstances. This law applies to all animals except fish, and Hadith proves that statement to be valid. Meat from a dead animal is not good for your health, according to science, because there is a big difference between killing and slaughtering. While blood flows freely from an animal's body during slaughter, blood remains inside the body and may contain various viruses, hormones, germs, antibodies, and infectious organisms. When blood remains inside the body for an extended period, meat becomes impure and, if consumed, has a negative impact on the human body (Nusran et al., 2018).

Blood is also forbidden since it is the body's means of transporting harmful compounds, carbon dioxide, toxins, uric acid, keratin, and a large amount of hemoglobin, which is difficult to digest in the stomach. As a result, it is unfit for human consumption.

Figure 3.13. Halal foie gras, spring rolls, chicken nuggets, ravioli, lasagna, pizza, and baby food are among the processed meals and goods available from several food firms. Halal ready meals are a developing consumer market for Muslims in the United Kingdom and the United States, with an increasing number of stores offering them. If there is no alcohol in vegetarian food, it is halal.

Source: https://www.pixtastock.com/illustration/22934234.

Pigs are thought to be the only animals created by God to be scavengers, eating trash, and carrying various germs such as helminths, roundworms, pinworms, tapeworms, and hookworms. The eggs of these worms cannot be removed from pork by increasing the cooking temperature.

Muslims are instructed to eat food that is clean and safe. The source and purity of food, as well as how to cook, serve, eat, and dispose of leftovers, are all especially important in Islam. In many ways, the notion of Islam in eating is the same as the notion of Islam in other areas, namely, the concept of maintaining the soul, body, and mind's safety. Halal food is permitted since it is beneficial to both the mind and the body.

Eating haram has harmful consequences, whether it is done consciously or inadvertently. Whether it makes you sluggish in accomplishing your customary amount or quality of good deeds, hesitant to donate to charity causes, or inflaming your forbidden desires. You could be negatively impacted in a variety of ways. Our soul, body, and piety are all affected by the haram food we consume. There are, nevertheless, ways to make amends, such as taubah (repentance), salah, and sadaqah (voluntary charity).

Islam is more than a religion; it is a way of life, governed by procedures, norms, and etiquette in all aspects of existence. Food regulations are particularly significant because food is such an integral element of daily living. Muslims are required to eat for the sake of survival and good health, not to live for the sake of eating. Eating, like prayer, fasting, almsgiving, and other religious acts, is considered a form of worship in Islam (Mohsin et al., 2016).

Chapter 4

How Do You Assure a Restaurant Is Serving Halal Food

CONTENTS

4.1. INTRODUCTION

Most of the restaurants that serve halal food tend to be worshiped by many given the nature of the food they serve. Their foods tend to be trusted by most individuals including those that are not from the Muslim religion. As a matter fact, to show how famous and celebrated Halal food is through an article that was posted by a magazine company. In 2014, halal secret of pizza express made a headline in The Sun. this actually a fact that the pizza chain boldly displays in its website given the fact that halal food is trusted by many. There have been tabloids that are putting up halal food but the truth of the matter is that the halal-serving restaurants are not new and are rather very common. There are even selected subway stores that have been using halal meat in their sarnies since 2007. A fifth of Nando's tend to be Halal only meaning their menus basically are those of Halal. The Nando chains tend to show their Halal status in their windows, their websites and in their menus. According to KFC and Nando, the claims are that they can only set up new Halal shops in the locations in which there are non-Halal restaurants nearby. For a long time, restaurants have been trying hard to adapt their menus in order to suit the Britain's population.

Figure 4.1. KFC restaurant. The restaurant is opened worldwide and is famous as it serves Halal meat.

Source: https://www.adweek.com/commerce/in-the-chicken-sandwich-wars-kfc-has-a-major-advantage/.

The reason behind this is that, Britain's Muslim population is growing by the year. As such, in the line of trying to attract more population to a restaurant, making it Halal-friendly may be considered as the right way to go. Take for instance KFC. This restaurant has gotten the trust of many individuals given their reputation to serve Halal worthy food. Years after years, individuals have been going to KFC and there are new individuals still going to the particular restaurant. This can show that in order to get a restaurant running and to get new customers, Halal should be part of the menu. Furthermore, it will get people talking about the newly found restaurant. Satisfied customers are very important in ensuring the success of a restaurant.

In order to assure that a restaurant is serving halal food, one needs to listen to the masses carefully. As seen, individuals are important in spreading the word and they tend to believe each other more. Once a satisfied customer gets to spread, the word then more and more people will be seen to avail themselves in the particular restaurant. In most cases, the word from a Muslim believer is a strong on given the fact that they truly understand the contents of halal food. Once you see that Muslims are spreading word about a particular restaurant and is encouraging their counterparts to eat from the particular restaurant (Mostafa, 2020). This method of knowing whether a restaurant is serving Halal food is not that efficient but still does the magic to spread the word. For the case of the restaurant, serving only Halal meat may not be that appropriate given the fact that there are those individuals who would not want to eat halal meat. As such, there are those restaurant entrepreneurs that would want to cater for but not solely halal food. In this case, once you enter into such a restaurant, you ask for the Halal menu if one is interested in eating halal meat. Alternatively, in such a case scenario, a customer might choose to make their decision based on the demographics of the local area.

Choosing a restaurant based on the demographics of that particular area may be useful in knowing whether a restaurant is serving halal meat. It is with no doubt that in a Hindu community, there are Hindu restaurants and basically Hindus as the head of the restaurants. In a Jewish community, there are Jewish restaurants and it is with no doubt that in an area whose demographics is highly populated with Muslims, most surely, there would be halal restaurants in the region. With such a case, it would not be hard to spot a halal restaurant given the fact that majority them will be Muslim-based restaurants. This will surely show that the restaurant is serving Halal food.

Figure 4.2. Muslims in India. An area densely populated by Muslims has a restaurant serving halal foods.

Source: https://www.dw.com/en/indian-muslims-face-renewed-stigma-amid-covid-19-crisis/a-53436462.

The name of the restaurant is also quite important before deciding to enter a restaurant. The name of the restaurant communicates a lot regarding the restaurant. It is very difficult to find a restaurant that is named in a Muslim manner and yet do not serve halal food. Take for instance the Italian restaurants that are actually very common around the world. These restaurants basically serve Italian food alongside the local cuisines of the particular country they are found in. Apart from serving the local food products, these restaurants serve the Italian courses in most circumstances. As a customer in search for halal food, it would be quite important, or rather vital to locate a restaurant with a Muslim name. This is something that one can easily recognize as they are walking in a restaurant. If such a restaurant is not found within the vicinity populated by Muslims, then it would be important for the customer to assume that the restaurant only serves halal cuisines (Mostafa, 2018). In such a case, it would be wise to ask the individual attending to you for the Halal menu or for the case, there is a joint menu, order from the halal section. In the case where one is not sure of a particular restaurant, then it would only be fair to ask for vegetables. This is given the fact that vegetables fall under the halal consumables. According to Halal, vegetables are considered to be part of the food. In addition, mild and all the dairy products are considered to be halal. However, there are those non-halal animal-derived additives that individuals need to be careful about. Most of them are normally used for dressing the salads and in such a case; it would be wise for individuals to stay off salads given the fact that some of those dressings do not clearly define where they were extracted from.

Figure 4.3. Salad on a plate. Salads are served in halal restaurants but it should not include additives that are non-Halal.

Source: A Couple Cooks.

The name of the restaurant is clearly important given the fact that in order to be a halal worth restaurant, individuals need to be certified in order to operate as one. In order for a restaurant to be halal worthy, there are a number of set rules and regulations that have been set by the Muslims regarding the same. A restaurant has to prove that they can be able to follow the stated rules before they are allowed to operate as a halal restaurant. As such, by looking at the name of the restaurant, one would easily state whether the restaurant is Halal. However, in the case of doubt, it would not hurt a peak to ask individuals around the vicinity to tell you more about the restaurant. The word of mouth or rather an assurance by an individual who is conversant with the place can go a long way clear some of the doubts that an individual may have regarding the place they would want to take their meals. The reason as to why one can trust the name as they have been certified is because of the rules and guidelines. To fully comprehend the guidelines that have been put in place in the certification of a restaurant ne needs to understand the rules explained by the department of halal certification.

4.2. CERTIFICATION OF A HALAL RESTAURANT

Halal is an Arabic word, which simply means permissible. In the holy book, the Quran Halal is contrasted to Haram. The term halal is usually associated with the diet in Muslim culture especially meat. Which should be prepared based and according to their requirements. When the word halal is used, it could simply mean allowed, legal, lawful or permitted and when it is associated with food, it simply means the food has met their requirements. The term halal will be used in this based on food products, meat products, cosmetics, personal care products, materials that come in contact with food, pharmaceuticals and food ingredients (Mannaa, 2020). Muslims and Jews have very strict dietary laws, which are followed to the letter, and anyone seen to break is seen as a sinner or can be banished from their culture/ religion and seen as an outsider. The laws of diet in the Islamic culture are specifically derived from their holy book the Quran, the hadith which is the sayings of the Prophet Muhammad and in the Fiqh of the Muslim juries; Maliki, Hanbali, Shafi and Hanafi. When food and other products are classified as Halal it is very serious and it will have been scrutinized and carried out by a Muslim who is an expert in the laws of Islamic diet.

Figure 4.4. The holy Quran. Most of the Muslim dietary laws are from the Holy Quran.

Source: Umrah Packages.

This leads to Halal certification of products and the main aim of this is to ensure that Muslim communities both national and international are complying with the religious requirements. The concept of halal applies to a wide variety and range of products that are used in a daily Muslim life. When Muslims choose products that they will use in their lives be it at work, home or anywhere they are the product needs to be compliant with the processes and procedures as defined by the Islamic laws.

Most industries and producers turn a blind eye to these requirements and their goods and services do not end up being certified Halal and for some they are not aware of these requirements. With all these, they end up overlooking this segment of the population. The Department of Halal Certification EU (DHCE) tries to promote unified standards of these products, acceptance by the Muslim community and certification for the Muslims to fully accept and use these products like the rest of the population. With unified standards, this helps to bridge the gap between the Muslims and industries or producers. With the standards set and with a halal certificate then as a Muslim consumer it assures them that the product or service has followed the strict compliance to the Halal process.

The main reasons as to why halal certification is important is;

There is a broad market in the world. The Muslim community in the world is almost 1.9 billion people across 112 countries who are devoted Muslims. This leads to them believing that there is a wide market that is waiting for these products or services. It is estimated that the halal market size is worth a lot of trillions of dollars. With these figures many companies, industries and service providers would like to comply with the halal process and tap into the market. There is a high demand for halal products and services. With increasing population and spread of the Islamic religion in Christian dominated areas, this leads to a high demand. There is an increase in the population of Muslims in the Middle East, north and south of Africa, the west of Africa also, south of Asia, the former Soviet Union and china. These areas present a very lucrative chain for halal food products.

The Southeast Asia and the Middle East Asia account for almost 400 million and/or more that are Muslims. This makes them the two largest communities that are Muslim and have to consume halal products.

Figure 4.5. Halal certification marks. They are put of food products to show they are halal compliant.

Source: quora.

Muslims can only eat halal food and on the other hand non-Muslims can eat halal food if do so wish. With the rigorous scrutiny the products and food materials undergo it has led to more and more non-Muslims to prefer halal food as compared to similar products without halal certification. They view halal food as being healthier.

With a halal certification it guarantees the product, food or service that it has been checked and is seen to be compliant with the dietary requirements as in the holy books and complies also with Islamic lifestyle.

More and more industries are preferring their products be halal certified as it guarantees that the products have been checked and verified for safety and good health to the consumer. Tis then promotes the marketability of products.

For export products then the halal certificate then it means that it is taken to Muslim majority countries as a requirement. With the certificate, the products do not undergo rigorous testing as they are seen to have already been verified to their standards (Mathew, 2014).

Halal products have to be compliant and they are very strict. The requirement for one to be certified their products have to;

Be pure and clean. The raw materials and end products have to be very pure and clean. The processes these raw materials have to undergo before they become finished products also have to be extremely clean. The end products are handled hygienically and they are stored well and transferred in the same clean and pure way up to when they reach the final consumer.

Be safe for human consumption. The products especially foods and beverages have to be safe for the consumption of humans. The additives have to be certified for consumption and they should never have any side effects.

Be ethical and have integrity. Muslims believe that we should never be cruel to any animal and hence any meat product has to come from an animal that has not been cruelly treated even when being slaughtered. They always pray before slaughtering and have a way of slaughtering the animals they eventually eat. The product or service should not bring any harm to the environment or lead to unfair business practices, i.e., a product should never give unfair advantage to someone else in the same business. They believe competition should be healthy and fair.

Be universal. Halal is for everyone and it does not matter whether it from another religion such as Christians or Buddhists and even those who do not believe in supreme beings such as pagans. It is not limited to Muslims only, it is just an ultimate stamp that guarantees safety and purity and brings superior products and quality services to the consumer.

For products to become halal certified there is a process by which a company industry or service provider has to undergo in order to be given a compliant certificate. The process includes;

The applicant first calls or emails to request for halal certification. This is to ensure that the person has notified the certification authority of their intention. During this process, the applicant will gather all the information about the product and provide all the supporting documentation. This will include from the production of raw materials, where they are acquired or produced how they are transported, the process of manufacturing up to the product and any additives added in the process. Then the applicants submit and pays any fee that is required for application (Lubis et al., 2016).

The halal certification team reviews the information that has been provided and they have a timeline, which is three days after the applicant has applied. After the information is checked it is okayed. In case they are not okay with the information provided the team sends the applicants the questions they have. The applicant then replies by answering to the concerns of the team, address, their comments and answer any questions they might have. It is then given a go ahead if they are satisfied with the answers.

This then means the documentation part is complete and the applicant awaits to be contacted. At this stage the applicant has to ensure that reception of raw materials, storage of raw materials, preparation and packaging of products, finished goods storage are all halal compliant.

The applicant is then contacted for the team to perform level one audit. The team will then visit the company or industry. They will have informed the owner beforehand of their visit. They then examine the company if it is halal compliant. After examination they will then write a report on their findings. All this should be done within six days. They give the okay for a level two audit.

They then run a level 2 audit on the company and write a report on their findings and recommendations. This is to be done within nine days. If the company gets a clean bill of health and the findings are, all positive the report is then taken to a committee for approval.

In case after the level 2 audit the has a few recommendations to the applicant and they present their reviews so that the applicant can correct.

These are found in the findings of level 2 audit. After the applicant has corrected the relevant areas, the report is then taken to an approval committee.

An approving panel then studies the report carefully in the presence of experts to help in their decision-making. They carefully audit the report and very carefully scrutinize the recommendations from the auditing team. If the approving panel is satisfied with the team's recommendations, an agreement will be formed.

Figure 4.6. A slaughterhouse that is halal compliant. They have a clean workspace and they drain blood from all the meat.

Source: Shanghai one-stop engineering co.

The agreement form is then signed by both sides, i.e., the applicant and approving panel to seal the deal. After the signing and paying, any additional fee required. A halal certification will be awarded to the products that have passed. The applicant is then issued with a halal certificate. This then gives the applicant author to add a halal mark on the products from the company to show that the products are halal certified. Halal certified products have a halal mark or the letter "M."

In food, processing halal is involved and in the process of certification, there is careful analysis of raw materials, ingredients and any additives to ensure halal compliance. The department of halal certification EU (DHCE) has to review all the ingredients and sub ingredients for any consumable or non-consumable products to determine where they were derived from, i.e., either an animal or plant. They also review the processes and processing aids that was used in their production. For some instance in food processing there are emulsifiers and enzymes such as rennet and some various cultures, which must comply with halal (Khan et al., 2018).

The area where the food is processed is also assessed against the DHCE integrated Halal Standards to ensure that they have the highest halal compliance. This is mostly carried out during level 1 and level 2 audit and this is usually carried out on the site. This is where the verification of the documentation produced during classification is carried out. The HACCP record, cleaning records, pest management records (to check the chemicals used to kill pests if they are the recommended ones), product specification records, worker's standards, types of machines used, delivery dockets, etc. they also perform an inspection of the site to ensure that it meets their standards.

In terms of food, the most common is meat, and according to halal, there is a specific way in which an animal has to be slaughtered so as to ensure that it does not suffer. During the slaughtering process involves using a sharp knife to make an incision that will cut the front of the throat, the esophagus and the jugular veins but it should not reach the spinal cord.

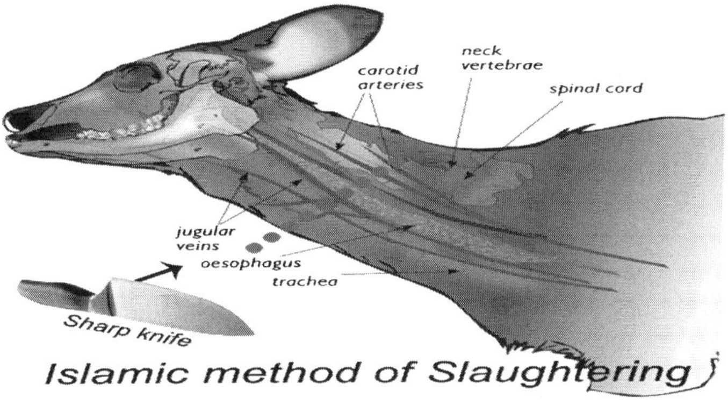

Figure 4.7. Halal method of slaughtering. They only cut once through the throat, esophagus and jugular veins but dot cut the vertebrae.

Source: ESDAW.

The head of the animal that is being slaughtered has to be aligned to qiblah. Qiblah is the direction towards Kaaba in the sacred Mosque in Mecca. Apart from the direction the animal should be slaughtered only upon the utterances of the Islamic prayer. The process of slaughtering should only be carried out by an adult Muslim and most preferably males. Any meat that is slaughtered by a non-Muslim is considered as non-halal.

Upon slaughtering all the blood should be drained from the veins and this is mostly carried out by hanging the carcass by the hind legs so as the blood will drain towards the throat. Any animal that has died without being slaughtered while still alive or died in the wild cannot be eaten and seen as not halal. To add to any animal that has been strangled, beaten to death using blunt or sharp objects, killed falling, and killed by a predator (this can be eaten only if a Muslim finds the injured animal and kills by slitting its throat using halal rules) or an animal that is on an altar cannot be eaten under any circumstances. Under halal these animals have suffered before dying hence, they see them as not fit to be consumed. Generally, in Islam killing of animals is only allowed or granted for two main reasons, to be eaten or to eliminate danger (a rowdy dog).

There are also several foods that are offered to Muslims and are from halal processed foods and products. These foods include; pizza, chicken nuggets, spring rolls, lasagna and baby food are just some.

Figure 4.8. Chicken nuggets that are fried and baked. They form part of the Muslim diet.

Source: Swasthi's Recipes.

The most common form of haram or unpermitted/non-halal food is pork. Meat from pigs. This is the only food that has categorically been forbidden from being eaten by Muslims. The main reason is that the Quran has forbidden it. Some foods that are seen not be in a state of purity are also considered to be haram. The criteria that is used to set them aside is where they were derived from, e.g., the cause of the animal's death and also how it was processed.

Muslims should also ensure that the non-food items they use is halal, e.g., cosmetics, and pharmaceuticals. This is because some of these products contain animal by products or sometimes they contain ingredients that are not permissible. Foods that are considered haram by Muslims include blood and intoxicants. The intoxicants can include alcoholic beverages (Krishnan et al., 2017).

In cosmetics, they should not contain animal products (if they do the animal should have been slaughtered the halal way). They should not contain alcohol, as it is known that alcohol has several negative effects on human skin. The beauty products should ensure that they are vegan (do not contain any animal product) and cruelty-free at the same time.

A Muslim can only be allowed to eat or consume non-halal food only during starvation and they are facing death.

All product in halal have been categorized into different scopes of certification and they labeled from A to J. these include;

- Scope A, this category is referred to as Farming 1(animal). The example in this category include fish, eggs production, production of milk, hunting, fishing, honey production, etc. this involves how animals are captured and how different products from animals are produced.
- Scope B, referred to as farming 2 (plants). These includes all edible plants such as horticultural products, cereals, spices, etc. these are plants that are produced for human consumption.

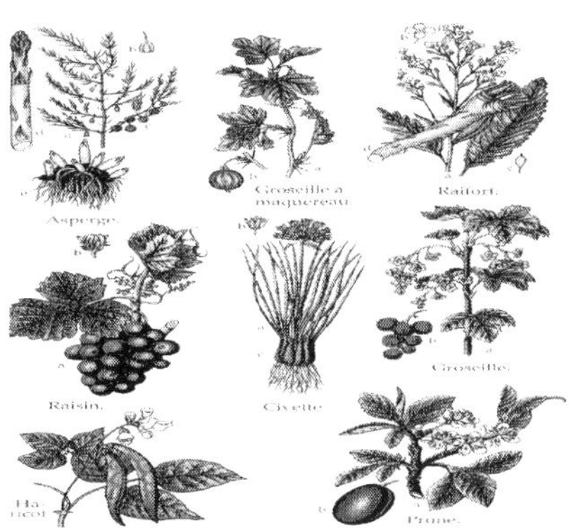

Figure 4.9. Edible plants. Scope B of Halal Certification is labeled farming meaning plants.

Source: Science Photo Library.

- Scope C, referred to as processing 1(perishable animal products). This will include all the activities that are carried out after farming 1. Animal slaughtering, dairy and products from fish. These are activities that are carried out after the farming in the farm. This mostly happens in industries of well off farms.
- Scope D, processing 2 (perishable vegetable products). These will include, fresh fruits, fruit juices, vegetables that are fresh from the farm. All these are directly from the farm and there are no additives.
- Scope E, processing 3 (products that have a long shelf life at room temperature). These include canned products such as beans, etc., snacks, drinking water, beverages or soft drinks, pasta, sugar, salt and flour.

The others include; feed production, food services from hotels, distribution, i.e., retail shops and outlets, services, e.g., financial services (Islamic), sewerage services, water supply, etc., transport and storage of goods, manufacturing of equipment's, chemical and biochemical manufacturing, packaging and packaging material manufacturing and lastly other material manufacturing such as cosmetics, leather, etc. (Karahalil, 2020).

In any event that the customer has a problem with any halal product or has a complaint the Department of Halal Certification EU takes all complaints and concerns from any consumer seriously. This helps the department have opportunity to improve and also maintain the high standards that they are trying to achieve. There are several stages and procedure to follow when one wants to file a complaint.

When filing a complaint or an appeal it should be addressed to the managing director with the complainants details, i.e., full names, details of the organization (if applicable), phone number and email address. State the nature of the complaint and attach any relevant documents.

The first stage after receipt of the appeal or complaint it is dealt with by a panel of at least two DHCE officials and headed by the managing director and after thorough investigations into the matter a response will be generated to be replied to the complainant or appellant within fourteen days of receiving the complaint or appeal.

In the second stage if the response to the complainant/appellant is not satisfactory, then the complainant/appellant can then lodge a complaint within seven days of receiving the response. Then the complaint can then be passed to the independent appeals and complaints board to look further into the matter.

Halal certification has various benefits both to the consumer and the producer;

- A halal certification provides the customer with an assurance that the product has undergone scrutiny and are at par with the sharia laws. Promotes trust among the consumers and in turn it boosts the customer satisfaction in the product.
- National and international acceptance. Many countries will buy the products.
- Stand out from competitors. This allows a business to have an advantage over the other as this is a big and growing market and one can use it as a marketing tool to advertise their product.
- It boasts of good quality. The product not only indicates it is a food product but it has fulfilled strict hygienic requirements and passed.
- For easier monitoring. It is easy to monitor the products as the halal certificate has to be renewed after a specified amount of time and this will ensure the company stay committed to remain halal compliant.

Just like most of the religions, the degrees of adherence within the Muslim faith is impeccable. This is because; these individuals tend to follow their rules to the latter. Some of the entrepreneurs that have decided on venturing into the restaurant business just want to serve the halal options. However, there are perks to this as there are those that are devoted to Muslim and for them to eat in your restaurant or diner, then, one needs to having a certificate that shows that they are a halal restaurant. This will mean that, they would follow the halal rules to the latter (Kamarulzaman et al., 2016). Alcohol is one item that does not fall into the halal menu. As such, to be a fully certified halal restaurant, it means that the restaurant needs to cut out some stock entirely which means there needs not be any alcohol in the restaurant. The belief is that, with no alcohol in the restaurant, then there would be no cases of contamination. As a customer who wants to make sure that the restaurant they are in is halal, then they should not see any alcohol in their counters. As a matter of fact, with alcohol I the counters, most of the devout Muslim believers may choose not to dine in the particular restaurant. All fruit, vegetables, grains, nuts, eggs and most dairy products (depending on additives) are with no doubt considered to be halal. The catch however is that, they need not come into contact with the non-Halal foods. As such, once the customer has been served the vegetables, they should not contain any forms of gelatin, stock or some emulsifiers and additives, which may not be Halal.

Figure 4.10. Restaurant's Halal menu. Looking at the menu can show whether the restaurant serves Halal food.

Source: Pinterest.

Looking at the menu to see the kind of meat they serve is also one way to tell if the restaurant is serving halal food. In the case where, the restaurant is serving meat that is haram, then it would be wise to take your things and run. If the restaurant is fully made for halal foods, yet there are foods that are not halal then the restaurant may be playing at something. One thing that should be understood is that Muslims take it to be vitally important how an animal was killed. As a matter of fact, there are those Muslims who would go to a restaurant and find that the butcher is not Muslim, then leave the restaurant. Not because it had bad revise but just because a Muslim is not taking care of the slaughtering. For this instance, it is the reason as to why; most of the halal restaurants have Muslim butchers to take care of the slaughtering. This will help in keeping the customers in and not out. In fact, there are those restaurants that are not halal, such as most of the grills that are not halal but would want to attract the Muslim customers. In such a case, they invite a Muslim to slaughter their livestock and in extreme instances, hire a Muslim to grill their meat. It is with no doubt that Muslims trust their own more than individuals of other religions to handle the food they choose to eat. As a customer in a particular restaurant, once you see this, then it is clear that the restaurant is halal.

The reason behind the fact that the Muslims are vigilant when it comes to slaughtering the animals is due to the fact that according to their beliefs, the animals need to be healthy and happy before they are slaughtered. As a matter of fact, before doing the killing, the person dong it needs to say a prayer to Allah. There are those animal rights campaigners who do not agree with the Muslim way of killing the animals given the fact that they do not see it as being humane. In their rules, in order to ensure that the animal is healthy and happy for slaughter, an animal should not see another animal being slaughtered. Furthermore, the animal should not see the blade as it is being sharpened. Researchers even claim that most of the animals that are killed in halal manner tend to be stunned before slaughter.

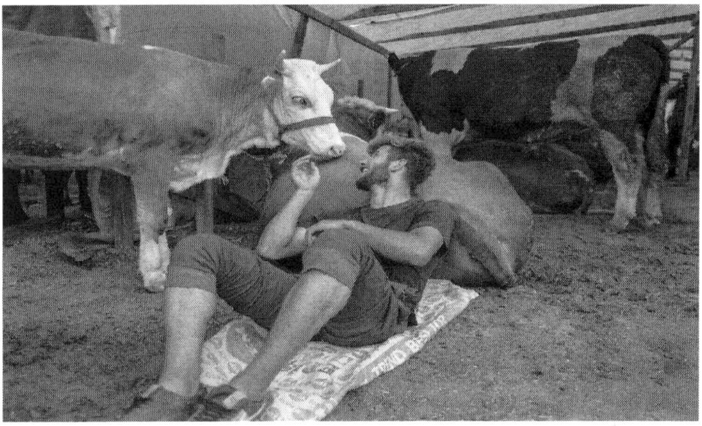

Figure 4.11. Animals before slaughter. According to Muslim laws, the animals need to be healthy and happy before slaughter.

Source: The Guardian.

Another way of ensuring that the foods that a restaurant is serving is halal is by looking at the suppliers of meat for the restaurant. This would only show that not only the restaurant is following the halal rules but also the suppliers of the meat. To get to be trusted, most of the restaurants have looked into wholesale halal meat suppliers. There are however difficult cases, especially in the commercial sector. In such a case, no sense is seen in having halal and no-halal production lines when the vast majority of consumers care about the food in a certain directing and few in the other direction.

Another way in which one may know whether a restaurant is serving halal foods is by observing the kitchen area. This is especially for these restaurants that serve both halal and non-halal foods. For such a restaurant, there is normally an area set aside to prepare all the halal dishes. Cross-contamination is a vital issue when it comes to the preparation of halal dishes. In order for the food to be properly halal, then it is required that it does not come into contact with non-halal products (Junaidi, 2020). As a matter of fact, the halal foods need to be stored, prepared and served in a different area in the restaurant's kitchen. In order to ensure that the halal foods and vegetables do not come into cross-contamination with the non-Halal dishes then it is required that the restaurant:

- Ensure all utensils, crockery, cutlery and surfaces are cleaned and sanitized before use.
- Store and cook Halal foods separately to your other foods – especially your meats, like pork. Ideally, use a different fridge and oven.
- Use a separate counter, chopping board and utensils for all Halal food preparation
- Clearly label all Halal dishes in their kitchen.
- Store and cook Halal foods separately to other foods – especially meats such as like pork. Ideally, use a different fridge and oven.

Once a restaurant follows all the above, they need to be certified. However, one needs to fully understand what halal is and the different kinds of food s that are categorized as halal.

4.3. HALAL FOOD IN RESTAURANTS

Human beings have been blessed by nature with a lot of resources and given options on how to utilize those resources rightly or wrongly in meeting their needs. Food falls under the basic needs of humans and its selection and consumption varies differently among regions, religions and cultures. Religion has stood out to be the most powerful factor influencing all sectors in life including the dietary patterns and habits of humankind. Halal is an Arabic word meaning lawful or permitted while the vice versa is termed as haram. Though the terms refer to universal aspects of life, the terms applies in relation to food products, meat products, food ingredients and food contact materials. Different religions have different interpolations of the terms halal and haram all discussing different life aspects. Verses from different Surahs, like Al-Baqarah have been referred to the Qur'an commands to take Halal food, before the performance of good deeds as it provides energy to both body and soul. Liquid and solid food items, such as water, vegetables and fruits have been described halal. All these items are originally lawful, unless contaminated with impurity (Jia & Chaozhi, 2021).

The halal meat from cattle has been chosen especially without vegetables, fruits, and other food items, because the Muslims and Jews are more cautious about meat and slaughtering procedures. Types of animals have been categorized, as some are Land Animals like camel, cow, buffalo and rabbit. Some of the birds include chickens, ducks, sparrows, ostriches, pigeons and quail. Some are doubtful birds like the crow and parrot. Out of marine animals fish and some are doubtful like prawn, starfish, crabs, oysters, dogfish and shark as decreed by certain Imams are halal food. Slaughtering has been mentioned as an essential requirement of Halal meat from land animals. The slaughtering process should be according to Islamic principles; cutting of blood vessels properly and mentioning Allah Almighty's name while slaughtering. Halal food generates great demand in the world particularly in the Muslim countries. Currently, international market of halal food runs into about US$580 billion annually. The culture of halal food has been accepted by people from different religions and its demand is increasing continuously.

The Islamic dietary laws are said to be defined in the Holy Quran by the Habit saying who is the last prophet Muhammad and additionally in the Fish (Jurisprudence) of the Muslim juries such as the Hanafi, Shafi, Maliki and Hanbali. The classification of food products as Halal is a very serious and can only be carried out by a Muslim who is an expert in the Islamic dietary laws on foods or drinks that are lawful, permitted or allowed for consumption by Muslims.

4.4. CODEX GENERAL GUIDELINES

The Codex Alimentarius Commission accepts that there may be negligible differences in opinion in the interpretation of lawful and unlawful animals and in the slaughter act, according to the different Islamic Schools of Thought; they have different interpretation of halal food. As such, these general guidelines are subjected to the interpretation of the proper authorities of the importing countries. However, the certificates granted by the religious authorities of the exporting country should be accepted in principle by the importing country, except when the latter provides justification for other specific requirements. Firstly, are the matters relating to the scope of the guidelines may entail measures taken in labeling of the foods. These apply to the use of the term halal and equivalent terms in claims as defined in the General Standard for the Labeling of Pre-packaged Foods. It includes its use in trademarks, brand names and business names. The guidelines are intended to supplement the Codex General Guidelines on Claims and do not supersede any prohibition contained therein. The term halal should thereby be used to refer to food permitted under the Islamic Law. Still, halal food can be prepared, processed or stored in different sections or lines within the same premises where non-halal foods are produced, provided that necessary process are taken to prevent any contact between halal and non-halal foods. In addition, halal food can be prepared, processed, transported or stored using facilities, which have been previously used for non-halal foods if proper cleaning procedures, according to Islamic requirements, have been observed (Ismail et al., 2018).

All food is considered Halal except otherwise which are referred to as Haram. The haram foods includes swine/Pork and its by-products such as gelatin, alcoholic drinks and intoxicants, reptiles and insects, carnivorous animals, birds of prey and certain other animals, food containing ingredients such as gelatin, enzymes, emulsifiers, and flavors are questionable such as mashbooh. This is because of the origin of these ingredients is not known. Additionally the foods products must be free from the following Pig or dog blood, blood part or by-product of human body, e.g., human hair in L-Cysteine Carnivorous animals (except fish). Birds with talons or birds that feed by snatching and tearing, e.g., eagles and other similar birds, Reptiles and insects should be avoided. Animals that live on land and in water (amphibians) like frogs, crocodiles and other similar animals are also avoided. Birds and cattle, which have died, by any means other than slaughtering according to the Islamic Law are prohibited. Animals which are generally considered as repulsive such as lice, maggots, mice, rats, spiders and other similar animals are also considered unclean.

AmalMerge

HALAL And Food Safety Institute

GUIDELINES
FOR THE PREPARATION OF
HALAL FOOD AND GOODS
FOR THE MUSLIM CONSUMERS

Figure 4.12. General guidelines for the use additives in halal food.

Source: www.fao.org.

Animals permitted under the Islamic Law such as Cow, Sheep, Lamb, Goat, Poultry, etc., which are not slaughtered according to the Islamic Law are not considered as halal. Additionally, Wine, Ethyl Alcohol or Spirits, Intoxicating and hazardous plants, any product or by-product including any product used temporarily as a substitute or for trial which contains or is derived from any one or more of the above products are not allowed. However, minute quantity, whether as an ingredient or sub ingredient or as a processing aid or as a releasing agent or as a glazing agent or as an additive or as a color in any other form, is Haram for Muslims.

Intoxicating and hazardous plants except where the toxin or hazard can be eliminated during processing. All alcoholic drinks, all forms of intoxicating and hazardous drinks, food additives derived from Slaughtering as well as lawful land animals that have not been slaughtered in compliance with the rules laid down in the Codex Recommended Code of Hygienic Practice for Fresh Meat are banned. When a claim is made that a food is halal, the word halal or equivalent terms should appear on the label. In accordance with the Codex General Guidelines on Claims, claims on halal should not be used in ways which could give rise to doubt about the safety of similar food or claims that halal foods are nutritionally superior to, or healthier than, other foods, as all food are considered Halal except the following which are (Haram Bashir et al., 2019).

Common food ingredients and additives that are permissible are mostly from animal or plant sources or produced synthetically. The ingredients which are made from plant or produced synthetically are Halal. All food ingredients and additives produced from animals which were not slaughtered according to Islamic rite or from the pig are Haram and not suitable for Muslims to consume, and any food product, ingredient or additive containing alcohol or produced with the use of alcohol is Haram and unsuitable for Halal use. Some of the food ingredients and additives include for example Acetic Acid that Occurs naturally in plant juices and can be prepared synthetically and can be obtained from animal tissues. If it is made from animal tissues, then it will not be Halal. Secondly is the adipic acid which occurs naturally in beets and can be prepared synthetically is also considered as a halal additive.

The other is the Agar agar additive that naturally occurs as seaweed, used in place of gelatin. The additive from the source plant is considered halal otherwise haram. Beta-apo-8- Carotenal (C30) (Apocarotenal) (E160e) is another additive that is orange/yellow in color derived from plants but may utilize gelatin or lard to dissolve in water. If lard or gelatin made from animal other than fish is used then it will not be suitable for Halal use. Casein which is a protein of milk used in the manufacture of cheeses is precipitated by acid or by animal or vegetable enzymes is considered halal if only plant enzyme is used. Another additive is the chocolate liquor Syrup made from chocolate and used for chocolate flavored products. It is not liquor or alcohol but because it is a liquid, it is called liquor. The liquor is suitable for halal use. Dextrose also known as the corn syrup, made from starch, used as a sweetener or coloring agent is also suitable for halal use. E153 Carbon Black, color obtained by charring bones, meat, blood, wood, vegetable, etc., If charred from wood or vegetables then it will be suitable for Halal use. Lastly, E322 Lecithin additive, an emulsifier originally obtained from egg yolk but commercially prepared from soya bean oil, which is also suitable for halal use while those prepared from other products are considered haram.

4.5. HALAL TRAINING

In efforts to increasing the understanding and consequently the demand for halal food, the Department of Halal Certification EU (DHCE) has prepared a series of Halal Training Programs on foods and dietary for human consumption. The training programs are based on Islamic Law and cover different issues in the halal food such as defining what foods are Halal that are lawful and permissible as well as the unlawful and prohibited called Haram, the concept of Halal, importance of Halal for Muslim consumers, the Halal market, product research and development, Halal certification, internal Halal training among other topics (Indrasari et al., 2020). The training programs are designed for professionals, Muslims/non-Muslims who are associated with the Halal industry, those who wish to join the Halal industry and even those who would like to improve their existing Halal production in their individual businesses and enterprises. Besides companies or enterprises that wish to deliver Halal, training to their employees can have an expert train them from their location since it is more of a personalized trainings.

Arranged visits to abattoirs and processing plants to aid understanding and see how others implement the DHCE standard/procedures in the real world also go a long way in helping comprehend the halal food processing processes. Trainings are imperative in the engagement of halal food so as to ensure that all guidelines are followed strictly. Otherwise lack of proper training may cause food to fail to reach the standards require by the halal food for human consumption.

Figure 4.13. Muslim slaughter. The butchers need to be humane according to Muslims.

Source: ABC.

Halal requires that the animals intended for human consumption should be slain in a certain manner such as they should not be physically weak or having any form of blemish that may term them unclean. Halal slaughter is one of the more humane methods available to the meat industry and the only method acceptable for Muslim consumers worldwide. The conditions for Halal slaughter are such as the animal to be slaughtered must be from the categories that are permitted for Muslims to consume. It has been reported that as a norm and law Muslims do not consume meat from pigs that is pork. Moreover, the animal must be alive at the time of slaughter without any forms of stunning and or unconsciousness of animals. Stunning through a gadget with a non-penetrating round head, in a way that does not kill the animal before its slaughter is permitted (Henderson, 2016). A sharp knife is used to slaughter the animal, which must not be able to kill due to its weight otherwise if it kills due to the impact the meat may be prohibited for human consumption. The windpipe, food-tract and the two jugular veins must be cut. The slaughtering must be done in one stroke without lifting the knife. The knife should not be placed and lifted when slaughtering the animal. Slaughtering must be done by a sane adult Muslim. Animals slaughtered by a Non-Muslim will not be Halal. The name of Allah must be invoked at the time of slaughtering by saying Bismillah Allahu Akbar, which means, "In the Name of Allah; Allah is the Greatest."

If at the time of slaughtering the name of anyone else other than Allah is invoked, then the meat becomes haram. However, if a Muslim forgets to invoke the name of Allah at the time of slaughtering, the meat will remain Halal. However, if he intentionally does not invoke the name of Allah, the meat becomes Haram. The head of the animal must not be cut off during slaughtering but later after the animal is completely dead, even the knife should not go deep into the spinal cord. Skinning or cutting any part of the animal is not allowed before the animal is completely dead. Slaughtering must be made in the neck from the front to the back. The slaughtering must be done manually not by a machine, as one of the conditions is the intention, which is not found in a machine.

The slaughtering should not be done on a production line where pigs are slaughtered. Any instrument used for slaughtering pigs should not be used in the Halal slaughtering. Some of the customary and desirable practices when slaughtering halal food includes water should be offered to the animal before slaughter, and it should not be slaughtered when hungry. The knife should be hidden from the animal, and slaughtering should be done out of sight of other animals waiting to be slaughtered. Animals should be killed in a comfortable way. Unnecessary suffering to them must be avoided. The animal must be slaughtered by the use of a sharp knife thus; it should be re-sharpened before slaughter. While storing, processing and transporting halal meat, chilled meat or frozen for export to Muslims should be stored in separate cold stores other than those in which pork or other non-Halal meat is stored. Meat minced or processed for Muslims should not be minced in the same machines used to mince pork or other non-Halal meat.

Figure 4.14. Why should we eat Halal meat.

Source: Amalia Cahaya Putri-Medium.

Halal foods are certified by various organizations such as The Halal Food Council of Europe (HFCE), Halal Certification Germany (HCG) as well as Halal Food & Quality in Spain. The religion aspects are not the only aspect that halal food considers but also the food is accompanied by other beneficial features. This other reasons for halal food have found their ways into winning the hearts of many who do not follow Islam. One of the benefits is the care for animal rules implemented in the processing of animal meat. Animal welfare has become a major topic in current culture and it is fair to say that many modern farming practices do not consider this. Issues of overcrowding the methods used in slaughtering the animal place animal care secondary to just getting a food product out there. The halal method is much different to these types of farming methods (Hanzaee & Ramezani, 2011). Halal dictates that all animals should be respected and treated well before they are consumed. During rearing, they are offered the space and care needed to live their lives as healthily and naturally as possible. Even during slaughter, great care and respect are shown to the animal. No animal may be slaughtered while in the sight of other live animals. The aim is to make the process as stress-free as possible for the animals. This has health benefits too, as this lack of stress prevents the release of hormones into the animal that can affect the meat that comes from it. Animals raised under the tenets of halal experience high levels of care.

Secondly, the halal food is accompanied by tremendous health benefits that some are not even documented. As reported from past studies, the method used for slaughter prevents the release of harmful hormones in the animal's body. However, the practice of draining the blood from the carcass is also an important aspect of the process. In draining the blood from the animal, the halal method ensures the purity of the meat that you eventually consume. Importantly, it also means that there is no uric acid in the meat. Uric acid can cause issues with your kidneys, skin, and blood. Non-halal meat often contains this acid, particularly in poultry. However, the halal method ensures that the acid is drained completely, which means it cannot have the harmful effects that are associated with it.

Furthermore, hygiene is a crucial aspect of the halal process. It is all about ensuring there are no impurities in the meat. As a result, incidences of food poisoning and other hygiene-related issues are much lower in halal meat than they are in other types of meat. Halal accreditation is known beneficial not only to consumers but also to manufacturer /producers as well as the government/authority. Halal certification convinces Muslim consumers on products they purchase and consume. Furthermore, halal certificate may protect consumers from deceptive and fraudulent, while non-Muslim consumers may also get benefit from the high quality products. For that reason, halal products, of course, are profitable by improving their competitiveness and marketability. For the government and halal authority, halal accreditation is an effective tool to monitor halal products in the market as well as supervising their production, during storing and transportation. Therefore, collaboration and better understanding among involved institutions is essential (Han et al., 2021).

With a Muslim population more than about 1.6 billion, and based on the estimated expenditure per capita for food of about US$0.85/day, it is estimated that the market for halal products is about US$ 550 billion/year. Conversely, halal food trade in the recent market is only at least US$ 150 billion/year. As the many of the countries have significant Muslim community, Asia becomes an important market for halal food that contributes more than 60% of total marketplace. Indonesia and India are known having predominantly Muslim population in the world. Generally, the major global halal food products are being imported from countries such as Australia, New Zealand, Ireland, the United States, U.K., Brazil and Canada among others.

As in many countries are becoming increasingly concerned about rising health care costs associated with preventable diseases, Islamic law has established the preventable way of particular diseases by forbidding any harmful substances. Basically halal requirements meet the conventional quality standard, such as ISO, Codex Alimentarius, Hazard Analysis and Critical Control Point (HACCP), Good Hygienic Practice (GHP), etc. Additionally, implementing halal requirement will produce the better quality products compare to those that only implement conventional standard. Therefore, halal products basically not only subjected for Muslim consumers, but also appropriate for non-Muslim community.

To the Muslims According to past reviews, companies are answerable to numerous groups of stakeholders and paying attention to adequate degree of their welfare might be crucial to the companies' survival. stakeholders are defined as "entities or individual that can reasonably be expected to be significantly affected by the organization's activities, products, services; and whose actions can reasonably be expected to affects the ability of the organization to successfully implement its strategies and achieve its objectives." Then, they may include shareholders, employees, lenders, suppliers, customers, government and the society at large. On the other hand, stakeholder theory suggests that the organization success is dependent upon its ability to manage the relationship with stakeholders successfully. A company is implied to have contract with various stakeholders (Debney, 2016). However, in other studies argues that not all stakeholders are equal and there is an existence of a hierarchy of stakeholders. The more powerful the stakeholders, the more companies have to fulfil their needs and demands and tend to disregard the concerns of less powerful groups. In accordance to a past study, companies need the stakeholders' support to be in existence for the foreseeable future since stakeholders have the power on the resources of the companies. Thus, if Muslims consumers hold the power on the companies' resources namely sales revenue, the importance of providing halal food to them should not be taken lightly since it is crucially important to Muslims market.

In conclusion, Muslim consumers need to heighten their power, as stakeholders to ensure their needs and demands will be considered by companies. In doing so, halal related matters should always be considered as top priority in choosing food products. Wide range of social media such as Face book, Twitter, What's app and others should be utilized to the benefits of Muslims by informing others of any unethical activities by any company. Any confusion with regards to the ingredients should be clarified firmly with the companies. Changing the purchasing behavior by taking more conscious act upon halal issues would demonstrate the seriousness of Muslim consumers in making sure the food products that are served to them are halal and according to the Islamic principle. As the stakeholders, make them as one who holds greater power and control over companies' resources. It leaves them with no other choice but to fulfil the needs of Muslims consumers.

The halal food also faces some challenges with major issue being that it requires earnest attention is pertain to the Halal literacy of the consumer. According to Connor, the consumers' understanding, awareness, and familiarity with the food they consumed are built upon many factors that consist of personal sentiment, societal, and other environmental factors. As evidenced by the study conducted by Hashanah and Hifza , despite the fact that the majority of consumers today are highly educated and can easily access any type the information, their level of Halal literacy vary. There is great resistance among some of the consumer because they misunderstood the true meaning of Halal. Some of them tend to associate Halal with religious ritual, especially the slaughtering and for this reason; the consumers feel unpleasant towards the product claimed to be Halal, due to the lack of knowledge on this subject. The universal concept of Halal in food production holds the notion of being clean, healthy, and free from any kind of contamination not only from pork and alcoholic substances (Damit et al., 2018). Undeniably, the Halal principles are religiously related concept; however, the principles connote healthy and hygienic cuisine and appeal to the health-conscious people. Promoting the Halal concept and making it easily acceptable to all types of consumer, it should not be viewed as offensive to any religious belief as Halal should be understood as a good standard in producing the product where it put forward the theme of hygienic and safety to the product.

Most of the time, consumers are unable to determine which foods are Halal simply by reading the label on the packaging of a product, this is due to the fact that some producers used specific terminology of the component in their product, in which the terms are most probably unfathomable by the average consumer. Therefore, some consumer tends to be suspicious of the substance used in the product because of their unfamiliarity with the content. The substance can only be recognized after going through a stringent examination of the product by certain bodies. Additionally, the rapid developments in food technology have spurred the advancement of the world food market today. The issue of genetically modified (GM) food is one the recent development in food technology that bugging the consumers mind. Genetically Modified foods are known as a source of food that has been modified genetically in the part its genomes. In a layman terms, a GMO food is foods that have been artificially altered to mimic the natural foods. The issue regarding GMO is clearly justified under the Malaysian Standard "Foods and drinks containing products of genetically modified organisms (GMOs) or ingredients made by the use of genetic material from animals that are non-halal by the Shariah law are not halal." Despite the government aspiration in supporting the development of GMO, the public, particularly the Muslim consumers have raised their concern over the ethicality and the halal state of the GMO. With regard to the issue of GM food, the consumer are becoming more concern of consuming the Halal product that uses genetically modified elements as it elicited suspicious thought over the ingredients used in the food.

Consumers were also being deceived by images and words used on the product packaging. There are some products in the market that used Arabic words and displayed images attributed to Islam to deceive the consumers. A study by Shari and others revealed that certain unethical company purposely used the Arabic-sounded or Islamic-signaled brand names, even to the extent of displaying selected Quranic verses to trick the consumer into believing the product to be Halal. Furthermore, some consumers take for granted the Halal word or the Halal logo without questioning their authenticity. On top of that, some unethical manufacturer tends to use Islamic images on the product packaging to imply that the product is Halal. There even dare to misuse the term "Sunnah" on the product packaging to induce consumer positive acceptance of the product. The consequences of the labeling exploitation can lead to confusion among the consumer and may also jeopardize the company's future. There by various interventions are needed so as to minimize or eliminate the challenges as well as in maximizing the benefits in the enterprise (Cuesta-Valiño et al., 2020).

Once one has fully understood the rules and guidelines of halal and the benefits that are accrued from serving halal food, it is important to spread the word. A customer can only trust that a restaurant is serving halal food or rather becomes aware of the same once the restaurant spreads the word by the use of the media.

4.6. GETTING INFORMATION FROM SOCIAL MEDIA

To create a culture of transparency in any restaurant, then owners tend use social media to help in the process. As a customer who is in search for a halal restaurant, it is quite important to make social media a friend. This is due to the fact that social media tend to be influential and where individuals write reviews about a place anonymously. One thing that should be understood by most restaurants is that, most of the restaurant-goers tend to take seriousness on the contents of the foods that they eat. The ethics regarding animals and the welfare practices are gaining attention in the human population. As a matter of fact, there is always a sense of relief when they are making positive conscious choices regarding the welfare of animals. The restaurants need to show that they are proud of the suppliers they get their produce from and furthermore be proud of the quality food that they are serving. It is notably unwise to give away trade secrets but it is not harmful if the restaurant discloses some information to their website for the purpose of informing their customers. However, it should be understood that there is no room for providing false information sine at the bottom of the website there is a small space for customer reviews. This is where the fate of the restaurant lies.

Figure 4.15. Social media reviews of a restaurant. Social media reviews can destroy or build a restaurant.

Source: Software advice.

At that point, as a customer, one may know whether a restaurant actually serves halal foods or if it is actually fraud. One should consider looking at the rates that the customers gave to the restaurant and also look at the tweets that have been posted regarding the same. In the Muslim community, word of mouth is very important and as such, once one of them decides to tweet about a particular place then it means that they know about it. If it is your restaurant, then pray to Allah that what is tweeted brings about a positive impact to your restaurant (Battour & Ismail, 2016).

Chapter 5

Halal Food Certification

CONTENTS

5.1. INTRODUCTION

Do we live to eat or we eat to live? Most individuals who believe in the universe, that they survive through fate, hold onto the thought that they live to eat; whereas individuals who believe in a greater power than them, more of a supernatural being, or God – hold onto the thought that they live to eat, and that, whether they eat or not, the supernatural being will help in their survival, in one way or the other. However, when it comes to food, the believe that different human beings hold onto, does not really matter; cause after all, in one way or the other, they will have to eat.

Food is basically anything that a living creature ingests into its body. Different types of foods come from different sources; some foods might be obtained from plants, others from animals, and others from fungi materials. To human beings, different foods contain different nutrients; hence it is important that the type of food being consumed to be balanced from time to ensure that the human body has just the right supply of nutrients. Consumption of balanced food nutrients promotes good health in a human being by ensuring that the body cells have the required amount of body energy; the body is strong enough to fight diseases and maintain life; and that the body is strong enough to support growth (Bergeaud-Blackler, 2015).

In living creatures, there exists different feeding behaviors which keep on evolving based on the rate of climate change which affects the habitats of all living creatures in diverse ways. Human beings fall under the category of omnivorous feeding mechanism. Omnivorous creatures obtain their food from different ecological regions. The omnivorous feeding mechanism represents a group of living creatures which feed on both plants and fellow animals.

Since time immemorial, human beings were known for their habit of obtaining food through two main different ways. The first one is through hunting, whereby they would go hunting for wild animals in forests and rivers; however, not all animals were edible, so they had to be vigilant of the animals they were after. The second method is agriculture. However, the first human beings did not start off with agriculture rather they were gatherers. Through gathering, it is believed that they were able to master the art of differentiating the edible and non-edible foods. Due to increase in human population, the gathers moved to agriculture whereby they would replicate the type of foods they used to gather; so as to ensure that there is enough food for all population.

As time eloped, and as the human race evolved, the hunting process had its own challenges, which pushed the human race to choose agriculture as their main source of food. With agriculture, they were not only able to grow different edible plants, but they had the chance of rearing animals depending on the climatic conditions of their regions. Rearing of domestic animals promoted the growth of wild animals whose populations had previously been declining due to increased hunting activities; which created a balance in the ecological niche.

With increase in the human population, they had to distribute themselves in different geographical regions. The geography in each settlement region affected the type of agriculture in that; each geographical region had only a unique set of plants and animals which could survive in it based on the topography of that region and more so because of the climatic conditions of that region. The geographical differences also brought about different cultures. With different cultures, different medicinal plants, dishes, food spices were born.

Human beings are known to be social being, hence, with time, they have managed to interact either through trade, marriages or through education which is the latest field known to be bringing people from different regions together. The interactions of human beings brought about the exchange of different cultural ideas. The exchange of cultural ideas does also include the exchange of food traditions and practices.

5.2. FOOD CERTIFICATION

The diversity of foods in the world has brought about the need of ensuring that the food being produced and sold to fellow human beings is safe and secure for consumption. Unsecure food is known to cause effects of food poisoning which if not treated immediately is fatal. For this reason, Food Certification process has been introduced in all parts of the world (Bergeaud-Blackler, 2015).

Food Certification is a term used to refer to the process of awarding a food safety certificate which verifies that the foods being sold by a certain individuals or produced by a certain food processing industry, is safe and secure for consumption. The food safety certificate is awarded after the completion of the food safety training course. Food safety training course specializes in equipping its learners with the several skills such as the likes of; one, how to properly clean and sanitize all surface and utensils used when handling foods; how to maintain high levels of personal hygiene; how to handle food in accordance with the legal recommendations in the law of the land; how to store and prepare food following the right recipe and in regards to the cooking temperatures, cooking environment and the appropriate equipment to use; understanding the process of food contamination and the possible effects that contaminated foods will have on the consumers; understanding ways of preventing food poisoning and also mastering the skills of offering first aid to customers who have suffered from food poisoning; and last but not least, understanding the art of using the right pest and disease control of food being produced in the farm, to ensure that, they do not have any toxins from the chemicals used to prevent pests and diseases.

The training and certification of food handlers ensure that, a business thrives well for the trainings guarantee long-term health of the business. Lack of food certification is believed to bring about effects which not only affect a business, but the operations of the entire country. For instance, employees suffering from either food poisoning or food allergies will not be able to give their best at their place of work, which leads to job loss, and lack of enough labor in the work place; affecting the economy of a country.

5.3. HALAL FOOD CERTIFICATION

Some of the regions in the world specialize in bulky production of different types of food; and for this reason, there exists several food certification organization which specialize in awarding of certificate to farms and industries which supply them with different food types which they distribute in different parts of the world. Halal food certification is one of the most common food certification organization specializing in the countries in the Middle East parts of the world.

Halal food certification upholds the integrity in food production by ensuring that, the foods being produced are suitable for the consumption by the Islamic community and that the production procedure is not harmful in anyway. The term 'Halal' is an Arabic word used to mean lawful; whereas Haram is also an Arabic word used to mean forbidden or harmful. It is mostly used during the halal food certification process to verify that the food production procedure is not harmful, (*it is not haram*).

Figure 5.1. An image showing halal logo.

Source: https://www.vectorstock.com/royalty-free-vector/halal-logo-emblem-halal-sign-certificate-vector-14043589.

The halal food certification procedure is mostly based on the Islamic beliefs drawn from the Holy book, the Quran. The halal food certification laws drawn from the Quran include: one, the meat foods are only to be distributed if the animal was slaughtered by the male gender, otherwise, the meat is considered to be haram according to their beliefs; two, still under the slaughtering of animals, a sharp knife out to be used and the cutting should be specific across the jugular vein, the carotid artery and the windpipe of an animal, and not in any other place; three, a Quranic verse, referred to as the Tasmiya or Shahada ought to be read out loud during the slaughtering process; four, dead animals are not to be slaughtered for meat, only healthy and alive animals are to be slaughtered, and before slicing the animal into small pieces, enough blood ought to be drained from carcass, mainly via its main veins; five, the consumption of meat from dead animals is considered a taboo. The halal food certification laws drawn from the Quran are mostly related to production of meat foods.

The Halal food certification is assigned only by the government of the respective nation. For instance, in India, which is one of the countries located in the Middle East regions of the globe, Halal certification is assigned by the government after an individual or even an industry has completed the training process. However, since the government has several other tasks to accomplish; the Indian government has established several public and private bodies which oversee the process of awarding halal certificates. Some of the private bodies in India assigning Halal Food certificates include: the Halal India Private Limited, the Halal Certification Services India Private Limited, the Jamiat Ulama-E-Maharshtra-A state unit of Jamiat Ulama-E-Hind, and lastly but not least, the Jamiat Ulama-i-Hind Halal Trust (Bergeaud-Blackler, 2015).

The halal certification does also cater for the certification of cosmetics and pharmaceutical products. The main reason why cosmetics and pharmaceutical products in Middle East fall under the category of certified products through the halal food certification is because most of them are made from plant and animal products; and if not certified, they might lead to serious effects. For instance, cosmetics such as the likes of lipstick use pig fat as their raw material; other cosmetics do also used by-products from animals such as the likes of chicken, goats, sheep, among others as their raw materials during their manufacture. Since the cosmetics use raw materials obtained from animals, which are also consumed by human beings, they ought to be certified under the halal food certification. By certified cosmetics and pharmaceuticals using the halal food certification means that, no haram procedure has been used according to the Islamic community. For instance, the manufacturing of lip balms from pig fat, the halal certification ensure that the fat was obtained from a healthy and alive pig, not a dead one.

Halal certification has grown its roots in different countries across the globe, and it is no longer restricted only in Middle East countries, but also in other continents. The factor which has contributed to the establishment of the halal certification across the world is trade. Other countries will at one point trade with Islamic nations in different commodities, and the food commodities ought to be certified before exportation or importation in Islamic nations. Still, the current world in which we live in, supports immigration, whereby, individuals from different parts of the world are able to co-exist together in a peaceful manner. Halal certification ensures that the members of the Islamic community who reside in Non-Islamic nations are able to feed on foods certified according to their religious laws and beliefs. The halal food market has been estimated to control almost a quarter of the global market; and for this reason, many companies are looking forward to ensuring that their products are certified under the halal certification so as to meet the global market demand and supply chain, and avoid being left out.

Figure 5.2. An image showing a halal certificate.

Source: https://www.kbhc.info/.

The halal certification does also require the certification of the tourism sector, a certificate referred to as the Halal Tourism certification. Almost every international tourist hotel across the world ought to be certified under the halal tourism certification. The halal tourism has been put in place so as to ensure that hotels and restaurants serve halal-certified foods to their tourists of the Islamic community. Nations in Middle East, have to uphold the halal tourism certification by ensuring that their facilities such as the likes of swimming pools and spa, are separated into three categories; one for the children, others for the women, and others for men.

Due to the growth and popularity of the halal food certification process, several issues have been raised across the world. One of the issues is the rectification of the manufacturing process if a product is to be certified under the halal food certification. Second, the price of halal certified products due to the cost incurred during the certification process. Individuals who are not members of the Islamic community might face the challenge of unemployment due to the laws of the halal certification process in that; only male Muslims are required to slaughter animals, making it hard for Non-Muslims to get a job in the halal slaughterhouses. Most individuals who are not of the Islamic community view the halal certification as a discriminating process for it leaves them out, by strictly adhering to the Islamic laws (Zulfakar et al., 2012). For instance, international hotels which are not located in Islamic nations might regard the Halal Tourism certification as a burden to them, since not all of their guests are of the Islamic community, and you might find that, only a small percentage of the Islamic community spend time in the hotels, with a large percentage being made up of individuals from other religious communities. Despite the fact that halal certification is popular in the entire globe, there exists no standard halal certification process; which brings the conflict of interest where, a halal certification process in one nation might not be recognized in another nations and the products might end up being rejected.

The good thing with halal certification, products which are halal certified are not prohibited in other parts of the world or to Non-Muslims. The halal food certification process in all parts of the world tries to consider several factors. One, the quality of the products being certified ought to meet all the Islamic standards which go hand in hand with the consumer needs and preferences. During halal certification, it is required that the consumers be enlightened on the differences between halal and haram products. The enlightenment process could be done either through advertisements or any other activities. Some members of the Islamic community like their foods which they consume to be processed in a certain way. The requirements of the consumers have to be put into consideration hence the formulation of different strategies which ensure that the demands of the customers have been met before the product is certified under halal food certification. The halal certification does also cater for the advertisement of their certified products. The running of advertisement projects under halal certification ensures that the right advertisement procedure is used based on the cultural practices of different Islamic communities. The halal certification process helps in taming business by ensuring that they do not con their consumers through the use of the exaggerated product prices.

The basic steps followed during the halal certification process are three. The first one is the validation of the production process of a certain product before it is even certified. The second step is the verification of the manufacturing process and ensuring that the manufacturing process was in accordance with the laws of the Islamic community. The third and last step is that of issuance of certificate if the firm has passed the test.

Halal certification process is critical mainly because of three reasons. The first one is that it promotes consumer confidence, the second one is that it promotes the competition of products in the globe market and the third one is that it promotes the quality of products. With consumer confidence, as the name suggests, a product certified under halal food certification is more preferred for the consumers have confidence in it that it is secure and produced under the strict Islamic rules. Consumers will be able to consume more of halal certified foods and prefer them to other food product. Halal food certification provides a bigger market for industries which are under the halal food certification (Wan Hassan & Awang, 2009). As state earlier, products certified under halal certification make up fifteen percent of the global market, meaning that, companies which certify their products under halal certification will have a bigger market to supply their products. Furthermore, food products certified under halal certification will be more promoted in Global Islam, bringing in more profits for the companies which manufactured them. Halal certified food products have their own way of standing out, not only in Islamic nations but also in other nations across the globe. The ability of halal certified food products in the market, limits the competition making more money for the manufacturing and processing companies. When it comes to quality, halal certified food products are considered more to be of high quality compared to other food products, not only because of adherence to the Islamic community beliefs, but also because they promote the hygiene and sanitation during food production and processing.

In most parts across the world, halal certificates are mostly awarded to individuals who own either a food production firm, or meat production firms, or even organizations which specialize in production of cosmetics and pharmaceuticals for they also fall under halal certification. However, it is not only food related organization which are able to obtain the halal certification, but also all the other organizations which created under the Standards and Metrology Institute for Islamic Countries (SMIIC).

Personal care products aside from cosmetics, do also fall under the category of halal certification. It is believed that the personal care products available in different market places do make their way into our body system; and for this reason, they ought to be consumed, for everything the body takes in is could either help it become better, or it could destroy the body, entirely. For instance, feminine hygiene products such as the likes of sanitary towels, baby diapers, baby wipes, are all required to be certified under the halal certification. Such products do come into contact with the human body and they ought to be tested to ensure that they are made using raw materials which not affect the body either directly by just coming into contact with the body or indirectly by releasing some chemicals from the materials which they are made up of.

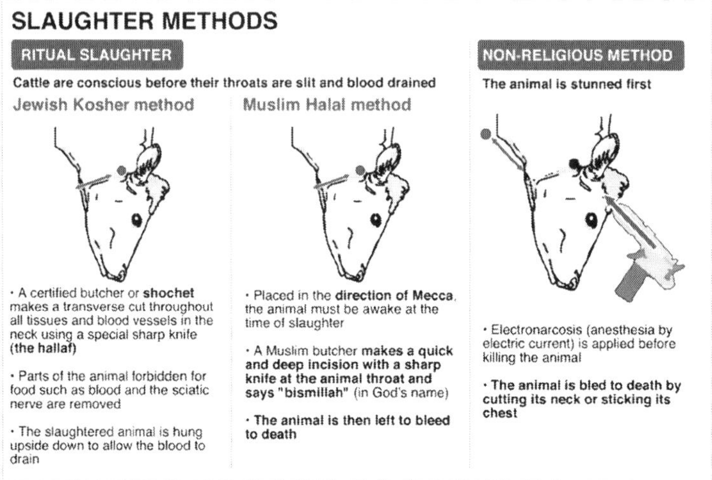

Figure 5.3. An image showing the slaughtering halal laws.

Source: https://theconversation.com/regulating-the-sacred-why-the-us-halal-food-industry-needs-better-oversight-34108.

5.4. HALAL FOOD CERTIFICATION PROCESS

As severally stated earlier, the halal certification process follows certain steps before completion. In each and every step, special terms are used to help in elaborating the way forward. The first word commonly used more so during the verification process is the Adequacy audit. As the name suggests, adequacy audit is a thorough inspection done on documents submitted by individuals interested in obtaining a halal food certification. The adequacy audit is done to ensure that the documents are accurate, and exactly the required ones, and avoiding any chances of fake documents during application process. Audit is the other term used to during the halal food certification process to refer to the process of ensuring that all the necessary processes which occur during the certification process are fulfilled. Audit criteria refers to the laid down guidelines and procedures to be followed during the auditing process. Audit evidence is used to refer to records and documents used to proof that the auditing process did take place and that everything was executed in the right way. An Auditor is a trained person approved by the halal certification board to be in charge of the auditing process. An auditor might have been trained in a higher education institution; however, upon employment to the halal certification organization; he or she must undergo another training which helps them understand the way the halal certification organization operates, the norms and the haram among other things relevant during the auditing process. A certificate holder is the individual who passes the auditing process and qualifies to be awarded with the halal food certificate. Certification is the process by which, a halal organization officially recognizes an individual or an industry to be fit to hold the halal food certification so that they be able to market their products through halal global market and ensure that the products they produce are produced under the halal laws (Shafii & Khadijah, 2012).

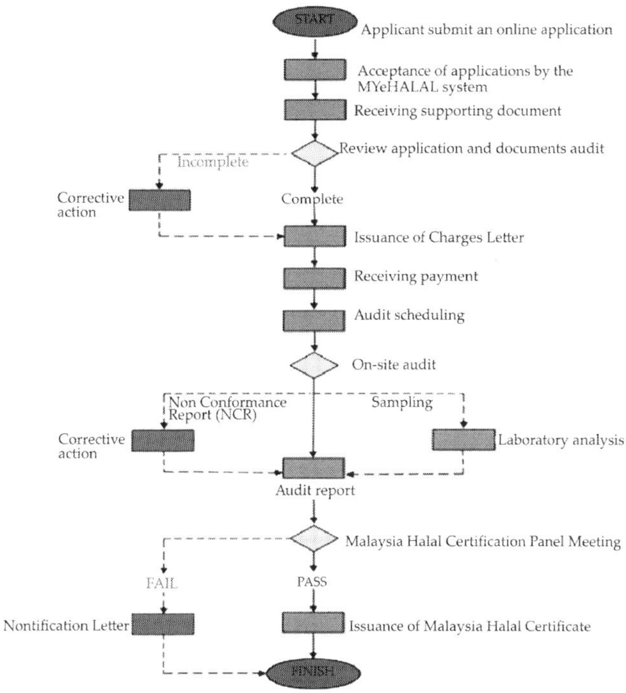

Figure 5.4. An image showing a brief description of the entire certification process.

Source:https://www.researchgate.net/figure/Flow-chart-of-Malaysia-halal-certification-process_fig2_315726466.

A committee is a group of individuals selected by the halal organization to verify the auditing process and approve the awarding of halal certification to the qualified applicants. Compliance in halal certification means that the holder of a halal certificate strictly adheres to the laws of halal during production and manufacturing of their products. A compliance audit is a process conducted regularly by the halal organization in industries which have been certified under halal certification; to verify that the industries are strictly adhering to the laws agreed upon during the certification process. Conformance is used to refer to the automatic adaptation of industries to the laws of halal certification, to the extent that there is no need for regular compliance audit. A Corrective Action Request is a document issued to applicants who are yet to meet the requirements for halal certification advising them on the areas to rectify before they re-apply. A follow-up audit is the process of examining individuals who were awarded the corrective action request to verify that they are doing their best to rectify the necessary process in order to fully qualify for the halal certification.

Food, during the halal certification process is a term used to refer to the anything that is consumed by human beings; be it any type of fluids, or solid materials, whether they are consumed in their original raw form or after some modification of either cooking or manufacturing, they all fall under the category of foods. A food analyst is an individual within the halal food certification organization who is quite knowledgeable on all types of foods and helps during the auditing process to ensure that the food being produced is right and follows the laws of halal certification. A lead auditor is the supervising auditor who is responsible for monitoring the auditing process done by the other auditors; he or she is the consultant auditor among all other auditors. Non-conformance, as the name suggests, is used to refer to the behavior of already certified organizations not carrying out their food production activities in accordance with the halal laws. An on-site audit is used to refer to the process through which the production field is inspected by halal personnel. A package, is used to refer to the storage of manufactured food materials; and packages ought to adhere to certain rules and regulations (Shaari et al., 2019). A permit, is quite different from a certificate; a permit allows an organization to label their products using the halal label, whereas a certificate, proves that an organization has qualified to be awarded with the halal certificate. A permit holder is the individual or the organization which has a solid proof of being awarded with a halal permit. A place of business is a term used to refer to the location in which the already manufactured food is being marketed to the consumers. Place of business can also be used to refer to the location where food materials are manufactured. Prepare is the process in which raw food materials are modified, either through cooking or through manufacturing process or treating the food using certain chemicals. Pre-requisite requirements is a term used to refer necessary steps which ought to be followed during the process of food production, ensuring that food is produced within a clean environment that strictly adheres to the laws and regulations of halal. A surveillance audit is a document used to refer to the approval document which allows officials from the halal organization to carry out an on-site audit.

Organization which have been certified under the halal food certification, have the obligation to label their products with the halal label, before they are exposed to the market; a move which helps in identifying the certified products under halal, which are okay for consumption by the Muslim community. The halal label on products communicates a certain information to the consumer. One, the labelled product, if it's a meat product, is not from an animal which has not been slaughtered in accordance with the laws of the Islamic community. Two, the product is not made up of any raw material considered to be prohibited in the Islamic community. Three, a label communicates the message that, the instrument used in the production process of a certain product is free from any substances which are considered impure in among the Muslims. Last but not least, a halal label communicates the message that, the product has not been in any kind of contact with the anything considered to be impure.

5.4.1. Application Procedure

The application process can be submitted for either a specific type of business or a certain place of business. In most nations, more so in the Middle East parts of the world, the application is done via the Ministry of Religious Affairs; since, halal certification is more of a religious activity and less of an official government affair. Upon completion of the filling of the form, several documents ought to be attached to the application form (Samori et al., 2016). Some of the documents include: a copy of an applicant's national identity card or a passport; the company's profile explaining what the company does, how it conducts its operation, the company's vision and mission; a copy of any other license the company holds; a copy of the business license which approves it carry out its day to day business activities; a copy of the business registration certificate which proves that the company is legally approved by the government to conduct its activities; a documents stating the name of the business and the type of business which it specializes in; a document stating the address of the place of business which proves that the address is real and not a fake one; a document stating the names and the different types of products being produced in a certain company; a document highlighting the elements used in the manufacture of the food products; a document stating the name and address of the elements supplier; a sample of the material used to package the food products; a document highlighting the processing and production procedures followed during the production of food; a copy of the Hazard Analysis and Critical Control Point document; a copy of the International Standard Organization document; a copy of the Good Hygiene Practices document; a copy of the Good Manufacturing Practices document; a copy of the Total Quality Management document; a copy of Veterinary Health Mark document; a copy of the Veterinary Inspection Logo document; a map document showing the location of the place of business.

غرفة التجارة الدولية للحلال والصناعات في الفلبين

Halal International Chamber of Commerce and Industries of the Philippines, Inc.

701 Jafer Place 19 Eisenhower Street, Greenhills, San Juan City, Metro Manila, Tel.

APPLICATION FORM
(Halal Certification)

Initial ☐	Renewal ☐	Scope extension ☐
TYPE OF CERTIFICATION SCHEME BEING APPLIED FOR HALAL CERTIFICATION:		
1. Product Certification ☐	2. Establishment ☐	3. Abattoir ☐

A. APPLICANT'S BASIC INFORMATION

NAME OF COMPANY/ESTABLISHMENT: PROWORLD, INC.				
OFFICE ADDRESS: 57 Evangelista St. Cor. 21st Ave., Project 4, Quezon City				
PLANT ADDRESS: 57 Evangelista St. Cor. 21st Ave., Project 4, Quezon City				
SALES OFFICE ADDRESS: 57 Evangelista St. Cor. 21st Ave., Project 4, Quezon City				
TYPE OF OWNERSHIP: (Please Check)		NAME OF OWNER/PRESIDENT:	COMPANY WEBSITE:	
Single Proprietorship		Roman Dexter D. Sio, Jr.		
Cooperative				
Partnership				
Corporation	*			
CONTACT PERSON/AUTHORIZED REPRESENTATIVE		DESIGNATION	CONTACT NO.	EMAIL ADDRESS:
Susan D. Mamaradlo		Sales and Marketing Assistant	0917-6974419	susanmamaradlo@yahoo.com

1. PRODUCT CERTIFICATION:
   1.1. PRODUCTS TO BE CERTIFIED HALAL: (Product name on the label)

Figure 5.5. Sample of the Halal Application form.

Source:https://www.scribd.com/document/423487897/APPLICATION-FORM-for-HALAL-CERTIFICATION-docx.

A complete application form, which has been attached with the above mentioned documents should be submitted to the Halal Food Division; a body in the Ministry of Religious Affairs. Upon successful submission of the application form, applicants should be able to keep a copy of all the required application forms for reference purposes during the audit process. After the application forms have been vetted by the auditors, they are then submitted to the inspection committee, which has the final say. Once the inspection committee has finished the approval of the application documents, the auditors are authorized to go ahead and do inspection on the place of business (Rejeb et al., 2021). All the expenses incurred during the entire application process are catered for by the applicant. The applicant is also the one responsible for catering for the travel expenses spent by the auditors as they inspect the place of business. Upon completion of the inspection of place of business, the auditors should submit a report to the committee accompanied with a laboratory certificate verifying that the place of business is safe of for food production. The committee analyzes the report and then approves the awarding of halal food certificate to the applicant.

The awarding of the halal food certificate to a company, is accompanied by the issuance of a Permit, which allows the company to label its products with the halal label. A permit is issued after the applicants have cleared all their application fees.

In most cases, some business evolve and change their way of doing business, hence there arises a need to change some few things in the document. However, no changes are to be done within an organization which has been certified by the halal organization; until the business owners have sought approval from the halal organization. The submission of the request for approval document is submitted to the halal division. The committee analyzes the application form then authorizes the auditors to carry out a compliance audit. The auditors later submit a report to the committee, which decides on whether the company will be approved to make the necessary changes and move to its new line of food production and carrying out business.

The change of the name of businesses, which have been certified by the halal organization, requires that company inform the halal certification organization. This is because, failure to inform them, the permit will no longer hold, in that, the company not be recognized as a legit holder of the halal permit. The letter informing of the change in business name is to be submitted either before or within a duration of thirty days since the change of the company's name. The letter is to be send to halal division under the Ministry of Religious Affairs. The letter ought to clearly state the reasons for the change in name of the business, and the exact date on which the company name was changed.

Several fees are paid during the application process for the halal food certificate. For an applicant to be approved, they ought to pay a fee of thirty dollars for the awarding of halal food certificate. As stated earlier, the awarding of halal food certificate is followed by assigning of halal permit, which cost fifty dollars. Both the halal certificate and the halal permit are issued immediately after both fees for each document respectively, have been cleared. Halal certificates are only valid for a period of one year upon which they expire and ought to be renewed. The halal certificates ought to be renewed thirty days before the expiry date. The renewal of halal certificates costs thirty dollars.

5.4.2. Requirements For Awarding of Halal Certificate and Halal Label

Apart from the application form and the necessary documents which are to be attached to the application form; applicants should ensure that they have fulfilled other requirements before they get to the level of filling the application form. One, the company should only apply for a halal food certificate only if it specializes in producing halal food products, which are not haram according to the Islamic community. The elements used in the manufacture of different food products should be permitted according to the Islamic religion (Rezaee, 2019). Before application, the company should have a history in production of food products in accordance with the halal laws on food production. Companies within the same locality which are interested in applying for the halal food certificate, should be able to come together and be under one halal audit committee. The committee will be responsible for inspecting the all the companies and verifying that they are fit for certification and issuance with a permit allowing them to label their products with the halal label.

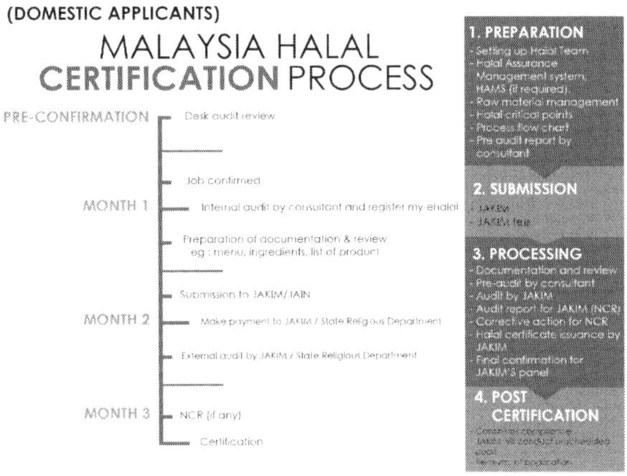

Figure 5.6. An image showing the Malaysian halal application requirements.

Source: http://halalanquality.com/index.php/halal/halal-certification-procedures.

The packaging process ought to be done within a clean environment which ensures that the product does not come into contact with any haram components. This not only applies during the packaging process, but from preparation of the products, to their handling, to their processing, and also during the transportation process. During the transportation process, only products which are halal according to the Muslim community and are acceptable according to their beliefs. The different equipment used in the manufacturing process ought to be cleaned thoroughly and the companies should ensure that they are free of any contaminants at all times. Each food producing company looking forward to applying for the halal food certificate should ensure that their employees practice high personal hygiene; and that their work ethics are top notch. Companies should have certain requirements in place, which act as guidelines during the employing period. One, each employee ought to undergo a medical examination before employment and sign an agreement of regularly going for the medical examinations. Before a company applies for the halal food certification; the employees should take part in a training session which enlightens them about the principles of food production according to halal organization. Sick days amongst employees are to be taken seriously for the chances of low food quality being produced if the employee is not feeling well are quite high. Direct contact with the different elements used in manufacturing of food products and the employees should be limited; and in cases which it is a must for the employees to directly come into contact with the elements, the employees ought to practice high levels of hygiene. The halal community requires that, only manufacturing elements are to be present around the production area. Activities such as smoking, eating, drinking among others are strictly prohibited within the company's vicinity. Not even medicines or any kind of drugs are allowed to be anywhere close to the production unit (Rahim & Abd Rahim, 2020). Food producing companies are expected to have its staff operate while clothed in full attire depending on the company's design; the same rules also applies to individuals who are only visiting either for company tours or inspection purposes. Personal effects such as the likes of jewelry, watches, among others are prohibited; meaning that employees should only be dressed in official working attire provided by the company.

5.4.3. The Auditing Process

As stated earlier, auditing process involves the inspection of the place of business; verification of required documents; after which, the general committee either approves for the next step of awarding of the halal food certificate, or the declining of the request of certification. Apart from the above mentioned steps; the auditing process is quite long, and several other procedures are followed.

HALAL CERTIFICATION CHECKLIST FOR FOOD PREMISES AND FOOD MANUFACTURER

SECTION A: Company Profile

Please Tick (☐) one where applicable.

REQUIREMENTS			TICK ☐	EVIDENCE / REMARKS
Company Registration	Security Commission of Malaysia (SSM)		☐	
	Business License from Local authorities		☐	
Certification Scheme	Food Products / Beverages / Food Supplement		☐	
	Food Premises/ Hotel		☐	
	Tick ☐ where applicable.			
Industry Categories	**Micro**	Annual turnover less than RM 300,000.00	☐	
	Small	Annual turnover between RM 300,000.00 and RM 15 Million	☐	
	Medium	Annual turnover between RM 15 Million and RM 50 Million	☐	
	Multinational	Annual turnover exceeds RM 50 Million	☐	
Hotel Kitchen Categories	4 star and above		☐	
	3 star and below		☐	
Food premises Categories	**Small**	Annual turnover less than RM 500,000.00	☐	
	Medium	Annual turnover from RM 500,000.00 and RM 5 Million	☐	
	Large	Annual turnover exceeds RM 5 Million	☐	
Other Certification / Quality standards	Good Manufacturing practices (GMP)		☐	
	Good Hygiene practice (GHP)		☐	
	HACCP		☐	
	BeSS		☐	
	Mesti		☐	
	Others : Please Specify ________		☐	
Tenure of Operation Prior to application				
Product/Menu Listings	Please attached full listing on separate paper		☐	

Figure 5.7. Halal auditing checklist.

Source: https://www.academia.edu/31128541/HALAL_CERTIFICATION_CHECKLIST_FOR_FOOD_PREMISES_AND_FOOD_MANUFACTURER.

Preparation for auditing is the first executed upon reception of an application later from either a company or an individual. Since the halal division in most nations, more so in the Middle East parts of the world, is under the ministry of religious affairs; the minister for religious affairs makes the move of appointing a certain number of people who make up the team of auditors. The lead auditor, who will be responsible for leading the rest of the team is also appointed by the minister of religious affairs. Once the team of auditors is complete, the applicant is informed of who they are; and enlightened on their role. The auditors go further ahead to lay down the plans of the entire auditing process; and the lead auditor reaches out to the applicant to agree on the dates for different auditing activities, including the auditing of the place of business or the places of businesses, for applicants who own more than one line of food business.

Compliance Audit Procedure follows after the preparation process. As the name suggests, at this level, several documents are prepared and signed by both the lead auditor and the applicant, proving that; they both agree to work together, and that the applicant will comply with all the auditing requirements. Compliance audit procedure exists to ensure that the entire auditing procedure is smooth and that both the applicant and all auditors have a good relation. With compliance, the entire auditing process takes the shortest time possible. Guidelines for the compliance audit procedure are clearly stated in the Guideline for Halal Certification and Halal Label (Park & Lee, 2021).

Adequacy audit is conducted immediately after both parties unanimously agree to work together. As stated earlier, in the adequacy audit, the auditors verify whether the applicant submitted all the required documents attached to the application later. They later prepare the adequacy reports which acts as a proof that they verified all the submitted documents.

Upon completion of the adequacy audit, the auditors are believed to be ready for the on-site audit. The on-site audit is done only when the adequacy audit proved that the applicant submitted all the required documents. The applicant is informed before the on-site audit whereby the auditors visit the place of business to inspect the conditions of the environment, manufacturing equipment among others. A guideline on the steps to be followed during the on-site application is also sent to the applicant prior to the auditing day. The program clearly indicates the arrival time the visit day; all the inspection activities to be conducted during that day; the recording of reports and comments after the inspection; the date and time when the first meeting before inspection will be done; and the date and time of the last closing meeting after inspection. Once the auditors approve that the applicant met all the requirements based on the inspection; the auditing process can proceed to the next step. However, if the inspection proves that the applicant is yet to meet the inspection requirements, the auditors present the applicant with the Corrective Action Request document. The corrective action request document is quite detailed for it informs the applicant on the exact areas the make corrections and the level of correction expected of them. If the changes to be made are not that complex, an applicant is expected to reach out to the auditing committee within a period of three weeks, informing them of the changes made and inviting them for a second visit to verify and approve the changes. The auditing committee is allowed to take a maximum period of six months before they respond to the applicant by rectifying the corrective action request document; and instead giving the applicant an opportunity to proceed to the next step. The second inspection done by the auditing committee after an applicant reaches out to them and invites them to verify the changes made, as requested in the corrective action request document is referred to as the follow-up audit.

Once the follow-up audit is done, the auditors compile a report which is presented to the general committee which is responsible for determining whether the applicant is to be awarded with the halal food certificate or the certificate should not be awarded to them. In places which pass the first on-site auditing, their reports are immediately submitted to the committee; whereas, places of business which have had both the on-site auditing and the follow-up auditing, the auditors present both reports, the report compiled during the on-site auditing and the report compiled after the follow-up audit. Submission of both reports for places of business which undergo both inspections is done to ensure that the general committee is aware of everything that transpired during the entire inspection period. Some of the companies have to send their products to the laboratory during the on-site auditing. The certificate of laboratory analysis obtained after the testing of the products, is also submitted alongside the other reports to the general committee (Omar & Jaafar, 2011).

5.4.4. Types of Auditors

The team of auditors appointed by the minister for ministry of religious affairs is made up of different types of auditors. Each type of auditor is responsible for a specific task and they all report back to the lead auditor appointed by the minister for the ministry of religious affairs. The first type of auditors is the compliance auditors. As the name suggests, compliance auditors are responsible for verifying if applicants are complying with the rules and regulations of halal division. Compliance auditors are the ones responsible for assigning of the corrective action request document; which informs the applicants that they need to change their way of doing things within their place of business. It is compliance auditors who do the follow-up audit to confirm if the recommendations they listed in the corrective action request document are being followed and the necessary changes have been made. After a place of business has been awarded with the halal food certificate, the halal organization does do frequent check-ups. It is the compliance auditors who are responsible for following up on the activities of certified place of business; they do conduct the compliance audit to verify that the company is still a worth-while holder of halal food certificate for it strictly adheres to the rules and regulations of halal food production. All the duties of a compliance auditor are clearly listed in the Guideline for Certification of Halal Compliance Auditor. Compliance auditors are selected from the highly ranked government agencies known to employ highly qualified personnel.

The second type of auditor is the surveillance auditor. As the name suggests, the surveillance auditors are responsible for conducting the main surveillance activities. Surveillance auditors conduct the first on-site audit to inspect the place of business, and verify if the applicant is qualified in that they meet all the requirements for halal certification in terms of food production. Just like compliance auditors, surveillance auditors are selected from the highly ranked government agencies. They are first taught on the principles of the halal certification before they are employed to work for the halal organization. The minister for the ministry of religious affairs is the one responsible for selecting the most qualified surveillance auditors from the government agencies. The qualifications and the selection process for surveillance auditors is clearly stated in the Guidelines for Halal Surveillance Audit.

YARSI UNIVERSITY, INDONESIA & WORLD HALAL AUDITORS COUNCIL

THIS

CERTIFICATE OF INTERNATIONAL HALAL AUDITORS

In recognition of the successful completion of the requisites and nomination of
Yarsi University, Indoncsia & World Halal Auditors Council
on the 2nd of may in the year 2017
by virtue of their authority, hereby confers upon Ridzuan Ng
the This Certificate of International Halal Auditors

with all the honors, rights, and privileges thereto pertaining.

Figure 5.8. A halal Auditor's certificate.

Source: http://www.diploma-degree.com/118755-This-Certificate-Of-International-Halal-Auditors.

Each halal organization should have both surveillance auditors and compliance auditors. At no circumstances are compliance auditors allowed to still serve as surveillance auditors or the surveillance auditors serve as the compliance auditors. However, both surveillance and compliance auditors have to work together as a team and deliver the best results in terms of all auditing activities.

5.4.5. Finalization Process of the Halal Food Certificate

As stated over and over again, after the auditing process is complete, the auditors present a detailed report to the evaluation committee. The evaluation committee goes analyzes the results of the entire auditing process and confirms if the applicant will be awarded with the halal food certificate. The last process is that, the committee approves the issuance of Halal Food certificate and Halal Permit to the applicant. Both surveillance and compliance audits will continue to be conducted after every six months to ensure that the place of business still operates in the right way according to halal laws.

The number one rule during the entire application process is that: both the auditors and the evaluation committee, should ensure that they maintain high levels of confidentiality in terms of the documents and other information about the applicant; whether the applicant qualifies for certification or not, they deserve privacy of their personal information.

5.5. BENEFITS OF HALAL FOOD CERTIFICATION

The halal food certification is considered sacred in that it offers so many benefits, not only to the Muslim community but to all individuals who consume halal certified food products.

The halal food label on food products in the market guarantees that the food product was produced in accordance with all the Islamic culture rules; in a safe and clean environment, and promotes the confidence the consumers have in the product. Halal certified food products prevent the effects of food poisoning. This is because, even after certification, the halal division does follow-up on the certified companies to inspect if they are still complying with the rules and regulations in the halal certification; which maintains a production chain of safe foods which are not halal in any or have come into contact with any halal laws (Nurrachmi, 2018).

Halal certified foods are in high demand across the globe. Companies which supply halal certified food products are likely to stand out compared to other companies which do not supply halal certified food products; giving them the benefit making more profits in the market which further boosts their business and makes them grow and expand.

Halal certification ensures that there is consistency in the production of quality and safe food products. The surveillance audits and the compliance audits which are done after every three to six months ensures that the place of business does its best to maintain halal standards of food production. With such inspection, the chances of production of low quality food products are eliminated; promoting food security in the market and the trust people have on the food products.

The halal certification does do a thorough auditing process before awarding the applicants with the halal food certificate and halal permit. The auditing process serves as due diligence for it guarantees that the company is truly capable of operating in accordance with the halal laws. If the company does not meet the halal requirements during the application process, they are given a grace period of a maximum of six months which helps them upgrade their production standards. The grace period is to ensure that, the halal division does not make a mistake in awarding a halal certificate and that the company is really capable of observing all of the halal's food production laws with no compromise.

As stated earlier, the halal certification all employees within an organization to be educated on the halal laws and regulation. Such training ensures that the consultation system within the organization is top notch. This means that, the subordinate staff members are able to consult the high rank staff about some of the laws and regulations of halal and seek guidance to avoid making any mistakes during the production process. A top notch consultation system within a company has a quality food production chain; for all the staff members share one thing in common and they are able to help each other even in times of difficulties of following the halal laws.

Apart from ensuring that food production adheres to the beliefs of the Islamic community and general hygiene standards; the halal food certification acts as a food insurance to the different food production companies. This means that, in case of occurrence of any disaster case within the place of business; the halal division will help the company in getting back to its feet and continue production of food products in accordance with the halal laws. Not all food certifications are able to serve as both food safety enforcers and food insurance companies; but the halal certification has such a higher advantage to them.

The halal certification promotes cost efficiency within a food production unit. For instance, in most Islamic nations, individuals only consume food products which have been produced in accordance with their cultures and beliefs; and in situations where the food products have broken one rule of the Islamic culture; the entire stock is gotten rid of, leading to losses to the company which produced such food products. However, with halal food certificate, even before the food products are stamped with the halal label, thorough inspection will have been done to ensure that they were produced in accordance with the cultures of the Muslims; minimizing the chances of mass destruction of food products. Another issue is that of contamination (Nusran et al., 2018). Food products produced in halal certificate organizations guarantee that high levels of hygiene were followed during the production process ensuring that, the chances of food contamination are almost zero; for with food contamination, it means that the food products have to be destroyed, incurring losses to the producing firm.

Most food certifications around the world are not standardized. Halal food certification is not standardized either; however, due to its popularity, it can be said to be standardized in a way. The halal certification process has been known almost in all parts of the world; and even countries whose large population is not made up of Muslims, they have adopted the culture of halal certification. This way, the procedures followed during halal certification in all parts of the world are similar to each, hence the justification that, the halal certification is standardized; even though there is not standard document of specific laws to be followed during the certification process in different parts of the world. The standardization of halal food certification process by word of mouth has promoted the trust all consumers have in products labeled using the halal label. Furthermore, the halal certification is recognizable in all parts of the world unlike other food certification; meaning that, even foreigners will be comfortable travelling to other parts of the world; for they are sure they can get hold of halal certified food products in any part of the world.

5.6. CHALLENGES FACING THE HALAL FOOD CERTIFICATION PROCESS AND POSSIBLE SOLUTIONS

Just like any other field in the world, the halal certification process does also have its own share of drawbacks. Most halal divisions in different parts of the world are doing their best to find solutions to the challenges and make the halal certification continue to stand out and be one of the most recognized, respected and valued food certification label, not only in Middle East nations, but across the globe.

Lack of enough manpower within the halal division officers is a great challenge. As stated earlier, the auditors and members of the evaluation committee are selected by the minister for the Ministry of Religious Affairs from government agencies after submission of an application letter by an applicant. This clearly shows that the halal division does not have such staff members already with them; and that they have to wait till an application is made, for the minister to select the most crucial staff members for the entire certification process. In most cases, some of the appointed staff members, might be so committed in their previous posts leading to the lengthening of the certification process. The laboratories used for testing food products among other components in a food company during the auditing process mostly belong to the government; and due to their high demand, it might take long before the test results are given back to the auditors for the compilation of a final report to be submitted to the evaluation committee. The challenge of lack of enough manpower can be addressed in several ways. The ministry of religious affairs could make it a priority to employ permanent auditors for the halal division who are highly qualified directly from the high learning institutions; instead of having to appoint new ones every time an application is made. Enough funds can be set aside by the government for the construction of laboratories; which are to be used only by the halal division for carrying out food test during the auditing process. The laboratories solution should be implanted together with the issue of staff members of the laboratories in that; during construction, the government will have set aside staff members to run the laboratory immediately it is commissioned. The above mentioned solutions will ensure that the certification process is conducted at a fast rate and that the entire process is smooth (Mohsin et al., 2016).

Some of the halal auditors in different halal division are believed to incompetent. Basically, halal auditors are required to be know it all when it comes to the operations of different food producing equipment, even the latest technologies; knowledgeable in the running of different activities within a food producing organization. However, the rapid increase of new technologies within food production sector; has left most of the auditors' incompetent. During on-site audits, most auditors who are not up-to date with the latest technology find themselves inquiring from the company on how a certain equipment operates yet it should be the auditors informing the company personnel on the right way of operating such equipment. The new habit of auditors inquiring from the company on their operations might lead to biasness; for the company staff might even give the wrong information to the auditors just to pass the auditing test. The solution to incompetent auditors should be frequent retraining of the auditors on the latest technologies and also perfection of their understanding of the halal laws and regulations; this way, the auditors will always be a step ahead of the companies, ensuring that they conduct a thorough audit on the firms and check all the possible areas which qualify a place of business for the awarding of halal food certificate.

Most halal divisions have failed in their responsibility of providing their staff members with detailed information on how to carry out their day to day activities. For instance, before the auditing process, most auditors are provided with only a brief description of what to inspect; instead of being provided with a full list of all the halal ingredients to be used during food production. Lack of detailed information on what to inspect leads to poor results during inspection, and some food producing companies might end up being certified yet they had not really qualified to be awarded with the halal food certificate. In addition to provision of brief information, the communication system in most halal division is poor. For instance, detailed information on the changes of halal laws is mostly made via associations. Not all staff members have joined the staff associations, meaning that, some of them will end up missing out on the information and the work they deliver will be of low quality (Mostafa, 2020). The solutions to this challenge is that, the halal divisions should take the auditing processes serious and always provide their auditors will all the necessary information prior to the auditing process; and if possible, the information should be provided even before an application has been submitted, so that the auditors take their time in familiarizing themselves with the information as early as possible. Poor communication should be addressed by the invention of a common platform from all necessary information will be shared to the staff members; for instance, in case of any changes, the division could conduct a general meeting to brief all the staff members on the changes.

Use of information management system is one of the major challenges facing the halal certification process. Most staff members have been complaining of the use of incompetent information system, which is not up to date; and in most cases, it crashes even before providing a staff member with the necessary information. This challenge can be addressed by upgrading the information system to the latest information systems in the market. With the latest information system, the chances of a system crashing are minimal, and staff members will always be provided with the necessary information.

Different halal certification bodies are facing the challenge of competition amongst themselves. As stated earlier, the halal certification process is not standardized; meaning that, the procedures followed might be similar since they all have the basis of following the Islamic religious beliefs, but they also do differ slightly from nation to another. A halal certification body in the nation of India might be less advanced compared to a halal certification body in a nation such as Malaysia. The competition comes in with the exportation and importation of halal certified food products. Since halal certified food products have been legalized in all parts of the world and they can be sold in any part of the world, the competition is quite high. For instance, back to our example of India and Malaysia; since the halal certification body in Malaysia is more advanced, most individuals will go for food products which have been certified in Malaysia and ignore the food products certified in India. The looking down on food products certified by the halal certification body in India demotivates them and lowers their morale of doing their best during the certification process. The issue of competition among products which have been certified under halal certification but in different countries can be addressed by standardizing the halal certification process such that; all the steps followed during the entire certification process are exactly the same in all parts of the world; eliminating the mentality of, products certified in this country are much better compared to products certified in another country.

The other challenge facing the halal certification process is corruption. Corruption has become worldwide pandemic affecting all parts of the world and all aspects of human life. Corruption in the halal certification process starts from the roots of appointment of auditors by the minister for religious affairs to the last process of analysis of the auditors' report before the awarding of the halal certificate and the halal label. Most applicant lie their way through the application process by filling in the application form with false details, and failure to attach all the required documents during the application process. When it comes to the auditing procedures, some applicants pay their way through the auditing process such that their documents are not thoroughly scrutinized. As for the on-site auditing, most companies pay the auditors to record the wrong details since the company is yet to be fully equipped and prepared for production of food products in accordance with the laws of halal certification (Mostafa, 2018). The analyzing committee is later corrupted to analyze the documents briefly and award certificates to companies which are not even close to producing food products in accordance with the halal laws. A case study on the proof of corruption in the halal bodies is that of South Africa. The halal certification body in South Africa is referred to as the Muslim Judicial Council Halal Trust. However, in the year two thousand and eleven, a video circulated in most social media platforms showing meat chucks which had been labeled using the halal label, yet thcy had not be produced in accordance with the halal laws of meat production. The disease of corruption in the halal certification process is a great danger for it could lead to not only destruction of the halal certification reputation but also death of large numbers of people due to food poisoning or feeding on prohibited meals according to their religion, which most individuals believe that it leads to the spiritual death of an individual; they no longer have an intimate connection with Allah. To solve corruption, it will take a lot of dedication and commitment, and focus on the end goal so as to overcome the challenges that will be associated with the journey to victory. Laws ought to be implemented to warn corrupt individuals of the consequences they will have to face and if possible, some of the corrupt individuals should be dealt with so as to serve as an example to the rest. For instance, instant resignation could work, or serving a period of a minimum of ten years in a correctional center could work. Such punishments should apply to all individuals despite their positions in the government.

The challenges facing the halal certification in all parts of the world cannot be addressed by only one individual or even one nation. An international body ought to be formed. For instance, the halal watch body in South Africa could be turned into an international body. The members of the body should be vetted on a regular basis to ensure that they still have a clear vision and understanding of what their main role is. Such an international body will have its headquarters in a certain nation, and the other branches in each member country. The body should serve as an international investigative body in the operations of all halal certification bodies; monitoring their day to day activities. If possible, every activity conducted to by all halal certification bodies should be digitized for easier monitoring and the security level should be top-notch. With such a body, all the halal challenges will be addressed from a global point of view for the betterment of the entire certification process in all parts of the world. However, no matter how good we become in making the halal certification process free of any malicious activities, the activities will never stop; so, the body should be ready to perfect its skills with each passing day so that it be ahead of the criminals.

In conclusion, Halal certification process might be viewed as a discrimination to other religions across the world; however, with further scrutiny, it has brought some light in the world. By viewing halal certification in terms of the enforcing of hygiene practices; growth of the global food market; opens our eyes to its benefits. All nations should embrace halal food certification and eliminate the belief that it is a discriminant process to other religions (Ab Talib et al., 2016).

Chapter 6

Halal Food Laws

CONTENTS

6.1. INTRODUCTION

The term Halal is used to refer to foods and other items considered lawful for Muslims to use. In the case of food, there are foods that fall under the category of Halal meaning that they are lawful for consumption by Muslims. Halal foods laws are laws placed that control the scope of Halal foods. In some cases, Halal food laws can be referred to as Islamic food laws. Some of these laws have been listed in the Quran while others have been established by Islamic Councils or Bodies. Islamic laws describe foods which Allah has allowed Muslims consume. Those that are lawful are called Halal while those that are not lawful are called Haram. Laws on foods that should be consumed and avoided are listed under commandments in the Quran (Mannaa, 2020).

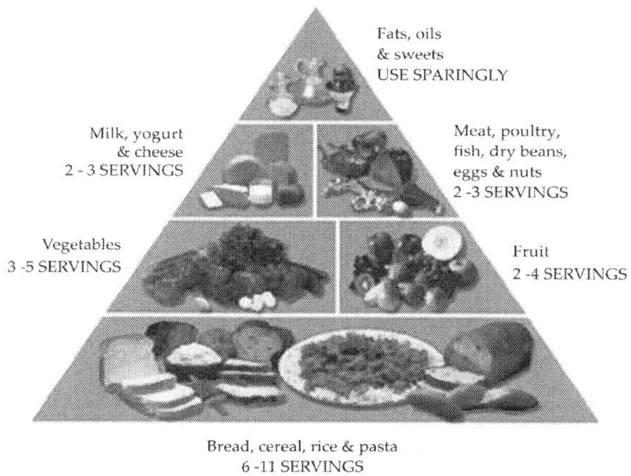

Figure 6.1. The Hadith is among the holy books containing laws on Islamic foods.

Source: https://www.askislampedia.com/wiki/-/wiki/English_wiki/Dietary+laws+in+Islam.

Other books containing Islamic statues on food include the Sunnah, Hadith and the holy book of Islam. There are laws derived from catalogue containing a description of the life of prophets such as Muhammad. Their teachings have been used in directing Muslims on how to live. The extent of guidelines placed by the mujtahids are different depending on the level of strictness. These laws are issued as fatwas and at times, they may not be considered as authoritative. These laws still relate to the Quran. There are certain conditions needed for food to be considered as halal or Haram.

Generally, it is forbidden for Muslims to consume blood, meat from animals that have not been slaughtered according to Islamic laws, pork and snakes among others. Individuals found consuming Haram foods are guilty of sin. However, there are certain considerations made that allow individuals eat Haram foods in certain conditions. Under this considerations, the individual is not guilty of sin. One of the considerations is when there is no alternative foods for consumption. Considerations are listed under the law of necessity. According to Islamic jurisprudence these laws make Haram foods permissible for consumption.

For Muslims who strictly observe Islamic laws, it is very important for them to ensure they are living right according to Islamic. Therefore, Halal food laws enable them know what is right and what is wrong. As most Muslims are concerned about what they eat causing them to look through ingredients used in preparing foods stuffs. Currently, there are enterprises seeking to create food stuffs that can be consumed by Muslims. This meat that all their products have to be prepared according to Islamic laws. For instance, animals have to be slaughtered according to Islamic laws and they type of animal slaughtered should be taken to consideration (Mathew, 2014).

Initially, Muslims would conduct their own research checking whether foods or products they were purchasing is acceptable. As there are many uncertainties with some foods and ingredients referred to as Mashbooh. It was difficult to know whether ingredients such as gelatin, enzymes and emulsifiers were lawful for them to consume. With the establishment of Islamic Councils concerned with halal foods, Muslims don't have to do much research work. The bodies state whether certain foods are acceptable for consumption or not. They also oversee production of these food stuffs. They also give certificates to companies producing halal food product. Companies bearing this certification are able to label their products with the Halal food label. These certificates are also given to restaurants serving halal foods. Bodies and councils in charge of Halal food handling the vary according to the country. For instance in America, there is the Islamic Food and Nutrition Council.

6.2. LAWS ON LAWFUL AND UNLAWFUL FOOD

Generally, Muslims can consume any type of food they desire. However, the Quran gives a list of foods that can be eaten and those that should not be consumed. All plants can be consumed though there is an exception of those that cannot be consumed. Those that can be consumed are referred to Halal and their opposite is Haram.

Figure 6.2. Muslims are allowed to eat halal foods.

Source: https://primefeed.in/news/3473417/halal-food-market-will-touch-a-new-level-in-upcoming-year-with-top-key-players-like-nestle-cargill-nema-food-company-midamar-namet-gida/.

Foods that can be eaten are listed in the Quran. According the holy book, Haram foods are not to be consumed as they are considered impure. Consuming them would result in an individual being referred to as impure. There are consequences of consuming Haram food. The Quran states that any individual guilty of consuming Haram foods will not be acceptable before God. Therefore their prayers or supplications will not be heard. In most cases, law observing Muslim follows Halal food laws. These laws indicate animals that can be slaughtered and those that should not be slaughtered. Halal food laws are as follows:

With regards to grain products, the Islamic community is allowed to eat rice, breakfast cereals, bread, pasta and all baked products that do not contain any form of Haram ingredients. Islamic laws forbid them from consuming any grain products made using Haram ingredients like artificial or pure vanilla extract, alcohol, lard or animal shortening. For fruits and vegetables, halal food laws allow Muslims eat all fruits and vegetables whether canned, raw, frozen or dried. The same applies for foods and vegetables that have been served or cooked with vegetable oil, water or butter. They are also permitted to drink all fruit and vegetable juices. However, the law forbids consumption of any fruit and vegetable made using bacon, alcohol, margarines containing diglycerides and monoglycerdies derived from animals, lard obtained from animal sources, gelatin and animal shortening.

Figure 6.3. Islamic laws indicate that there are consequences of consuming Haram foods.

Source: https://www.google.com/amp/s/www.wikihow.com/Eat-in-Islam%3famp=1.

Laws on milk and milk products allow Muslims consume ice cream, cheese and yogurt made using microbial rennet. This includes those made with microbial enzymes or bacterial culture. It also allows consumption of fresh or processed milk. Milk and milk products such as yoghurt, ice cream, frozen tofu and cheese made using ingredients like lipase, animal rennet, pepsin, pure or artificial vanilla extract or gelatin are considered haram therefore they are not to be eaten. Islamic food laws provide a large list of meat and meat alternatives that can be eaten as long as these products have been prepared according to Islamic laws. Some of the halal meat and alternative products include eggs and seafood. It is forbidden for Muslims to consume any form of pork or it products such as sausage, bacon, ham and deli meat. The same applies for all poultry and meat products that were not prepared in accordance to Islamic laws.

In the case of legumes, products such as dried lentils, beans and lentils are halal. The same applies for peanut butter, seeds, nuts, Halal deli meats and tofu. It is considered haram for an individual to consume products like canned lentils, beans and peas prepared using pork. The same applies for meat and their alternatives dishes made using pork, animal shortening or alcohol. Tea, coffee, carbonated drinks, cocktails, fruit juice and juice are among the beverages considered Halal. Liqueur, beer, alcohol and wine is forbidden for consumption or preparing dishes (Abderahman et al., 2021). Vegetable oils, butter, salad dressings, mayonnaise and margarine are examples of halal fats and oils. It is unlawful to consume fats and oils made using lard and animal shortening. Spices, coconut milk, chutneys, pickles and jam can be consumed or used in preparing other foods. However, candies and chocolate prepared using artificial or pure vanilla extract or alcohol. All desserts made using carrageenan or what are acceptable for consumption in exception of those made using gelatin. Sweeteners like chocolate liquor made with roasted ground cocoa bean syrup, honey, syrup and sugar are acceptable. Those made with alcohol should not be consumed.

Halal food laws also cover different food combinations. For instance, with main dishes such alternative dishes, Zabihah meat, pasta, rice and pizza that have not been prepared using Haram ingredients or foods are acceptable. Dishes made with Haram ingredients should not be eaten. The same case applies to sauces and soups, those made with halal ingredients should be eaten. For desserts and sweets, halal food laws require that they should not be made using pure or artificial vanilla extract or any Haram ingredients like alcohol.

Islamic laws strictly prohibit the consumption of Haram foods. They are considered impure. There are different kinds of food considered impure. For instance, the law prohibits consumption of blood. This is why slaughterers are required to allow blood from the animal to properly drain before other process are done. Meat obtained from animals such as moneys, dogs, pigs and cats. The same case applies for meat obtained from carnivorous animals having fangs such as wolves, dogs, lions, cats and tigers. Meat from domestic donkeys and birds having talons like eagles, hawks, vultures and falcons should not be consumed. Animals that should not be killed like snakes, mice and scorpions should not be eaten. Amphibians, reptiles and rodents are all considered Haram. There laws prohibiting Muslims from eating meat obtained from animals that were not properly slaughtered according to Islamic laws. This includes those that were slaughtered by non-Muslims and those that were slaughtered but not in the name of Allah. There are compromises made with regards to consumption of Haram foods. If a person is facing starvation and his or her life is on the line, they are allowed to eat Haram foods. This is because life is considered sacred under Islamic laws.

Consuming foods containing Khamr or intoxicants is unlawful. Laws laid down by prophet Muhammad prohibited Muslims from importing, exporting, trading or giving intoxicants as gifts to their fellow Muslims and non-Muslims. The laws further prohibit Muslims from working in factories, industries or organizations producing and selling intoxicants. Some of the intoxicants include paan, Khat, alcohol, dhoka and tobacco. In some areas laws against intoxicants are so strict that they prohibit a Muslim from sitting at a table where these intoxicants are served. Other substances that could cause intoxication such as marijuana, Heroin and cocaine are prohibited. Ingredients such as gelatin, Nutmeg, vanilla extract and asafoetida are prohibited as they are said to contain some alcohol concentrations. Villa extract is said to contain some alcohol in it. In the case of gelatin, it is prohibited as it is sourced from pigs. All forms of confectionary containing gelatin, nutmeg and vanilla extract are prohibited (Lubis et al., 2016).

Food products made from human body parts should not be consumed. An example of these products is commercial biscuits. Most of these biscuits are made using L Cysteine which is melted human hair. Hair consecrated to goddesses in Hindu temples are used in making global supply of L Cysteine. Most birds in exception of chicken are prohibited for consumption. This is because most birds have insects as a major part of their diet. In the case of birds of prey, they eat other animals hence prohibited for consumption. All food s contain blood or any Haram ingredients are unlawful. In most cases, Muslims run roadside shops offering chicken.

6.3. THE NECESSITY LAW

All Muslims are required to observe halal laws to avoid consequences of eating Haram foods. However, there is a necessity law that allows Muslims eat Haram foods or foods having Haram ingredients under certain conditions. For Muslims who live in areas where is food abundance, they may have to consume food alternatives of certain products that are not halal. There is a special case if individuals who are unable to get access to any halal food. It may be that they live in areas where there are no halal foods options and in severe cases, there are no food options. The individual is facing starvation. Islamic laws place much emphasis on the importance of life. Life is considered sacred. To ensure life is preserved, the necessity law was established. The law allows Muslims facing starvation among other issues to consume Haram foods to ensure their survival. With the necessity law, the individual consuming unlawful foods may not be considered guilty of eating Haram foods as the situation required drastic measures. Those who eat Haram foods and are not in such situations are against Islamic laws.

Figure 6.4. Necessity creates grounds in which halal food laws may not be observed.

Source: https://steemit.com/necessity/@juvyjabian/human-acknowledged-the-teachings-of-necessity-in-its-reasoning.

Under Islamic dietary laws, the necessity law is meant to ensure that life is easier for Muslims. It spares them from suffering from oppression. Under Islamic Judicial laws, the necessity law plays a significant role in removing restrictions. It demonstrates Islamic laws do not conform to human weaknesses or the ability to face life exigencies. The necessity allows Muslims do things considered unlawful according to Islamic laws as a result of compulsion of necessity. They break laws for them to meet the necessity and in the long run save a life from harm. Islamic laws define necessity as hard. This means that an individual encounters and excessive situation which could result in his life being in danger (Khan et al., 2018). Effects of necessity includes the individual getting hurt, his body being destroyed, damage on body parts, his mental health, destroy his family, finances or religion. In as much as all Haram foods and ingredients should not be consumed Muslims, the Islamic Judicial laws adopted the necessity law and have been able to quote a number of verses from different holy books. Proof is needed to help ensure Muslims understand the grounds of necessity laws.

6.3.1. Proofs of the Necessity Law in the Quran

From the Al-Qur'an 5:3, Allah communicates on necessities. In the Surah of al-Ma'idah, Allah forbids Muslims from consuming foods such as swine-flesh, carrion, blood and flesh. He also forbids them from eating foods dedicated to other deities. He forbids eating meat from animals that have been strangled, those that died due to a long fall, those killed due to beatings by a blunt tool, those killed and eaten by predators, those gored by horns and those sacrificed to idols. It is forbidden to alive conflicts by using gambling arrows as it is considered as corruption. Those who do not believe are prone to experience despair due stifling of the individual's religion. Allah instructs them not to fear such people but instead fear him. He further states that he has perfected the Islamic religion and grants favor upon those who choose the Islamic religion. The final Section of the verse talk about the necessity law where He says that those who are forced by hunger to sin by eating Haram foods should not worry as Allah is compassionate and forgiving. The verse is a clear indication that unlawful food can be permissible in light of an emergency such as extreme hunger.

Figure 6.5. The Quran contains a number of verses supporting the necessity law.

Source: https://www.whyislam.org/quran/originofquran/.

Another verse supporting the law of necessity is Al-Qur'an 2:173 where Allah says the He has forbidden his followers from consuming food consecrated to other deities, carrion, swine meat and blood. However an individual driven by necessity to eat Haram foods, he will not be considered a sinner. This is because Allah is compassionate and forgiving. The law gives the condition the individual should be driven by necessity not by transgression or cravings. From Al-Qur'an 6:119 the surah of Al-Qur'an Allah says that he has commanded that his followers should not eat meat with which his name has not been mentioned as he explained that it is forbidden in exception of a situation of the individual compelled by necessity. Though there are those who mislead others for their own desires depending on their own knowledge for it is Allah who knows transgressions (Krishnan et al., 2017).

6.3.2. Proofs of the Necessity Law From the Sunnah

Among different communities and traditions established grounds that the term necessity dictates considerations or expectations. Some of the exceptions have been listed by the prophets requiring people live free from harm. This means that Haram food will be considered permissible on necessity grounds to lessen the oppression while making life easier for human beings. Some verses supporting this necessity law include verses from the Sunnah such as Al-Qur'an 2:185 where Allah says that he desires ease for his followers and not hardship for them. As hunger is a form of hardship and creates grounds for Haram foods to be considered Halal. The same ideology is supported in Al-Qur'an 4:28 where Allah that he would lighten the burden for his followers as man was created weak.

However, it is crucial for Muslims to uphold halal food laws ensuring that the necessity law is not utilized as a pretext resulting in Haram foods being relished and causing individuals to eagerly embrace it or causing them to succumb their own desires. It is assumed that relishing Haram foods may establish one to surrender to prohibited food desires resulting in grave corruption. This is well explained in Al-Qur'an 23:71 where Allah says that if the truth fulfilled their desires where the Earth and the heavens as well as his inhabitants would all be corrupted. Though they are given reminders, from the reminders they turn away.

Figure 6.6. The Sunnah contains laws permitting the necessity law.

Source: https://www.dar-alifta.org/foreign/ViewArticle.aspx?ID=34&CategoryID=5.

To ensure that individuals do not incline to their desires. It hinders the exploitation of the necessity principle and preventing people from using the principle as a tool to realize the evil intentions. To control utilization of the law of necessity, the jurist of Islam established certain regulations that manage the utilization of Islamic laws. The following are some of the conditions stipulated by the jurists.

The conditions laid out by jurists required individuals understand necessity as a situation that can be unexpected and present. They gave the example of people who were sailing in an overloaded ship with the knowledge that there was a prediction of expected hard weather in different weather forecast stations the following day it was prohibited to throwing away some of the ship's load to the sea despite the weather the forecast. However, if there is a sudden change in the forecast result in the weather becomes rough to an extent that they have the option to throw away some of the lad or face death then the law of necessity will require that they throw away some of the baggage or luggage to ensure that the lives of every individual on the ship is saved. However, the law requires that all affected passengers who have lost their luggage be compensated for their loss.

There are conditions requiring the individual to ensure that the necessity being recorded is real hence not imagined. This implies that the individual should be facing a real prospect of losing their life, body part, finances, mental health, religion or family. In this situation the magnitude or nature of the necessity is established by righteous or certified jurists. An ordinary person is not involved in determining whether the necessity is real. This condition prohibits one from taking an interest-bearing loan in order to help another individual improve or expand another's business or increase their profits in the pretext of protecting wealth sanctions of the Shariáh. Individuals are also forbidden from getting involved in interest-bearing loans to allow them but a new car or furniture. It is prohibited for a female Muslim to travel alone in an aim of acquiring an education in the absence of a close make relatives. This is because these goals can be realized through other legal means and are not extremely necessary (Karahalil, 2020).

The necessity law should be the last resort and should be used when there is no other way of eliminating necessity other than taking part in Haram acts. Being the last resort, it is important for the individual to ensure that they have tried to look for other permissible solutions for his necessity as it is considered Haram to resort to unlawful solutions for issues for the problem at hand if it could be solved through Halal methods. A case example is when one is using a commercial insurance to ensure that their wealth is protected. This act is considered unlawful. This is because if the given insurance is a necessity, it can still be achieved through co-operative insurance. The same case applies for foods laws. As lack of food is considered a necessity, one can still out to consume alternative halal options. This is demonstrated in Al-Qur'an 5:2, where Allah commands that people should help one another in piety and benevolence however people should not help each other in transgressions and sin.

The magnitude of the necessity law permitted is dependent on the magnitude of the necessity. A starving individual, for example, is allowed to eat Haram foods such as pork or other Haram products if there is no other source of food. The conditions require that all measures taken should not result in serious human effects. For instance, a person suffering from starvation should ensure that they do not consume foods stuffs containing elements harmful to human health. This includes consumption of poisonous foods or fruits which could result in death. It is very important for Muslims to ensure that they deal or use the necessity law with high level of caution as well as total piety and above all they should place a high regard for limitations and restrictions placed by Allah. Individuals should ensure that they are not quick to take part in Haram acts and things in light of a difficult situation. Instead, the individual should ensure that they take time to carefully and properly analyze the situation at hand. By so doing they are able to look for other alternatives before that take part in Haram.

6.4. LAWS ON PREPARATION OF HALAL FOODS

6.4.1. Cleanliness

Among the most important elements of halal laws is cleanliness. The halal laws place a high regard for cleanliness. There are numerous benefits of cleanliness. Islamic dietary laws strongly emphasize the need for cleanliness and hygiene. This has resulted in different aspects of hygiene being taken into consideration. Some if the aspects of hygiene include hygiene of the premise, equipment, personal hygiene of the individual and dressing used by individuals. Much emphasis is placed on the level of Hygiene in areas where good is prepared and processed. One may also state that both Toyyiba and Halal are founded on the basis of health and hygiene. Islamic dietary laws require that food be prepared in clean environs to ensure that food and food products generated are good for human consumption. This is achieved when food is clean and free from poisonous or harmful elements.

Figure 6.7. Islamic dietary laws require high level of cleanliness and hygiene.

Source: https://www.mpofcinci.com/blog/guide-to-sanitary-and-hygienic-design/.

It is important to note that cleanliness and hygiene have different meanings. With regards to cleanliness, major emphasis is placed throughout the Quran. The need for cleanliness covers different sectors. Islamic dietary laws require that food should be halal, the kitchen used in preparing food stuffs should be clean and all cooking and serving utensils should be sterilized. Those cooking should also be clean. Chefs are required to wear hair nets and protective clothing such as aprons. These materials should all be clean. It is also important to ensure that the kitchen is clean to avoid halal food becoming Haram. Halal foods can be considered Haram in the case where they come to contact with ingredients or elements considered Haram. Cross-contamination with such elements renders them unable to be consumed. In a bid to ensure that Halal foods remain halal, it is important for chefs or concerned individuals to ensure that halal food products are kept away from Haram products (Kamarulzaman et al., 2016). It is important to ensure that all cooking materials such as utensils and cookware are frequently cleaned. The same case applies to hands. They should be maintained clean throughout the cooking process. Those involved should ensure that unclean or Haram items are used in preparing halal foods. There are certain practices done in Islam among them being purification practices with regards to food. In this case if a chef plans to prepare a halal cuisine, they are required to use or purchase a set of cookware specifically made for preparing halal foods. The chef should ensure that these cookware does not come in contact with Haram ingredients or elements. Certain terms are used in identifying elements free from prohibited materials, dirt, filth or things or substance considered unclean according to Islamic laws.

With regards to cleanliness and hygiene there are certain aspects that received much emphasis. They are as follows:

Areas used to manufacture, prepare and sell foods and beverages should be clean and free from all components that can cause infestation from cockroaches, flies, lizards and rats among other pests. Employees of food factories must have good health and are required to wear protective clothing to help prevent possible contamination due to dirt or other contaminant. Companies are required to obey all standard operating procedures for good food hygiene. It is also required that all tools and equipment used in processing food should be clean and this is achieved through frequent washing and cleaning of utensils. One standard procedure is rinsing of these tools using clean water. This should be a basic activity apart from cleaning using water and other relevant cleaning agent. It is also required that all toilets and washrooms within the premises that are a possible source of harmful germs and dirt should be clean regularly. Individuals using different kinds of cleaning agents should ensure that they clean their hands after using them. Employees are also required to clean their hands after visiting toilets and before initiating food processes. Cleaning and sanitation in every aspect of food production is done to minimize and prevent harmful contaminants.

6.5. LAWS ON HALAL COOKING

For Halal foods to be made, there is need for Halal cooking. There are laws that govern halal cooking in restaurants to ensure that Muslim customers are served Halal foods. The same concept applies in Muslim homes. To better understand the term Halal cooking, we need to understand that the term Halal is used to refer to acceptable or lawful while its opposite, Haram, is used to refer to things that are unacceptable or unlawful. Therefore the term Halal cooking is used to refer to the process of cooking without the utilization of any ingredient considered Haram according to Islamic dietary laws. This means that chefs should abstain from using ingredients such as pork and alcohol or any products containing by-products of substances considered Haram. In some cases there may be impressible ingredients like birds of prey, blood and animals of prey having fangs eaten in certain parts of the world. Those cooking should ensure that such ingredients do not make it to the table.

Figure 6.8. Islamic dietary laws require halal ingredients be used in making halal foods.

Source: https://esmmweighless.com/five-essential-rules-of-cooking/.

In some areas, halal laws are very strict limiting individuals from coming to contact with Haram ingredients. Some of the laws on cooking are as follows:

With regards to preparing and eating Halal foods, there are some guidelines. The first and basic laws for Halal cooking is that all ingredients used during the cooking process should be considered acceptable under Islamic dietary laws. This means that all ingredients used should be considered a halal ingredient. Chef should ensure that Mashbooh ingredients are not used. All Haram ingredients should be replaced with alternative halal ingredients.

With regards to cooking methods, there are no laws that prohibit the use of certain cooking methods. However, methods requiring the used if halal ingredients such as pork, animal carcass, birds of prey, alcohol, human body parts, animals with claws or fangs and all other ingredients considered haram should not be done. For instance, if the cooking method requires the use of alcohol which will not be completed burnt off or using bouillon or broth obtained from animals that were not slaughtered according to Islamic laws should not be used (Junaidi, 2020). One is required to use other alternatives such as making their own broth. Islamic dietary laws do not limit the type of tools that can be used in the kitchen. Every equipment can be used in preparing halal foods. The issue may be the case where pans, dishes or pots used were used in making non-Halal foods. For those who share kitchens with individuals who prepare non-Halal foods are required to clean all tools thoroughly before use. This is to avoid cases of halal foods being prepared in equipment used in preparing non-halal foods. In most cases, it is advised that one should purchase cookware specifically meant for cooking halal foods.

A major issue with Halal cooking is the use of ingredients. Those cooking halal meals need to know where to source ingredients. Currently there is an added advantage that enterprises are producing halal products. The individuals should ensure that the product bears the halal label. In areas where such products are not available, the individual will have to look out for halal and Haram ingredients. For instance, with meat, not every meat sold in butcheries is halal. Individuals will have to confirm with butchers whether it is halal or not. The individual should inquire the animal the meat was sourced from and the manner it was slaughtered. In cases where the halal certification or stamp is present, the individual should check it to ensure authenticity.

Figure 6.9. There are no specific method considered Halal.

Source: https://www.eatright.org/food/planning-and-prep/cooking-tips-and-trends/culinary-lingo.

One should look out for dates for certificate renewal checking if the certificate is up-to-date. This applies for halal food products sold. This is because there are enterprises that got the certificate but have not updated it and have started mixing food operations. Above all it is important to ensure that halal foods do not come into contact with non-halal foods.

For those in Mediterranean countries, they should not assume that all foods sold are Halal. This is why it is important for Muslims to check whether the ingredients contain and element considered Haram. The should check if the product was made using ingredients such as pork, alcohol or any other Haram foods. Halal cooking requires the individuals cooking to be keen so as to ensure that they are preparing entirely pure halal foods. There are question about food preparation methods that use halal methods but the final product contains Haram components. For instance when using milk, if milk is used to prepare a dish that resulted in fermenting of the milk should the food be considered Haram or Halal (Jia & Chaozhi, 2021).

6.6. LAWS ON HALAL MEAT

Most Islamic dietary laws focus on meat as there are numerous controversies with regards to meat. Some of these laws have been directly derived from the Quran and the Sunnah. These holy books have listed animals that are considered Halal and Haram. Those that are Haram are explicitly forbidden for consumption by Muslims. There are animals that should not be killed. Some of the animals that have been explicitly forbidden for consumption include domesticated donkeys and pigs among others. Islamic dietary laws does not permit the consumption of animals born and living in water. All of these animals in exception of fish and some sea foods are considered haram. With fishes, all are considered Halal in exception of those that die naturally in water bodies without any external causes. Islamic laws permit the consumption of fish that died as a result of external course such as colliding with stones, heat, cold or being thrown in water shores.

Figure 6.10. There are certain fish varieties considered Halal for consumption.

Source: https://en.shafaqna.com/49308/common-halal-and-non-halal-sea-foods/.

Although in Surah al-Ma'idah, V:53 Allah forbids the consumption of meat from swine, blood and dead meat, on the aspect of dead meat the verse does not specify whether it applies for land or sea animals. This would result in all sea-animals being forbidden for consumption. However, Islamic jurists made an exception with fish. This because a number of Allah's messengers have mentioned fish as explicitly permissible for consumption. Among the jurists is Sayyiduna Abd Allah ibn Umar who says that the prophet once said that there are two kinds of dead meat and two kinds of blood permitted for consumption. They include dead meat of locust and fish while the two kinds of blood are those of the spleen and liver.

For sea food, jurists have not been able to prove whether other sea animals can be consumed. The law only places an exception for fish. The proof being that the neither the messenger of Allah nor his companions ever eat meat obtained from sea-animals other than fish. This shows that fish was permissible. If other sea animals were to be considered permissible it would have been consumed by the messenger or his companions. With regards to fish that died due to natural causes in the sea, the messenger of Allah said that whatever is given up by the sea or left as a result of tides one may consume it. However, if the fish dies in the sea and floats then it is considered Haram. In some areas, Muslim Jurists have forbidden the sake of naturally dead fish in food markets. This resulted in a general law listing all sea animals as Haram in exception of fish. Consumption of fish is permitted even though it has not been Slaughtered according to Islamic dietary laws. The law prohibits consumption of fish that died due to natural causes and began floating on the water surface (Ismail et al., 2018).

The other law on meat affects land-animals. I'm this category, there are those that do not have blood in their system. These animals are considered Haram. Examples of such animals include ants, hornets, scorpions, flies, beetles and spiders. Such animals are considered to be impure and a natured individual is expected to detest eating of such animals. Laws against the consumption of such animals follow the command of Allah in his holy book where He commands them to eat what is just and prohibits evil. In this sense, he allows consumption of foods considered pure and forbids the consumption of impure foods. As animal that do not have blood are considered impure, they should not be consumed. However, there is an exception with locusts. In the Quran, there are records of the messenger of Allah consuming locusts. Under this pretext, consumption of locust is considered permissible. It is also evident when Ibn Abi Awfa said that he fought with the messenger of Allah in around 7 battles and would eat locust with him. The general law forbids consumption of all animal that do not have blood in them in exception of locust.

Figure 6.11. There are laws that prohibit consumption of animals that don't have blood in them.

Source: https://www.gutenberg.org/files/33874/33874-h/33874-h.htm.

The next category is of land-animals that have in them however, the blood does not flow. These are animals that don't have flowing blood. All animals in this category are considered Haram. Example of such animals are chameleon, snakes and lizards. The other category is concerned with pests. Islamic dietary laws forbid the consumption of all animals considered as pests. They include jerboa, mouse and hedgehog among others. Animals under this category are prohibited for consumption are they are considered impure according to the verse of Surah al-A'raf. The other law covers land-animals that have blood flowing in their bodies and survive on leaves and grass. These are animals that do not feed on other animals. All animals under this category are considered Halal. Examples of these animals include deer, camel, sheep, buffalo, cow and goat. There are some concerns about other animals who fit under this category. This include the likes of horses. Islamic laws permit the consumption of the animals in exception of donkeys as its meat is considered haram (Indrasari et al., 2020).

There are numerous verses supporting the consumption of meat obtained dorm these animals. For instance, Surah al-Nahl, V:5 says that Allah has created cattle for humans that they may get warmth and other benefits and eat their meat. The same is also demonstrated in Surah al-Mu'min, V:79 with says that Allah made cattle for humans that they may use some for food and some for riding. In the Quran, the term al-An'am is used by Allah to refer to cattle. The term is used in referring to non-predatory animals. Among the list of non-predatory animals is horses. Consumption of horsemeat is not well embraced by all. This is because horses are regarded a certain level of honor as it is much needed in Jihad. There are jurists who consider horse meat as Halal. As there are some who consider horse meat as halal, it can be considered permissible though it is best for people to avoid such meat.

Figure 6.12. Donkey-meat is considered Haram therefore it should not be consumed by Muslims.

Source: https://www.eg24.news/2020/07/after-helwans-hawawshi-6-signs-reveal-the-difference-between-donkey-meat-and-wa.html.

However, for animals like mules and donkeys it is forbidden for one to consume meat from such animals. Form Surah al-Nahl, V:8 we learn that Allah has created donkeys, mules and horses for riding and for show. He has also created other things that men have no knowledge of. In the other verses, non-predatory animals were created for consumption. However, in the case of donkey and mules, they were created for adornment and riding. If these animals were permissible for consumption, Allah would have mentioned it in the verses. Other knowledge forbidding consumption of meat from donkeys and mules is when the messenger of Allah prohibited the consumption of donkey-meat on the day of the battle of Khaybar. In Sahih al-Bukhari, no :5205, Sayyiduna Abu Tha'laba says that the messenger of Allah forbade the eating of meat from donkeys.

In Sahih al-Bukhari a story is told where an individual came to the messenger of Allah and told him that the donkeys have been slaughtered and eaten. A different man came and told the messenger that the donkeys have been destroyed. This resulted in the messenger of Allah ordering a caller to announce to all that Allah and him messenger prohibit consumption of donkey-meat as it is considered impure. This resulted in pots used in boiling donkey-meat being turned upside down while the meat was in it.

In the case of mule-meat, it is said that there are numerous verses narrating that the messenger of Allah prohibited eating of meat from donkeys, mules and horses. However, with regards to mules there were certain exceptions made depending on the animal involved in creating the mule. The mother of the mule is taken to consideration. If the mother of the mule is a donkey, then meat from the mule is considered haram. However, if the mother is a cow or any other halal animal, then the mule-meat would be considered Halal. In the case where a horse is the mother, then laws regarding consumption of meat from horses would be used (Henderson, 2016).

There are meat Laws on animal under the category of terrestrial predators and beasts. This include animals that use their teeth in hunting. Examples of such animals include dog, lion, wolf, tiger, cheetah, cat and leopard among others. All animals under this category are all considered Haram. Therefore, their meat should not be eaten. There also laws regarding birds of prey. Examples of such birds include kites, eagles, bats, hawks and falcons. All these animals use their talons or claws in hunting animals. Proof of this laws is in Sahih Muslim, no:1934 where the messenger of Allah forbids consumption of meat from birds having talons and fanged birds of prey. This means that all animals be it birds of prey or beats that use their talons or teeth to hunt other animals are all considered Haram.

Figure 6.13. Birds that feed on crops and grains are all considered Halal and permissible for consumption.

Source: https://poultry.extension.org/articles/poultry-management/raising-meat-chickens-in-small-or-backyard-flocks/.

There is also another category of birds who do not hunt other animals instead they use their beaks in eating crops and grains. This category is made up of animals such as crows, chickens, sparrows, doves, pigeons and ducks. All these animals are considered Halal. In Sahih al-Bukhari, no: 5198 Sayyiduna Abu Musa al-Ash'ari says that he saw the messenger of Allah eating chicken-meat. This renders chicken-meat permissible. There is a law regarding halal animals consuming Haram things. The law directs that if an animal consumed impure things to the extent that it's meat and milk have bad odor then it is forbidden for an individual to drink the milk and eat its meat. The law has an exception. If the animal eats both impure things and other substances and its meat and milk do not get a bad odor, then it is permissible for an individual to consume its milk and meat.

This is well elaborated in the al-Fatwa al-Hindiya which says that chicken-meat is forbidden for consumption if a large portion of its diet is made up impure things which end up penetrating to the meat resulting in it having a bad smell. The final law with regard to Halal meat is with regards to mixed parents of the animal in question. For instance, if the animal is born of a mother considered Halal while the father is considered haram the animal will be considered Halal. This is because the mother is taken into consideration. The opposite applies. If the mother of the animal is considered haram, its offspring is considered Haram. This case is mostly applicable in animals that inter-breed such as mules. If its mother is a donkey, the animal is considered Haram and if its mother is a cow it is considered Halal (Hanzaee & Ramezani, 2011).

Consumption of food following these laws, Muslims will be right according to Islamic laws. From the laws above, the following is the list of animals considered Halal: Buffalo, camel, goat, stag, sheep, gazelle, cows, antelope, deer, rabbit, ducks, quail, wild-ass, heron, parrot, locust, nightingale, francolin, lark, partridge, ostrich, dove, sparrow, goose, rooster, pigeon, stork, starling, chicken, peacock and all fish of different kinds such as prawns. Animals considered as Haram include cats, leopard, wolf, monkey, hyena, scorpion, lion, cheetah, Tiger, hedgehog, jerboa, swine, squirrel, bears, domesticated donkeys, snake, dog, jackal, turtle, crab, tortoise, elephant, fox, crocodile, weasel, bat, falcon, kite, hawk, rat, vulture, mouse, beetles, mosquito, spider, fly, wasp and lizards.

6.7. LAWS ON FASTING IN RAMADAN

Among the Halal food laws, there are laws concerning the Ramadan fasting. The Islamic calendar year is founded on a lunar cycle made up of 12 months of either 30 or 29 days in each month. The ninth month of the Islamic calendar is called Ramadan. The Islamic calendar is quite different from the Gregorian calendar. The Islamic calendar is shorter by 10 years resulting in the shift in the period of Ramadan. Different religions have different perspectives of fasting. For the Muslims, fasting meant that one had to abstain from beverages and foods. They are also to abstain from smoking, medication, water and gum from dawn to sunset. During this period there are two main meals consumed one immediately before dawn while the other after dawn. Food eaten immediately before dawn is called Suhur while that consumed after dawn is called Iftar.

The two meals are consumed with relation to two of the five prayers done by Muslims daily. Laws do not restrict them from having other snacks or meals during the night. Though the fasting causes hunger and thirst among individuals, the fast is said to bring spiritual peace among Muslims as during to this period there is great intensification in acts of worship. Meals consumed differ from one community to another. This is because there is a broad diversity in the Muslim community. This makes it quite difficult to describe the kind of meals termed as Iftar and Suhur. In some cases, Iftar foods can be common breakfast foods while Suhur foods can be those left over from the before dawn meals or ethnic foods. In the case of Iftar, most communities have social gatherings where buffets are held. The buffet is mostly made up of traditional foods.

In most cases, once that fast has been broken Muslims take a cup of water and a few dates. There others who consume bread, fried pastries, legumes, salads and bread. During the fasting period, traditional desserts become more frequent. There are those who break their fast with water while others may take milk and juice. Consumption of beverages having caffeine as well as soft drinks are reduced. As it is a holy month, it is important for Muslims to ensure that what they are consuming is Halal. The fasting period requires one to be pure. With regards to food, one can attain purity by ensuring that they consume foods considered pure according to Islamic laws. This will require every individual be careful in checking the type of ingredients used in making their foods. All ingredients should be halal (Han et al., 2021).

The fasting period is such as vulnerable as any form of mistakes has its own consequences. For those who consume impure food, fasting could be in vain as Haram foods has rendered them impure. This means that their prayers and supplications may not be heard by Allah. As the fasting period is aimed at improving spirituality, it is important for Muslims to adhere to Islamic dietary laws. If they are not sure about certain foods, they should opt for alternative food options. The amount of foods consumed may be reduced or increased depending on the individual. With regards to medication, there were issues with ingredients used in making medication. However, medicine is useful in ensuring the survival of an individual more so those suffering from diabetes it considered Halal according to the law of necessity. In most cases, patients work with dietitians in choosing a food plan that can supplement consumption of certain medicines and foodstuffs.

In most cases the dietitian with create a diet focused on ensuring nutritional care used during the fasting period. Strategies used in the diets need to ensure that all Islamic dietary laws are adhered to. Some of the strategies are as follows: meals consumed before dawn and after sunset should focus on ensuring satiety. Food portions should be controlled more so during Iftar buffets. Sodium amount should be reduced while increasing the rate of water intake. Food options should all be Halal and packed with nutrients. They should ensure that their patient's weight is managed and also avail a variety of options of halal foods rich in fiber to be incorporated in the diet. Most traditional dishes prepared during this period though halal are mostly made up of fat and sugar. Dietitians offer a variety of options on the type of cooking methods to be used. Patients are taught to Manage their own conditions while at home and if need be, they are given miner supplements.

6.7.1. Halal Foods and Dishes For the Ramadan Period

There are different foods consumed by different Muslim communities. For instance, in South Asian some of the ethnic halal dishes consumed include Falooda which is a drink made using tapioca seeds, milk, vermicelli and rose syrup. There is a finger fry food called Chaat eaten as an appetizer or snack. It can be sweet or savory depending on the individual's preference. There is Lassi, a drink made using spices, salt, yoghurt and pepper. In some cases, fruits can be used to add flavor (Debney, 2016). There are savory mini cakes called Idli eaten during breakfast hours or as a snack. These cakes are made of rice and black lentils. Among the most common appetizers is Papad which is a crispy water that can be consumed as a snack. There is a stew called Hakeem made using spices, meat, wheat and lentils. Among the most common traditional foods known as Roti which is a flatbread made of wheat flour. Finally, there is a pastry made of meat or spiced vegetables know as samosa eaten as a snack or appetizer.

For the Arabic community some of the common ethical dishes include Katayef which is a pastry that looks like a pancake. It is made with nuts or cheese and fried or baked. Once cooked it is dipped in syrup. Khoshaf is a salad made of dried nuts and fruits. There is a rice pudding called Muhalabyeh and Qamaruddeen which is an apricot juice. Most of these ethical foods are made using Halal ingredients as most are founded on Islamic dietary laws.

6.8. LAWS ON ISLAMIC SLAUGHTER OF ANIMALS

With regards bro meat, there are several concerns resulting in Islamic Jurists Councils creating laws in fasting. The manner in which the animal is slaughtered will determine whether it is identified as halal or Haram. There are several prerequisites to be adhered form Islamic laws on fasting to be fulfilled. Most of these prerequisites are taken into consideration before animals are slaughtered. Among the prerequisites is that the animal to be slaughtered should be considered Halal according to Islamic dietary laws. The individual slaughtering the animal should be a Muslim. It is also crucial to ensure that the individual is of sound mind and should be an adult. For meat to be considered Halal, it is required that the individual slaughtering the animal invoke the name of Allah.

Figure 6.14. Halal food products are required to bear the halal food label.

Source: https://www.freepik.com/premium-vector/halal-food-label-collection-with-flat-design_2606281.htm.

Laws of Islamic slaughtering of animals are obtained from the Quran. It is required that only the name of Allah be invoked before the slaughter. If the name of another deity is mentioned before the slaughter, then the meat will be considered Haram. It is crucial for slaughterers to ensure that the name of Allah is mentioned before each animal is slaughtered. In the case where the slaughterers forget invoke the name of Allah then the sacrifice is considered void as the meat cannot be eaten. This is why Islamic Jurist Councils consider the mentioning the name of Allah an obligation during the slaughter process. In some cases, this laws is referred to as the Supreme law.

Under the Supreme law, if the name of another deity is mentioned then it is prohibited for Muslims to consume such meat. This is in line with verse 5:3 of the Quran which says that it is prohibited for individuals to consume swine, carrion, blood and meat from animals that were slaughtered after the name of another deity (Damit et al., 2018). The same applies for animals that were slaughtered or killed using blunt instruments, those that died due to strangling, those eaten by wild animals, those that died by falling from a high level and those slaughtered on an altar. It is also demonstrated in al-An'am which states that Muslims are forbidden from eating meat on which the name of Allah has not been invoked. This means that meat sourced from an animal slaughtered by a non-Muslim who did not invoke the name of Allah before the slaughter if the animal is forbidden for consumption.

Different countries have established different laws on Islamic slaughter. This is so as to enable traditional methods of slaughter be used by different religious groups. Some of the regulations on traditional methods of slaughter used in the USA have been established through acts. Among the acts on halal slaughter is the Humane Slaughter Act which requires certain conditions be met before religious slaughter of animals is done. In the case of Islam, the act allows for halal methods of processing meat. Most of these Acts require that the animal experiences minimal pain before it is killed. In most cases, slaughter houses are encouraged to use electronacrosis as a slaughtering technique.

The slaughter process is usually considered as an act of subdual and not mercy. The Quran says that Allah brought all things to existence and therefore the source of life. This requires slaughterers to be more sensitive to animals. During the slaughtering process, it is required that the animal be treated properly. Those slaughtering animals are required to use the phrase "In the name of Allah." This phrase is said so as to dedicate the animal to Allah. There are scholars who says that reciting the phrase is a form of acknowledging that he provides and sustains and therefore has a right over everything on earth. There are so e who say that it is a form of praising Allah. It also shows that food should not be taken as a show of gluttony or sin but instead thanksgiving to Allah.

Islamic dietary laws require that once the animal is brought in the slaughter house, the slaughter process should not cause any form of pain to the animal. Usually the animal is laid down and dealt with gently. The Quran requires that the animal's head face the Qibla. In this state the slaughter is considered Sunnah. The slaughterer should ensure that the blade and other slaughter equipment be kept sharp and hidden from the animal's sight. The blade should be seen when the animal's jugular is felt. Islamic Jurist Councils decided on a conventional method of slaughtering animals. This method requires large arteries, trachea and esophagus found in the neck region be cut using a non-serrated blade (Adekunle & Filson, 2020). The law also required the individual slaughtering the animal to ensure that the nervous system of the animal is not tampered with. This is because it could result in the animal dying before the exsanguination has occurred. It is also required that the head of the animal is not decapitated as the blade is swiped. This is because it results in blood draining rendering slaughterers unable to continue with other processes. The law requires that the animal's blood be allowed to drain before other processes are done. In some countries, Committees in animal slaughter require that the animal be rendered insensitive to pain. This has resulted in methods such as electronacrosis being used and the animal's meat considered Halal.

Laws on slaughter enforced by Islamic Councils and Committees need to be humane for them to be considered permissible in the country. There are laws that require animals to be slaughtered in secluded areas individually to make the act more humane. The same case applies for poultry houses and Slaughter houses. This avoids one animal seeing another animal being slaughtered. This act is referred to as makruh. Slaughtering animals one at a time may be time consuming. This is why some slaughter houses have automated the slaughter process by using an abattoir. It has allowed the slaughter of multiple animals while meeting certain conditions with regards to animal slaughter. This method of slaughter is within the confines of Islamic laws hence meat obtained from these animals is considered Halal. This is because the animal didn't die due to Haram methods. The method has also proven useful and effective in allowing blood drain from the animal's body. This helps Muslims adhere to laws forbidding the consumption of blood. There are still some concerns on whether all the blood is drained from the animal's body allowing the meat be rendered clean. Islamic laws require that most of the animal's blood be drained.

6.9. LAWS ON HALAL CERTIFICATION

Currently there are numerous enterprises offering halal foods to customers. This applies to restaurants and food production companies. By law, it is required that these companies have a certificate showing that they have been certified to produce or sell these products. The same applies for slaughter houses. Those that follow the halal slaughter procedure need to bear a certificate to prove that. For companies that have these certificates, they have a benefit in their end in that they are able to get more consumers to trust their products. Different countries have different boards in charge of certificate allocation. These Bodies set grounds for which certificates will be awarded to companies. They also determine whether the business is fit to receive a halal certification (Cuesta-Valiño et al., 2020).

For instance, a with slaughter houses, the body will send a representative who will check whether the slaughter houses have met all Halal requirements. This means that they have followed all laws on Halal slaughtering. It is advisable for consumers to purchase products from certified companies. This way they are sure that the products they are purchasing have been ensured. For companies or organizations to acquire certification, it is crucial that they apply for a certificate with a relevant body. There are some requirements when applying for certification. The member of certificates to be applied for is dependent on the type of business or company and the location of the company. If it has numerous branches, they may be required to make numerous applications.

Bodies involved in application for halal certificates include the Ministry of Religious Affairs, the Halal Food Control Division and the Department of Syariah Affairs. Halal certification for businesses is obtained under Appendix 1 of the laws set by the bodies. When filling the forms, the companies or enterprises are required to fill-in required information that is accurate and up-to-date. Alongside the application forms they are required to attach their passport or the Identity card of the applicant, the business profile, a copy of the business registration certificate, miscellaneous license if the business and business license. They are also required to indicate the name of the business; it address and information about the type of business being ran. They should give information on the type of product being produced and ingredients used in making the products. All information about the business should be given. Once that is done, if the company has qualified the relevant body will award it a certificate.

However, if there are any changes made in the business for instance a new product is being produced then by law the company is required to give this information to the relevant body. By law, all companies given a Halal Certificate a halal certificate are required to come with the guidelines listed by relevant bodes. They should ensure that only halal products are produced and sold. If the company starts to produce different products, then the relevant body is granted the permission to revoke the certificate. For instance, if the business was known to produce halal meat products and they start producing and selling non-Halal meat products, the relevant bodies can cancel and revoke the license.

There also guidelines on how long the certificate is considered valid. Once the time has ran out, the business is required to apply for a certificate renewal. This may require them to pay a certain fee to the halal certification body. Companies whose Certificate have not been renewed are working out of line. It also places consumers at risk as they could begin adding Haram ingredients in food.

6.10. LAWS OF FOOD LABELS

Most halal food products bear the halal food label. For companies to get this label in their products, they are required to make an application to halal bodies concerned with giving of labels. There are laws requiring companies place labels on their products making it easy for consumers to identify whether it is halal of not. It is required that all products bearing this label have Halal ingredients. The business should meet halal standards. The same applies to the products they sell. Application for the labeling is made to the relevant body (Bergeaud-Blackler, 2015).

These companies are prone to receive more visitations and inspections from members of the Halal food board as they are required to ensure that products are worth of the label. The company is granted power to revoke labeling rights given to companies if they do not comply with the set agreement. The board can also sue the company for misconduct.

Chapter 7

Islamic Slaughter: Islamic Halal Meat Preparation and Supervision

CONTENTS

7.1. INTRODUCTION

With the rapid expansion of the Muslim community, Halal has always been important in the mass market. Halal food and halal certification cover not only spiritual requirements, but also commercial and cultural needs, according to a study of restaurant managers' views on halal certification. Halal is an Arabic term that means permissible or permitted; haram, on the other hand, means unlawful or forbidden. Halal and haram are Muslim words that refer to all aspects of life and are often used in fruit, meat goods, food additives, and food communication materials. Muslims, as well as the rest of humanity, are commanded by God to consume halal foods.

Owing to the large request for animals killed in this fashion and the assertion of some Muslim groups that animals be slaughtered while completely alive, the slaughter of animals for adherents of the Islamic faith is both ethically and economically significant. The global production for butchered meat for Muslim consumption is substantial, and it is expected to rise even more so in the future (The Economist, 2009). According to The State of the Global Islamic Economy Study, conducted by Thomson Reuters in collaboration with Dinar Standard, the quantity of funds spent by Muslim customers on Halal food and beverages accounts for 16.6% of global food and beverage spending.

Figure 7.1. Halal meat hanging in a Moroccan butcher shop.

Source: https://tasteofmaroc.com/islamic-slaughter-zabihah/.

This is about $1.1 trillion, and it is projected that by 2018, the valuation will have risen to $1.6 trillion. Because of the obvious economic advantages of the Halal industry, many food companies in the West have joined the Halal market. Nestle, one of the world's largest food companies, also has Halal clearance for about 150 production facilities around the world. To be deemed fit for Muslim eating, the animal may well have been reared in conditions that allow it to articulate three natural behavior, and the processing of such animals must be done in a humane manner, according to Islamic law, the Shariah.

The Quran (Islamic Holy Book) and Hadith are used to establish Shariah law (traditions of the Prophet of Islam, Mohammed). The Hadith that follows is one of a number of Ahadith that stress the defense of animal health during Halal slaughter.

Figure 7.2. The Quran.

Source: https://www.learnreligions.com/quran-2004556.

With over 1.4 billion Muslims in the world, Islam is one of the world's fastest rising religions. In comparison to a general population growth rate of 1.6%, the Muslim population is projected to rise by 35% by the turn of the century. As a result, Muslims are making their political and social influence felt, for example, by seeking proper nutritional labeling and quality control of food items.

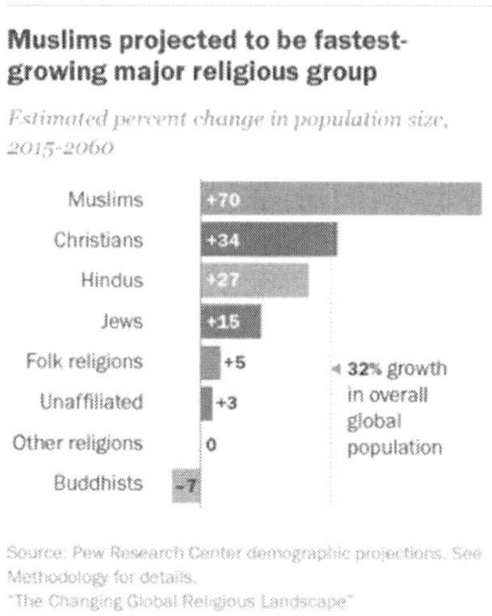

Figure 7.3. Islam is one of the world's fastest rising religions.

Source: https://www.pewresearch.org/fact-tank/2017/04/06/why-muslims-are-the-worlds-fastest-growing-religious-group/.

The accelerated spread of Islam has resulted in an increase in demand for ceremonially slaughtered, halal meat. Halal meat processing, on the other hand, is not easy. Even among Muslims, the exact ritualistic conditions of the process of slaughter are disputed. The process technology used can be significantly influenced by the various methods of butchering. If Halal (permissible) food comes into contact with or is polluted with non-Halal food items, it may become Haram (not permissible).

Food products have been tainted with meat from other animals, non-Muslim customers have been fed with Halal foods unwittingly, and foods meant for Muslim consumers have been tainted with residues of pork DNA, according to recent media reports. These have heightened concerns raised about the origins of food, especially meat-based products that are subject to religious slaughter requirements. Despite the popularity and desire for Halal food around the world, there is relatively little scholarly literature on the topic. One of the only Halal-centered research was published in 2012, and it highlighted the need for appropriate functionality in Halal food (Battour & Ismail, 2016).

This paper fills the void by delving into the slaughter process surrounding Halal food processing. It investigates the mechanisms in place to ensure quality protection, preserve tracking, and avoid cross-contamination of Halal and non-Halal meat. The following section offers an outline of the legal and logistical aspects that regulate food production: an in-depth review of the relevant laws is beyond the reach of this article, and it is therefore insufficient in order to understand the chapters content.

This paper discovers that product tracing is not enforced, there is intentional inability to conform to Hazard Analysis and Critical Control Point (HACCP) systems, Halal food products are inappropriately defined and sold, and there are several instances where there is actual, and significant risk of contamination of Halal products by in-depth surveys and interviews of the organization. The literature review is divided into three parts, each of which represents how food supply chains have reacted to growing issues, as well as a study of the challenges of Halal food production: food security, and the introduction of programs to increase quality and safety; traceability, and changes in food monitoring and process transparency; and pollution, and the understanding that identification is complicated, as well as the fact that foods processed in compliance with religious standards bring additional difficulty. Following that, an outline of the Halal food preparation religious criteria is given. The methodology chapter also goes through the case identification process as well as the data collection and interpretation approaches used.

In 2017, the global Muslim population hit 1.8 billion people, and this number is growing every year. Halal food markets are expanding at a breakneck pace, paralleling the rise of the Muslim community. In 2017, Muslims spent US$1.3 trillion on food and beverages, which equals the entire halal food industry spending. Today, the halal food market contributes for about 16% of the global food sector, and it is expected to account for about 20% of global food future trade deals. In Europe, the food industry has started to engage in halal food processing.

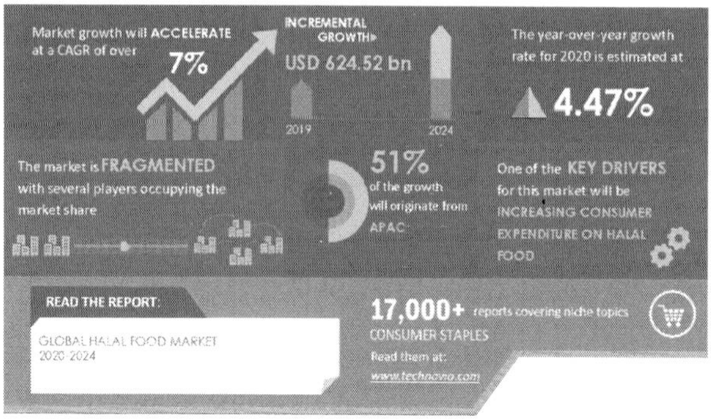

Figure 7.4. Technavio has announced its latest market research report titled Global Halal Food Market 2020–2024.

Source:https://www.businesswire.com/news/home/20201008005101/en/Halal-Food-Market-Increasing-Consumer-Expenditure-on-Halal-Food-to-Boost-the-Market-Growth-Technavio.

Some European distributors have introduced fresh halal meat to their menus, and some European manufacturers are selling their goods to the Islamic world. The Netherlands, which ranks first in the world for halal food warehousing and transportation, acts as a conduit for halal food to the European economy, the Middle East, and Africa. As per the 2015 DinarStandard composition and analysis survey, the top halal meat exporters to Organization of Islamic Cooperation (OIC) states are Brazil, India, Argentina, Russia, and France, accounting for 28.5% of the overall halal meat industry.

The top five halal meat suppliers are Saudi Arabia, Malaysia, the United Arab Emirates, Indonesia, and Egypt, accounting for 42% of the global halal meat industry. For all goods manufactured to satisfy the needs of Islamic customers, Halal requirements should be followed. These requirements are linked to food production's sources, history, and processing methods. Halal food is classified as food processed in accordance with halal practice. To Muslim customers, Shariah law criteria split food into permissible (halal) and banned (haram) categories (Bashir et al., 2019). Haram animals include:

- Animals in a state of death.
- Pigs.
- All animals killed without Allah's name being proclaimed over them.

- Tusk-bearing species.
- Primates, snakes (with the exception of spiny-tailed lizards), and amphibians.
- Donkeys, mules, and Lycaonpictus (horses are permitted) (African wild dog).
- The vast majority of bugs.
- Only marine species that are dangerous to people's welfare.
- Blood (from every animal) and blood-based goods.

The Arabic term "Zabiha" refers to the bleeding of animals for meat processing in accordance with Islamic ceremonial slaughter parameters, also known as halal slaughter. Several unofficial halal approval bodies have sprung up in the Western world in an effort to reassure Muslim customers that goods bearing the halal seal follow the standards of Islamic dietary law. To be applicable to consumers, regular certificates must meet halal standards. The World Halal Council (WHC) is the world's largest certification body, overseeing 41 halal licensing bodies from all over the world Al-(Ansi & Han, 2019).

The Organization of Islamic Cooperation (OIC), which has 57 member states, has established general halal food standards for its members all over the world. Despite the fact that these halal validation agencies are uncontrolled and frequently work under different halal rules, many Muslims regard them as enforcement agencies of halal dietary laws, particularly in states with a small Muslim community where there is a possibility of cross contamination with non-halal commodities (such as pork).

Figure 7.5. The Organization of Islamic Cooperation (OIC).

Source: https://www.kaiciid.org/who-we-are/our-partners/organisation-islamic-cooperation.

Many scholars from various perspectives have recently examined the concepts of halal meat, halal control points (HCPs) in meat production, the composite of Islamic dietary and Hazard analysis and vital control points (HACCP) principles, and religious against legal interpretations of halal slaughter. In the meat industry, new technical strategies and procedures are increasingly being introduced in order to be more cost-effective and hygienic, to meet rising market demand while still adhering to animal protection standards.

Nonetheless, in certain ways, these technical means may be incompatible with halal standards. The aim of this analysis is to illustrate the consistency of current technical techniques with halal slaughter practices.

7.2. SLAUGHTER HALAL

The term Halal is an Arabic term that refers to anything or conduct that is legal under Shariah law. The slaughter of animals for Muslim eating, known as Zabiha/Dhabihah, shall adhere to such guidelines outlined in the Quran and Hadith. Since the following Quranic verse orders Muslims to ingest only Halal meats, many Muslims view consuming Halal meat as a religious act:

"O you who have believed, eat from the lawful things which We have provided for you and be grateful to God if it is (indeed) He that you worship" (Quran, 2:172).

For Muslims, not all ingredients are allowable. The following verse explains what is Halal and Haram for Muslims to consume; it is important to note that at the end of the verse, God makes it clear that these dietary rules do not exist in true necessity conditions:

"Dead animals, blood, swine flesh, and that which has been dedicated to other than God, and [those animals] killed by strangling or by a violent blow or by a head-long fall or by the goring of horns, and those from which a wild animal has eaten, excluding what you slaughter, and those sacrificed on stone altars, and that you seek decision by divining arrows. That is grave disobedience. This day those who disbelieve have despaired of [defeating] your religion; so fear them not, but fear Me. This day I have perfected for you your religion and completed My favour upon you and have approved for you Islam as religion. But whoever is forced by severe hunger with no inclination to sin then indeed, God is Forgiving and Merciful" (Quran, 5:3).

It's important to remember that declaring any food, or something else for that matter, Haram is against Islamic teachings unless God expressly forbids it (Quran, 16:116). Muslims who behave in a way that contradicts the aforementioned verse are considered idolatry worshippers, as shown by the following verses:

"If God had willed, neither we nor our ancestors would have associated (anything), nor would we have forbidden anything." Similarly, those who came before us denied until they tasted our retribution. Do you have any information that you might share with us? You don't do anything but make assumptions, and you don't do anything but falsify (Quran, 6:148).

Say (O Mohammed): "Bring forward your witnesses who will testify that God has forbidden this. and if they testify, do not testify with them. and do not follow the desire of those who deny our verses and those who do not believe in the Hereafter, whilst they equate (others) with their Lord" (Quran, 6:150).

Figure 7.6. Recently the Hyderabad based Muslim seminary Jamia Nizamia, started in 1876, issued a ban on Muslims eating prawn, shrimp, and crabs, calling them Makruh Tahrim (abominable). According to Islam, there are three categories of food: halal (allowed), haram (prohibited), Makruh (strictly to be avoided as abominable).

Source: https://www.firstpost.com/india/muslims-and-food-what-can-be-eaten-safely-and-what-should-be-avoided-as-per-islamic-law-4336851.html.

So generally, the butchering of animals that is permissible according to Shariah law must meet the following conditions:

- The animal must be a Halal acceptable species.
- The animal must be alive at the point of slaughter (Quran, 5:3, 6:118–119, 6:145, 16:115).
- The name of Allah must be proclaimed in the process of butchering (Quran, 6:118–119, 22:34, 22:36).
- The person who is bleeding the animal must be above the age of maturity and emotionally sound. While it is better if the slaughterer is a Muslim, the Quran allows Muslims to eat meat killed by Christians and Jews (Quran 5:5).

There are other guidelines that do not actually make meat Haram if they are not followed. It's also worth noting that certain of these secondary standards are almost difficult to meet in commercial settings, such as:

- Orientating the animal to face Qibla (The Grand Mosque in Mecca).
- Sharpening the blade or knife out of sight of the animal.
- Slaughtering animals out of sight of other animals and shielding animals from the sight of blood.
- Slaughtering in one single movement of the knife. This requirement is particularly difficult to achieve in cattle. As stated above, the Quran forbids Muslims from declaring food as Haram unless it is clearly commanded by God. On the contrary, some Islamic jurists have declared some new slaughter technologies such as stunning, as Haram despite the fact that this is not mentioned in any of the scriptures.

Figure 7.7. The Kaaba (Arabic: ٱلْكَعْبَة, romanized: al-Kabah, lit. 'The Cube,' Arabic pronunciation: [ka.bah]), also spelled Ka'bah or Kabah, sometimes referred to as al-Kabah al-Musharrafah (Arabic: ٱلْكَعْبَة ٱلْمُشَرَّفَة, romanized: al-Kabah al-Musharrafah, lit. 'Honored Ka'bah'), is a building at the center of Islam's most important mosque, the Masjid al-Haram in Mecca, Saudi Arabia.

Source: https://en.wikipedia.org/wiki/Kaaba.

It must be noted that stunning is a relatively new technique which was discovered several centuries after the Quran was revealed, it is therefore not surprising that it is not mentioned in the scriptures. In a situation where a technology cannot be found in the scriptures, Islamic jurists must pass a seven judgement (Fatwa) as to whether that technology can be accepted as Halal or not (Al-Ansi & Han, 2019).

However, these jurists interpret Shariah law in a variety of ways. It is obvious that numerous passages in the Quran and a number of Hadith narrations emphasize animal welfare care throughout the animal's life. As a result, if stunning is objectively proved to produce instant loss of sensitivity and does not result in the death of animals prior to slaughter, one may claim that such a procedure meets Halal slaughter requirements because the scriptures do not designate such a method Haram.

Halal customers in most Muslim-majority countries frequently rely on HCB clearance stamps or certifications to certify food's Halal certification. However, these unregulated HCBs follow a variety of methods, and the level of expertise of some of these organizations has been questioned on several occasions.

Figure 7.8. Halal Stamps.

Source: https://www.dreamstime.com/illustration/halal-rubber-stamp.html.

The Holy Quran plainly states that Islam regards all animals to be equally precious as humans. It is also stated that provided proper precautions are performed, the Islamic way of killing (halal technique) is the least painful technique. This is to ensure that both the animals and the consumers gain the most.

Animal slaughtering must be carried out by a Muslim of sound mind and maturity who is fully aware of the basics and conditions surrounding this practice. According to the Department of Standards Malaysia (2004), slaughtering must be done with niyyah (intention) and the slaughterer must be fully conscious of his actions. The sole goal of slaughtering is to please Allah, not for any other reason. In addition, the animal must be halal and alive or judged alive at the moment of slaughter. The animals to be slaughtered must be in good health and have received approval from the appropriate authority.

According to the halal standard, all slaughtering lines, equipment, and utensils must be dedicated solely to halal slaughter. The massacre must be carried out using a sharp instrument, not one composed of bones, nails, or teeth. The "sawing action" of the slaughtering is authorized as long as the slaughtering knife or blade is not taken from the animal during the slaughtering (Department of Standards Malaysia, 2004). The Department of Standards Malaysia goes on to say that halal slaughter begins with a neck cut immediately below the glottis (Adams apple) for short-necked animals and after the glottis for long-necked animals.

In addition, the trachea (halqum), esophagus (mari'), both the carotid arteries and jugular veins (wadajain) would be severed to speed the animal's death and bleeding. The customary way of slaughtering in Islam is to slice the throat, cutting the carotid arteries, jugular veins, trachea, and esophagus without removing the head, as per scholars. As a result, the bleeding will be total and sudden. A skilled Muslim inspector who is committed to ensuring that the animals are appropriately killed per the Shariah must examine all of these procedures in order for the meat to become halal.

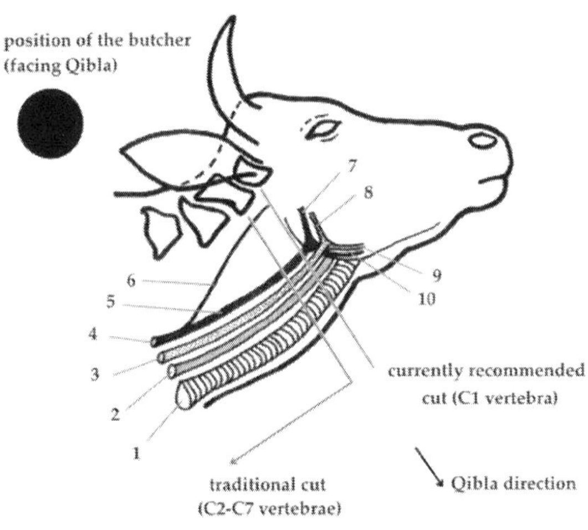

Figure 7.9. Method of slaughtering cattle.

Source: Department of Standards Malaysia.

Apart from halal, Islamic Law has explicitly defined haram as having universal application, with no favored groups or persons who, in the name of religion, are free to do anything they want according to their whims (Al-Qaradawi, n.d.). As a result, Muslims do not have the authority to make anything haram for others while making it legal for themselves. The three legal sources of prohibitions are the Quran, the Prophet's Sunah, and the Muslim scholars' consensus (Stork, 2004). The Quran reveals the following in this regard:

Why should ye not eat of (meats) on which Allah's name hath been pronounced, when He hath explained to you in detail what is forbidden to you – except under compulsion of necessity? But many do mislead (men) by their appetites unchecked by knowledge. Thy Lord knoweth best those who transgress.(Al-An"am [The Cattle], verse 119) .

Non-Muslims, according to an Islamic expert, are more inclined to feel that killing animals is cruel because they feel the animals would suffer and bleed to death. However, Islamic slaughtering guidelines clearly indicate that the knife used must be extremely sharp in order to make a swift, deep, and clean cut through the critical anatomy of a halal species animal's neck. The trachea, oesophagus, and major blood arteries are the primary targets. The knife should not be honed near the animal for animal welfare concerns.

According to another expert, halal slaughter causes ischemia of the brain and makes the animal numb to pain by immediately severing the veins of the neck. The quick flow of blood that drains from the animal's body is the outcome of this approach. Bleeding the meat also assures that it is of high quality. The jugular vein and esophagus are slashed with a single swipe of a sharp knife, interrupting the flow of blood to the brain and rendering the animal unconscious nearly instantly. It is also stressed that halal slaughter guidelines are founded on the twin principles of correctly draining the animal's blood while avoiding undue pain (Zulfakar et al., 2012).

Humane treatment is needed here, and strangling, hitting, piercing, or goring the animals is forbidden since it can injure them. According to scholars, representatives of the scientific community and the Association of Muslim Lawyers accept the Islamic method of killing as being compassionate because it causes significant hemorrhage and anoxia (lack of oxygen in the brain cells). As a result, it works as a strong painkiller, disabling the sensing center and rendering the animal completely pain-insensitive.

Figure 7.10. Wilhelm Schulze (10 December 1920, Leipzig – 30 December 2002) was a German professor of veterinary medicine, director of the University of Veterinary Medicine Hanover (1966–68, 1978–80 and 1980–81) and a specialist for pigs.

Source: https://globalhalaldatapool.com/halal_slaugher_humane/,

Professor Schultz and Dr. Hazim of Hanover University in Germany conducted an experiment utilizing an electro-encephalograph (EEG) and an electrocardiogram (ECG) to show that Islamic murder is a highly compassionate procedure. One group of animals was murdered using a halal procedure, whereas the other was murdered with a captive bolt. All animals had their EEG and ECG recorded to see how their brain and heart were doing during the procedure. The experiment, which astonished a lot of people, came to the following conclusion:

- The EEG showed no altering brain activity in the first three seconds of Islamic killing and hence no pain was felt by the animal during or after the incision;
- The EEG revealed a condition of profound slumber three seconds after that: unconsciousness. Because of the tremendous amount of blood that comes out of the body;
- The EEG detected no brain activity after the aforementioned six seconds, showing that the animal did not feel any discomfort;
- As messages fell at zero, the heart continued to beat and the body toppled vigorously with maximal blood from the body (a

reflex action of the spinal cord), providing in healthy meat for the customer.

The Malaysia (2004) Department of Standards has declared that amazement should not be advocated, but that the circumstances indicated above must be fulfilled if it is to be carried out.

- Slaughter should take place in accordance with the slaughter regulations of Islam;
- Animals are alive or are considered alive during slaughter (hayat al-mustaqirrah);
- The usage of stunning machinery should be reviewed frequently by the Islamic authority or the Halal Certification Authority and supervised by a skilled Muslim;
- The astonishment must not kill or permanently damage the animals;
- Gadgets for stunning animals of the category of mughallazah may not be utilized in stunning animals for halal slaughter;
- Type of stunning approved by the majlis fatwa (Fatwa Council) is an electrical shocking or any other stupendous stunning;
- The power stunner is of the kind permitted by the slaughtering appropriate authority;
- The type of stunning for slaughtering halal animals must be "head alone stunner," with both electrodes on the head area;
- Only "water bath stunner" is permitted to electrically stun the poultry;
- A trained Muslim and Islamic Authority or Halal Certification Authority supervises and monitors the intensity of the current utilized

7.3. FASTING OF ANIMALS PRIOR TO SLAUGHTER

It is stated that Muhammad, the prophet, says, "Let one of you kill him," implying that you must sharpen the knife carefully and feed, soothe and water before you kill it (as mentioned in Sahih Muslim, Book 21, Chapter 11, Number 4810). Therefore, according to Sharia law, animals are best nourished by allowing unrestricted access to food and drinking water throughout the wait for slaughter. Ruminants are suggested for fasting at slaughterhouses during transit and lairage to minimize the intestinal capacity and consequently the number of germs, minimizing the danger of carcass pollution during dressing.

The Council Regulation (EC) No 1/2005 does however specify maximum durations of speed/feeding and travelling for several animal species. Council Regulation (EC) No 1099/2009 reads, 'Animals not abducted and fed in reasonable quantities of food should be provided at suitable intervals within 12 hours of their arrival' This results in a pre-slaying time of up to 12 hours of feed withdrawal. Duration of journey is intimately connected to the problem of predators and hunger. When animals are readied for travel, energy and fluid balance must be kept in mind.

Heat stress is an important part of pre-transport and quick food. Rumen is the most important source of heat generation in cattle, 4–6 hours after feeding, owing to exothermic fermentation reaction by feed breakdown. It is important, therefore, to bring animals swiftly into the butcher, especially in hot weather sites, and transport diseases can also be avoided.

The European Union now concurred on the necessity to pre-slaughter animals. The rest of the world is changing in the time of pre-slaughter fasting for animal species in accordance with legislation in each nation (Wan Hassan & Awang, 2009).

A 12-hour pre-slaughter period is specified in the rules of the Brazilian Ministry of agriculture as a minimum duration for livestock and as a maximum for broilers. Long-run feed losses have a detrimental effect on several features of meat quality and raise physiological stress in lambs, therefore fasting over 24 hours has not been suggested as a result, when feeds are accessible for livestock up to 3 hours before pre-laughter, meat tenderness has not been adversely affected. Feed for pre-slaughter animals should, however, be provided under Islamic (Sharia) guidelines to guarantee animal welfare, whereas the feed must be withdrawn now.

It is vital to explain to Islamic lawyers that animal pre-slaughter for a limited duration (a few hours, depending to animal species) doesn't relate to animal welfare but has enormous technical advantages, which might persuade them to give a fatwa to allow it.

7.4. THE ACT OF BUTCHERING

The act of killing itself is preceded by proclamation of God's name. It can sometimes be seen that invoking the name of God at the moment of killing represents an acknowledgement of God's rights over all things and thankfulness to God for all the nourishment he gives.

Bismillah, or "In the name of God," as the most prevalent blessing. It is not acceptable in this scenario, as killing is an act of subduality rather than mercy, to employ the word "Bismillah al Ra Sustainable Al Ra Sustained.' In the name of God the Mercifully Beneficient. The animal is taken to slaughter and placed softly, according to Islamic tradition, that it is not injured. The head of the animal faces the Qibla, sunnah but not fard. The blade should be kept hidden until the last minute of the animal's jugular feeling.

Figure 7.11. Arabic Islamic Calligraphy of Bismillah.

Source: https://www.pinterest.com/pin/790663278325140867/.

These recommendations should also obey the regulations of the U.S. government which permit practice in the U.S. It is also obligatory for each animal, according to certain schools of thought, to be killed individually and in isolation. One animal must not see another animal butchered as it is macruh in a poultry farm or in a house for slaughter. The killing of several animals at the same time, utilizing a full-automated abbatoir, is regarded adequate within the Schi'a school (followers of the Ayatullah Sistani). This procedure corresponds to Islamic law and helps properly drain the animal's blood from it (it assures that the animal doesn't die with any Haraam approach). The reason is because in Islam it is banned to take blood itself [Quran 2:173]. It is not however obvious that bleeding, in order to maintain unclean flesh, eliminates all blood from the carcass. Indeed, Islamic scholars have ruled that "most" blood must only be drained from the animal.

7.5. STUNNING

Stunning is permitted, according to the UK Halal Food Authority. There are, however, several sorts of amazement; some are forbidden, some are allowed. The following are forbidden in accordance with the HFA:

- Stunning caught-bolt;
- Stunning percussion;
- Gas stunning.

The Halal Food Authority approves of two kinds of stunning:

- Bath with water. Stun – exclusively for poultry – when birds with electric stunner are drawn through water. They are sometimes not entirely stunned after the water bath because they lift their body up while resisting and do not make complete contact with the stunner,
- Electric-Tong Stun – for larger animals such as sheep, cows, camels, goats, and so on. When the bovine drops, the tong must remain linked to the head. Because the electricity may not get through the brain, the neck to neck posture should never be employed. It is extremely advised to use a head holder to keep the animal's head up when the body collapses (Ab Talib et al., 2016).
- Electronarcosis is also commonly employed on bigger animals to numb their senses before butchering, and the Egyptian Fatwa Committee has deemed it legal.

Figure 7.12. EU: Waterbath best option for poultry stunning, says EC.

Source: http://www.eat-halal.com/eu-waterbath-best-option-for-poultry-stunning-says-ec/.

As previously said, stunning is one of the most contentious technological processes in the halal meat business, and it is vital to examine it more. The word "amazing" does not appear in the Quran or Hadith literature. Stunning raises questions about whether the standards and ideals of halal killing described in Islam's main texts are being followed. The fact that the animal is not alive at the moment of butchery and is only somewhat exsanguinated owing to stunning raises such issues. The stunning of animals before to slaughter is a legal necessity in Europe, according to Council Regulation (EC) No. 1099/2009, and is used to render animals unconscious.

Any purposely produced procedure that produces loss of consciousness and sensibility without pain, including any technique that results in sudden death, is defined as "shocking" under Council Regulation (EC) No. 1099/2009 (1). Preventing anxiety, pain, suffering, and discomfort in animals before and throughout the killing process is the goal of stunning.

Discomfort and tension associated with constrained mobility, pain arising from the incision and activation of nociceptors in the wound, delay in time to loss of consciousness and accompanying misery, and blood aspiration into the respiratory system and accompanying anguish are all problems of slaughtering cattle and small ruminants without stunning. False aneurysms can form in halal-slaughtered animals (without stunning) as a result of delays in the loss of consciousness, obstructing blood flow. "Slaughter without stunning needs an exact slicing of the throat with a sharp knife to minimize suffering," according to Council Regulation (EC) No. 1099/2009.

Furthermore, animals that are not physically confined after the cut are more likely to experience a delayed bleeding process, resulting in extra pain. The most prevalent species murdered via this process are bovine, ovine, and caprine animals. As a result, ruminants murdered without being stunned should be confined individually and manually. Aside from religious considerations, stunning is not widely used owing to a variety of factors, including a shortage of stunning technology and materials, the high cost of the equipment, and a lack of professional training in the use of stunning knowledge and techniques (Shafii & Khadijah, 2012).

Animal slaughter without stunning necessitates the use of a highly competent team to manage the animals and conduct the bleeding. Employees who work with animals must be educated, according to the Canadian Food Inspection Agency to;

- Keeping an eye on the signs of loss of consciousness.
- The capacity to determine (in accordance with recognized animal welfare quality standards) that loss of consciousness did not occur during bleeding.
- If any anomalies occur, remedial efforts are taken to avoid the particular animal from suffering (e.g., post cut stunning).
- Understanding that as a correction step, introducing numerous or extra cuts or sawing movements (non-fluid movements) is not permitted.
- Checking that the animal is unconscious before hanging it up (using numerous indications).
- Assessment of animals after bleeding to confirm that they are dead before proceeding with other operations such as dressing or manipulation of the wound area for religious reasons.

If the person conducting the bleeding is inexperienced or inept, the time between restraint and cutting might be too long, causing unnecessary agony and severely impacting animal welfare.

Several nations (e.g., Sweden, Denmark, Norway, and Switzerland) have already forbidden the killing of animals without previous stunning, despite European legislation (Council Regulation No. 1099/2009) permitting religious slaughter, which is normally practiced without stunning. Indeed, supporters of pre-killing stunning, as well as supporters of religious slaughter techniques, all agree that stunning is the most compassionate technique. Muslims have differing opinions on whether or not pre-slaughter stunning is acceptable.

While it is recognized in certain places, such as Malaysia (where the Shf school of thinking is followed), it is not acceptable in Pakistan (where the anaf school of thought is followed). Currently, Muslims have three primary viewpoints on stunning before slaughter: acceptance under specified conditions (reversible stunning); rejection owing to contradiction with religious norms and inadequate bleeding (since blood is not deemed halal material); and not sure yet or requiring particular guarantees (Shaari et al., 2019).

According to an EBLEX poll conducted in England, 76% of Muslims (out of 1000 respondents) refused to have animals stunned before slaughter and opted to buy meat from providers that exclusively sold meat from non-stunned livestock. Despite its small sample size, this study demonstrates that even Muslims in Western Europe prefer to eat meat products that have been butchered using conventional ways and shun meat from animals that have been made unconscious before being killed.

Although various Muslim officials have given their okay to various stunning procedures, the European Union has yet to give its consent to stunning techniques used on cattle, which might result in economic losses for halal beef producers as customers switch to alternative international suppliers. For animal welfare concerns, Australian government rules demand the stunning of animals before to slaughter. Halal slaughter utilizing reversible stunning, on the other hand, is acceptable.

A limited number of slaughterhouses in Australia have even gotten approval from the local authorities to execute halal slaughter without stunning the livestock (only for cattle and sheep), but only if the animals are stunned immediately after the throat is cut (only for cattle). This implies that sheep are butchered without being stunned, even after a throat incision, unless they are in distress (e.g., vocalizing, butting, or attempting to run) or if unconsciousness takes too long, in which case they must be stunned immediately after the neck incision.

Because of animal welfare, stunning animals before to slaughter is common and sensible. It might be done soon after throat cutting to limit animal suffering till loss of consciousness while still meeting halal regulations, making it both compassionate and religiously right at the same time.

Reversal pre-slaughter stunning technologies are constantly expanding in the meat business sector, according to scholars, in attempt to optimize animal welfare during slaughter and fulfill halal slaughter regulations. The authors verified that new methods under development might be used in the halal meat sector, where they would be able to meet both halal slaughter and legislative criteria. Single-pulse ultrahigh current (SPUC) and microwave energy, for example, are in experiments performed and might be improved further to be employed as commercial stunning devices that fulfill halal slaughter regulations. Previous evaluations have properly highlighted some of these technological advancements. According to scholars, most Islamic experts and customers think that reversible shocking corresponds with the ideals of Islam, as per a poll conducted in the United Kingdom (Samori et al., 2016).

The Department of Islamic Development Malaysia has issued precise standards for halal preslaughter stunning that may be reversed. For broilers weighing 2.40–2.70 kg, for example, a voltage range of 2.50–10.50 V for 3.00–5.00 s is advised. In this aspect, the American method of immobilizing chicken (electrical stunning, ES) is more suited to halal criteria than the European one. In the United States, low-voltage ES (10–25 V) and high-frequency (500 Hz) systems are employed to immobilize birds. Because the voltage is so low, the birds may recover within 2 minutes of being stunned if they are not bled.

Irreversible stunning (120–150 mA per bird; 50–400 Hz) is employed in the European Union and symbolizes lethal stunning; hence it does not match halal meat rules. Despite the fact that the voltage of electrical stunning and the mass of the fowl have been established, some birds die as a result of the stunning procedure or a lag in the butchering process, resulting in inadequate blood drainage. Even within a same weight range, the capacity of chickens to endure the same voltage current and survive after electrical stunning varies. This is why in the halal poultry sector, stunning with an electric current is not permitted.

During water bath stunning, if a bird's wing or any other part of the bird comes into touch with the live water before the head, possibly painful pre-stun shocks can occur. According to European law, electrical shocks must be avoided prior to stunning, which may be accomplished by appropriately constructing the water bath to incorporate an entry ramp. Mis-stuns can happen when the flock is uneven in size, and smaller birds arch their necks or rise up owing to a pre-stun jolt, causing them to fly the entire length of the water bath stunner.

Researchers have observed the benefits of appropriately administered high-frequency pre-slaughter electrical stunning in grazing animals and poultry, including efficient bleeding and enhanced meat and carcass quality; it also conforms with the basic criteria of halal slaughter because it is reversible. In certain Muslim nations, non-penetrative percussive reversible stunning (provided it does not cause neuropathological alterations) may be an appropriate approach for halal slaughter. However, cattle were shown to have a high rate of subarachnoid hemorrhage, making this procedure controversial for the halal meat market (Rejeb et al., 2021).

Scholars discovered that while utilizing a non-penetrating captive bolt stunner on mature cattle (bulls), the ratio of mis-stuns was 18%, which is a severe welfare issue. To guarantee that the blow is adequate to knock the animal unconscious and avoid mis-stuns, European regulation allows this method to be used only on poultry, hoofed mammals, and ruminants weighing up to 10 kg of live weight. The risk of a skull fracture must be avoided. Experts verified that stunning before butchering can be used provided the following three conditions are met:

- The stunning must be recoverable; the animal must not be killed or permanently injured.
- Stunning should be done by a Muslim slaughter man or inspector under the supervision of a qualified Islamic authority or halal certification agency on a regular basis.
- The stunning apparatus used on pigs should never be utilized on halal slaughter animals.

7.6. THE ANIMAL'S BODY POSITION DURING SLAUGHTER

The right restraint of animals before to slaughter is critical for the effective execution of the butchering procedure, especially for halal slaughter without stunning. If the animals panic or get irritated by the constraint, the precision of the incision may be compromised during halal slaughter. The employment of less-stressful restraining techniques improves animal welfare and slaughter operating safety, as well as the supplier's quality.

When killing animals for halal purposes, they should be put on their left flank, ideally towards the Qibla (in thc direction of Makkah in Saudi Arabia). This implies that the butcher should face the Qibla at the start of the incision, and the animal's neck (incision site) should be rotated to face the Qibla as well. Animals should be chained and lifted only after bleeding and after the animal has lost consciousness, according to Islamic killing standards as described by Hadiths. In Islam, these are the traditional customs of animal killing.

Per the proponents, the goal of this murder posture (laying on the left flank) is to improve the likelihood of maximal blood drainage by the body's pressure on the heart, as Muslims are prohibited from consuming blood (Quran 2:173, 5:3, 6:145, 16:115). Some research back up the concept that sheep killed in the horizontal posture lose more blood than those butchered vertically.

The lifting of conscious animals by the hind leg, restricting in the upright or standing posture, restraining calves by inverting them on their backs, and lateral recumbency have all been utilized in contemporary halal slaughterhouses throughout the years. Because of their great weight and the structure of the gastrointestinal tract, cattle are still hoisted by the hind leg when fully aware in certain countries, such as Turkey. This causes tremendous pain and needless pain for the animals. The teachings of Islam, EU laws, and animal welfare all prohibit such brutal animal confinement (Rezaee, 2019).

A chin-lifting device designed to extend the neck to make easier approaches for halal incision performance in pens known as the American Society for Prevention of Cruelty to Animals (ASPCA). Blood inhalation into the lungs, inadequate bleeding (clamping of the blood vessels of the neck against the head restraint), and delayed loss of consciousness are all downsides of the upright restriction technique during halal slaughter (without stunning) of cattle. Although it is not recommended by certain Muslim organizations, the upright restraint method is nowadays frequently adopted by European halal regulators.

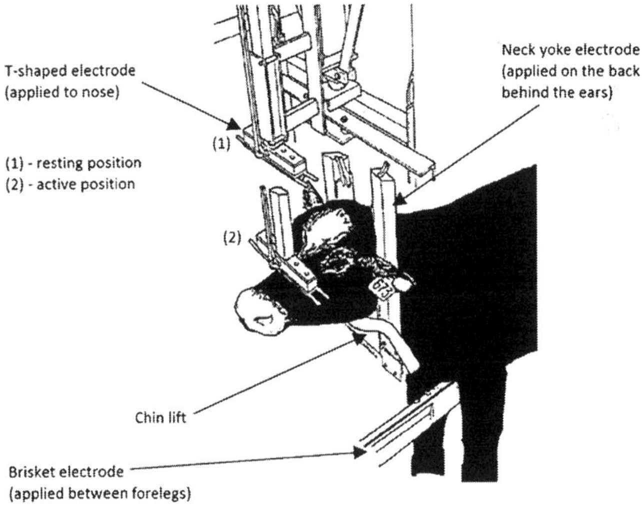

Figure 7.13. Illustration of equipment used for head-only or head-to-body electrical stunning of cattle.

Source: https://efsa.onlinelibrary.wiley.com/doi/full/10.2903/j.efsa.2020.6275.

Reporter reports have shown a bad animal welfare due to the constraint of the cattle on their shoulders, which prove that the trachea and larynx are contaminated by blood and intestinal matter according to the ritual incidence and depth. The restriction on cattle laterally recumbent is the preferred restriction technique for most halal slaughterhouses (90 degrees angular, laying on their sides), since it is the most adequate technique of meeting halal standards. Even though the animal has no difficulties with the stress on the diaphragm, aorta or main veins when the lateral retraction technique is employed, pressure can occur on other internal organs.

The restraint in a fully or partially reversed V-shape conveyor and a straight retaining system are used in the killing of red-meat animals. Vertical suspension of shackles is the typical posture of the poultry at slaughter. Scholars have evaluated and compared various animal restraint strategies for halal slaughter, such as 45% turn them around (i.e., by 90°), turn them backwards (180° turn), and keep them upright. The study showed that in animals with all containment methods, the greatest amount of struggles and vocalization have been seen, while when animals are turned on their side.

The study also indicated that when animals were turned on their faces, the proportion of animals sufficiently bleeding was the greatest, and when slaughtering was done straight with animals. The fact that the time to lose position (recumbent and hypotonic livestock) is shortest in a situation was linked to the adequate bleeding of the animals that turned on their sides during slaughter. A considerable variance in the amount of cuts across restriction systems has been found, with higher cuts in the upright position (9 cuts) on bovine animals compared to the inverter at 180° (5 cuts) and 90° (three cuts).

The delay between retention and cutting the neck of sheep that had been murdered without astonishment was lowest in manually reinforced animals on its side. Scholars] reported that bleeding is affected by the killing posture. They also observed that blood loss following the slaughter of lambs dramatically increased when corpses were hung out vertically instead of being held up in a v-sustainer. The changes in animal position and gravity are most likely to cause this higher bleeding of animals. In animals that hung vertically via confining the rear legs more effective bleeding was recorded also by livestock compared to animals bled horizontally (Rahim & Abd Rahim, 2020).

In a right (standing) posture and inverted posture, the European Food Safety Authority showed blood aspiration in the respiratory tract after cattle slaughter. It is known that people without machines used the halal killing technique manually in the past, so that the location of the animals during the halal killing (which is located on the left flank) and towards the Qibla might thus be appropriate. However in the case of chicken, when the pouls are retained and hung vertically and mechanically, criteria for the animal's posture are impossible to fulfill in halal slaughter. While "all animals save the camel" are defined by Islamic law, it is preferred but not obligatory to lie on the right side for halal slaughter of chicken according to fatwa.

No sector of life is excluded from the tendency of all modernism. Strategies employed in the past are not now applied and may not be acceptable in future, as we now deem to be sufficient. More than 1400 years ago, major religious restrictions and restrictions were enacted in the halal-meat sector. Some Muslims think that Islamic laws apply for all eras and locations without changes or modifications today, as they think these principles are divine. The Qur'an, Sunnah and Islamic intellectuals are the origins of the regulations and law on halal meat. Ijmā (legal consensus) and Qiyās (reasoning by analogy) are further sources of law that play a key part in the interpretation and use of slaughter procedures, such as the acceptance of a number of stunning techniques.

Compared to the primary and essential sources of Islamic law, including the Quran and Sunnah, Ijmas and Qiyas have a secondary priority. Moreover, in all Islamic legal schools (Madhhab), if Sunni interpretations differ from shia perceptions, these two sources of Islamic law do not have the same relevance or efficacy. There are therefore disparities in the appropriateness of stunning practices amongst Muslim nations. Muslims' rigorous obedience to these religious precepts based on the significance of their laws, especially the Qur'an and Sunnah or Islamic scholars The objective of this work is to emphasize the interconnections and regions of consonance and disconnection between the two elements, not to laud or criticize the regulations of Halal Meat or show the effectiveness of contemporary meats technology. These insights may be taken into account by the meat business and technology suitable for religious rules.

The reversible stunning of the animals, animal retention in the lateral recumbence (for grazing animals), and neck incision execution in a position higher than traditional low incision in the cattle are appropriate processing methods and procedures that comply with halal standards for the meat business, in order to limit the risk of false aneurysms. Un-stunned slaughter, which depends more on the workplace than on the technology, is more costly and time-consuming by hand (the manual killing of chickens); hence there is severe difficulty in rivals of existing slaughter procedure.

This paper does not address the technological operations carried out following slaughter, such as cutting of the skin, evisceration, division, washering and dressing corpses, meat cutting and use of meat cutting, due to a lack of religious (Islamic) scriptures in this respect. It is incredibly difficult and hard in practice for all Halal standards to apply since the many sects of Islam are lacking a unifying perspective. In the actual implementation of the principles and the laws of halal production, globalization and new technology have both harmful and good consequences (Park & Lee, 2021).

It is necessary to create technology that is not in conflict with religious principles while keeping pace with modernisation at the same time.Islam has advised its believers on acceptable and forbidden foods under Islamic dietary regulations. All aspects relating the regulations have causes behind them that might be discovered in the Quran and the Hadith.

There is a very tiny scope in Islam forbidden items, whereas those for allowable things are extensive.

There are also only a small number of sound and explicite text relating to prohibitions, while anything else not declared as legal or banned by nas (either the Qur'an verse or a clear, authentic and explicit Sunah) fall within the overall concept of allowability and in the favor of Allah. Countries that produce food already strive to accommodate the increased demand for safe, high-quality meals.

The potential for trading in halal products and services is enormous with a worldwide Muslim population estimated at 1.8 billion and expected to grow to 3 billion next year. Without connecting it with hygienic and nutritional factors the notion of halal massacres is insufficient.

In addition, animals have to be halal, safe to consume and have great nutritional benefits from a holistic standpoint. The questions of Halal slaughter continue to be a public discussion, while the protection of anials was thoroughly discussed in the Quran and the Hadith before and during the Halal slaughter. Furthermore, study data indicates that halal slaughter delivers excellent meat. Here halal food is not an automated procedure that consume without reasoning as it is linked considerably to the great personal priority given by religious affiliations to halal meat intake.

Chapter 8

Halal Food Marketing Supervision

CONTENTS

8.1. INTRODUCTION

Every country in the world tend to have different kind of resources und further have different cultures. In most circumstances, the resources that ae available do not meet the needs of the individuals of the society and in other instances, they may actually not be needed by the individuals in the region. Such conditions tend to encourages the trade between the regions so as to have the ability to export what is not required and further import the necessities. Ideally, international trade is the trade that take place with a foreigner, a foreign country or rather a foreign nation. Conversely, in the case where a country has limited access to a particular resource leads to the need of importation activities. In most cases, the existence of international relations tend to bring about harmonious relationships between the countries that are conducting trading. This ideally means that all the parties involved benefit from the terms of trade both economically and socially. These activities also allow for the availability of employment for individuals from the parties or rather the nations involved. According to Heckscher & Ohlin's (1991) theory, the fact of the matter is that, a country will only trade the resources that it has comparative advantage over. Taking for instance Indonesia, export preference has been encouraged in the nation. This was following the industrial era where the strategy in the country changed from import substitution to export promotion. There are cases of domestic consumers buying products from imported goods or those goods that are oversees or the case international consumers buying products from the local markets. This brings about very sharp competition existing between the products.

Figure 8.1. Trading of Halal food products. These both economically and socially beneficial.

Source: Korea.net.

In the case in which such trade occurs, there are standards in which the goods are required to conform to, the price, the quantity and the quality. They are normally set by the country of destination and in most cases are the determinants of the competitiveness of a product. Apart from the fact that export brings about a positive impact to the country, there are a number of complex problems that emanate from the same. They normally range from upstream to downstream which tend to be interesting whenever it is applied to scientific work (Omar & Jaafar, 2011). As a country with the highest number of Muslims in the world, it tends to have a very huge potential for halal food market for the various products. It is with no doubt that, there has been a growing number of Muslim population around the world and as such, there is the need for Halal food certification and labeling is one thing that is absolutely required for the case of the processed food products. The case is for the finished or the semi-finished products, which can be easily marketed either domestically or abroad. Some of the countries that are the largest recipients of Indonesian halal products in the world includes the United States, Malaysia, Philippines, Singapore and china.

According to number of government regulations concerning the labeling and the advertisement of Halal food, they are products that do not contain haram and its elements or any other product that is prohibited material to be consumed by the Muslim. The raw materials and other auxiliaries are also included in the foodstuffs that are to be consumed by the Muslims. The practices by halal are considered to be very sensitive issues to most of the food producers and the operators. This is due to the fact that there are many definitions of halal and is quite difficult to have the exact products. Furthermore, in the process of finding information that will be helpful in halal food processing gets to be challenging to the information seekers especially in organization. The biggest issue that should be addressed to the current society is that, there lacks historic data that one may easily rely on in the process of venturing in their businesses. The current societies should then leave a manual or a digital footprint that would easily help the future generations in their processes, that is, make it easy for them to avoid the confusions that are currently being experienced. Ideally, the suggestions by most of the individuals that are involved in the process of marketing halal food products is that it would be wise if they would work by networking with the collective food producers and operators. Through this, they would be able to work with each other in making personal visits to the halal premises to help each other in putting together the missing pieces.

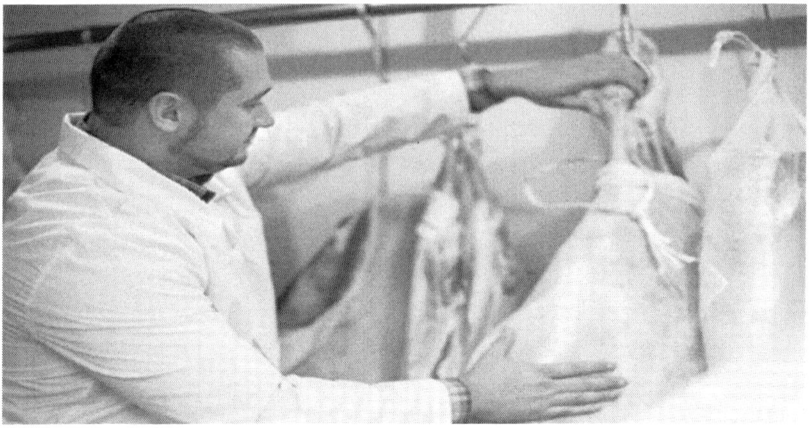

Figure 8.2. Distributor of Halal food products. Distributors and traders of halal food products need to work together with other traders so as to be well informed.

Source: Halal Watch World.

JAKIM is the Islamic body that is put in charge of the inspection of the halal certificates that are given to the food operators especially those that are working in the restaurants and those that are working in the marketing of the halal products. This body is normally appointed by the national government to issue Halal certificates to the new applicants and furthermore issue licenses to those that are willing to renew their own. This body has had the capacity to accredit several overseas Islamic organizations, which shows the vital role it plays in the Islamic community.

JAKIM has also been commissioned with the responsibility to study the documents that have been submitted by the applicants and furthermore inspect the products that are being manufactured, the premises and whether they are following the rules that have been stipulated. Furthermore, this body has taken up the responsibility to frequently educate individuals on Halal practices. They do this by conducting seminars each month.

Figure 8.3. JAKIM logo. the body is responsible for ensuring Halal guidelines are followed.

Source: Twitter.

JAKIM's Halal requirements tend to consider the safety and quality assurance by the products that are being sold by the individuals that have taken up the role. The products that are finally sold need to be clean, safe, well taken care of, with good presentation, served in a proper manner and furthermore, cater for the needs of every person. The body is in charge of ensuring all the requirements are followed. Furthermore, they do inspections and supervisions to ensure that the rules have been followed to the latter.

8.2. PRODUCTION PROCESS OF HALAL PRODUCTS IN INDONESIA

Indonesia remains the largest Muslim country globally with over 250 million people, about 90% of them being Muslims. This makes the country the largest market for Halal products and services in the world. The introduction of regulations and provisions for supervision is a good strategy for increasing demand for Halal products and services in the region as the Halal commodities win the hearts of the huge Muslim population in Indonesia. Recent studies showed that the current value of Halal products in Indonesia amounts to up to US$163 billion. Investors and manufacturers have thus been attracted to the market and are willing to penetrate the promising enterprise (Nurrachmi, 2018).

Products subject to this law include goods and services related to food, beverages, pharmaceuticals, cosmetics, chemicals, biological products, and genetically modified products. The law in the country was officially implemented in October 2019. There are a number of factors that the companies using Halal label need to consider. These are the guidelines that will help them in their production and marketing process. The first factor is that the animals need to be cleaned after they have been slaughtered. This is so because blood is not considered as Halal in the Muslim community. The second factor that the companies should consider is that the machines that are used in the production process need not have come into contact with any material that is regarded as Haram. The third is that, the water that is used in the cleaning of the Halal products should be clean and preferably running tap water. The final component is that the production process need not come into contact with anything that is considered unclean. Halal products and services are to those that one should be able to trace back to the Islamic cultures and community, considering the food that was eaten initially. This involves the entire process of production, which is from raw materials acquisition and handling, factory facilities, logistics, storage, the retail stores as well as in market outlets .A Halal certificate is a document that is issued to justify that Halal product sold to and used by the Muslim population are in conformity with Islamic Sharia laws. For businesses, Halal certification is the only way to label their products as Halal. The highest authority in issuing of Halal certificates is called the National Body of Halal Assurance. In Indonesia MUI are the highest authorities that deal with Islamic affairs under which the Food, Drug and Cosmetics Assessment Agency (LPPOM), and MUI Fatwa Committee falls under. Both of them are in charge of the Halal audit, assessment and declaration of verification and regulation of licenses for Halal products marketing. Evidently, to certify your Halal products in Indonesia makes a lot of logic. Halal labeling on products seems to be a lot more appealing to Muslims who try to avoid any possibility of consuming or getting into touch with Haram products. The practice of labeling of Halal products assist consumers in selecting the products that they would like to consume in line with their religious beliefs and preferences for the non-Muslims.

Figure 8.4. Science urged for Halal food.

Source: Bangkok Post.

While the procedures involved in the Halal certification of products and services in Indonesia might seem tedious and burdensome due to the paperwork to comply with the requests, the process could be a simple one with Cekindo's registration assistance which include gratifying Halal requirements associated to raw materials, products and manufacturing process and then with the implementation of Halal Assurance System, getting ready all documents required for the application of Halal certification. You will have to submit the documents to Cekindo, together with the Halal certification contract fee and registration fee. We will organize the documents for you to comply with the submission requirements, filling out documents as required by the LLPOM-MUI during the registration process, according to your certification status. You need to submit the dossier to Cekindo as well for LLPOM-MUI to process, Cekindo provides guidance for pre-audit, audit and post audit assessments, as well as lab analysis to ensure conformity, products fulfil has requirements and LLPOM-MUI lab analysis, MUI approves the products or materials and BPJPH issues the Halal certificate. The entire process of product regulation in Indonesia may take approximately about 60 days and may not apply if a products composition has to be modified (Nusran et al., 2018).

8.3. SANCTIONS FOR NON-COMPLIANCE

Sever criminal sanctions are reported to be introduced in the new Halal law and may be imposed on enterprises with Halal products as well as the LPH. For companies with Halal certificates that fail to maintain their products Halal quality will face up to IDR 2 billion fines or 5 years of imprisonment. Besides, LPH that fails to protect the trade secrets such as the Halal product formula, which they evaluate, will be subject to IDR 2 billion fines as well, or up to 2 years of imprisonment. This is the first time that criminal sanctions will be imposed on Halal non-compliance. According to Indonesian Halal law, products or materials with Halal certification from outside of Indonesia will need to be registered at BPJPH. Only then, they can be distributed and sold in Indonesia with legal Halal status. However, Halal certificates issued by foreign certification institutions that are not listed in the regulation will have to go through BPJPH assessments. The certification must be however authorized by the regulating bodies in Indonesia. During production, raw maerials are considered as the main ingredients. The materials that areadded in the production process are not considered as the main ingredient which in mostcases may be finished or semi-finished materials.

Figure 8.5. Halal industry certification bodies shaken.

Source: Salaam Gateway.

Those materials or the additives whose main function is to speed up or slow down the production process are what are known as the auxiliary materials. As a matter of fact, all the individuals that are involved in the halal value chain need to understand the importance of looking at the dangers that can be experienced through the consumption of particular goods instead of looking at their own interests. To the Muslims religion, the belief is that whenever a food is known to endanger ones soul then it should be forbidden from consumption. This makes the Halal products safe for human consumption, as they are free of all germs associated with unclean products. A written fatwa MUI that describe all the Islamic shari'a is what is described as a Halal certificate. They tend to include the Halal label.

8.4. INSTITUTE FOR FOOD, DRUG AND COSMETICS ASSESSMENT

Indonesia is very adamant on ensuring that the issuance of food as a way of Halal management protects the activities that are performed by the Muslims especially when dealing with the halal food and the products. Standards were set since 1996 and are in application up to date. The Acts regarding the Haleness of product was done by the body known as LPPM MUI, which was responsible for preparing the government regulations regarding the advertisement of the Halal food products and the Food Label. Up to date, it has been described that the products that are circulated in Indonesia including the foods and beverages need to be issued by the Majelis Ulama Indonesia through the LPPOM. This practice makes the certification of Halal products and services easier to go to different countries because the process has been standardized.

The main reason as to why there are standardization procedures is the fact that there is need to provide protection to the individuals and in the process ensure the safety and further the health of the consumers. The various societies that are involved are participating in the process in order to ensure that efficiency is increased and further help in realizing the or rather managing the quality of the system of the entire process. The process of certification is normally associated with ensuring that the certificates that are granted meet the required quality especially by the business standards (Mohsin et al., 2016). This shows the vital role that certification plays in basically continuing the activities of the standardization process. By the use of the certificates, it shows that there is a formal form of recognition in terms of providing assurance to the consumers that all the standards have been followed.

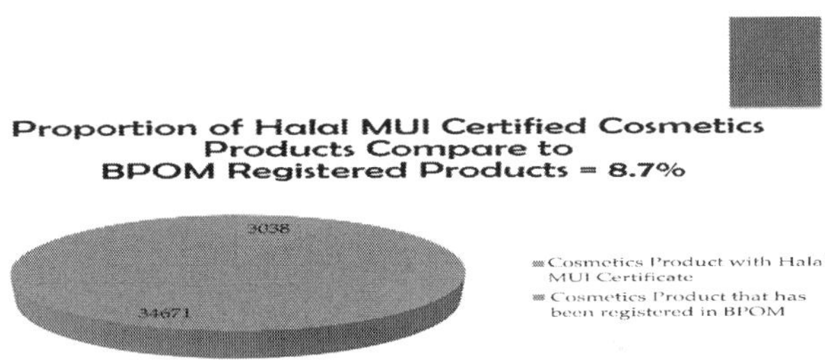

Figure 8.6. Halal Cosmetics Certification.

Source: SlidePlayer.

LPPOM MUI has a great vision of being a trusted Halal agency that promotes peace among the Muslims and further provide information that can be useful to the users of the Halal products.

Law involved in Halal product warranty is normally approved by an extraordinary power among the Indonesian Ulema Council. This can be easily observed by the articles that are useful in informing Halal products and in most cases are issued under the umbrella of fatwa Indonesian Ulema Council. This body is known for the deliberations of Ulema especially those that are Muslim Intellectuals, the officials that are involved with the Islamic scholars, which are competent in answering and solve some of the solving religious and social problems within the society. This is what is commonly determined as fatwa.

The word fatwa is derived from an Arabic word which is described as having the role of providing advice or the advice itself provided to the individual. This word is normally used to mean or rather help in describing the scholars and how they relate to various issues in the society especially the religious ones. This description provides the information that fatwa is not only relate to an individual's opinion and mere thoughts but involves the Ulema which cannot be neglected. Activities that are conducted within Fatwa are normally determined based on the Quran.in most cases, the determination process tend to be anticipatory, proactive and nonetheless responsive. There are a number of methods or rather procedures that are followed that need to be established before the determination of fatwa. The initial step is that, before Fatwa gets to be determined, it is rather crucial that the opinion of the school of thought is taken into account but should be within the jurisprudence of the Islamic religion. The second factor is that any problem that is experienced in the implementation of the law should only be said as it appears. As a matter of fact, there is no need to sugarcoat any of the problems since the belief is that taking care of the problem as soon as possible is important compared to making it sound better which may be the root cause of problems for the future (Mostafa, 2020). The third thing that must be considered is when dealing with issues where individuals tend to have different opinions. When such a case is experienced, the belief in the Islamic culture is that when there exists inconsistencies among the madhab, then the determination of fatwa is delegated to the schools in which case, it involves incorporating the conflicting propositions. The fourth case of the matter is that, when there has been no success in resolving the issue, and then fatwa determination is normally based on the strength of tarjih in the process of comparing the schools of thoughts. The method that is used in the process uses the principle of comparison. In the case where there is no legal opinion that is provided by the school of thought the determination is normally left in the hands of the collective community. What should always be noted is the fact that the decisions that ae normally made by the fatwa need be for the common good of all the individuals within this world. This shows that in the Islamic religion, the fatwa is a very important material that helps in keeping the individuals of the society in check.

The fourth chapter as stipulated in the Fatwa reports the authority and the territory of the fatwas for the Indonesian Ulema Council. It bears some characteristics and as such need to be taken into consideration. It is important to understand that the council has the authority to issue the fatwa based on the religious matters especially when it comes to dealing with the legal and the religious issues. The vital component in this is that, it considers truth and purity of the Indonesian Muslims.

Figure 8.7. Indonesia government ends MUI'S.

Source: HalalFoucus.net.

The concept involving that of national law according to the Fatwa is led to mean the positive law. In most instances, this kind of law is normally authorized by the constitution and are helpful in the formation of such laws. According to the constitution that was written down in 1945, it was clear that the legislators were not that relevant as most of the duties were carried out by the state organs, which included the president and the DPR. The institution was able to give authority to the two of the institutions. Ideally, the legal system of the nation, MUI fatwa is not considered to be part and parcel of the positive law. This can consequently mean that it is not part of the positive law that is widely used in Indonesia since it was established by an agency that is outside the state institution that is official. In order to establish a systematic law, it is normally based on a systematic hierarchy and as such considered systematic and juridical.

Looking on the idea of legislation, there may exist disharmony or battle of norms that arise among the countrywide legal structures with the fatwa set with the aid of using the MUI. Because primarily based totally at the explanation of legal homes that are constructed with the idea of Kelsen desires the legislators that are the legit to the state as stated within the country as it shapes better hierarchical law and legal norms present within the regulation which tend to be challenging within the legal and better norms (Mostafa, 2018).

The desire of ideas or arguments to harmonize the regulation is that the idea of legal harmonization is less complicated and realistic to put in force as compared to try and institute legal unification inside a rustic that has numerous legal structures or legal sub-structures, along with the plural

Indonesian legal system. The idea is that the means of harmonization in step with Hannu Honka is with the uniformity of guidelines or noticeable ideas among numerous structures and ideas of disharmony regulation. While the idea of harmonization via way of means of the Ministry of Justice of the Republic of Indonesia is as a systematic interest to guide the manner of harmonization of written regulation that refers, each on philosophical, sociological, monetary and judicial it is based within the theoretical perspective.

Figure 8.8. Halal Food in Indonesia.

Source: Switzerland Global Enterprise.

The reason of harmonization of the regulation is to make the primary concepts of various subsystems or legal structures made or observed in the intersection as a reference for the practice of law with a view to keep away from conflicts among the factors or the elements therein. Therefore, the means of harmonization of the regulation consists of adjustment of legal guidelines and rules, authorities' decisions, judges' decisions, legal structures and concepts with the intention of improving legal unity, felony certainty, equity, application and legal clarity, without obscuring and sacrificing felony pluralism.

Thus, the sample of MUI fatwa harmonization into countrywide regulation need to seek advice from the values of philosophy, sociology, and juridical as a mirrored image of the attempt in the direction of concord and conformity with legal guidelines and rules, each unwritten and written now no longer to disclaim the precept of felony pluralism. For the reason of harmonizing fatwas, the not vital element to not forget is how the concepts and especially the legal ones contained within the fabric of the MUI fatwa are capable of harmonize, synergize, and concurrently exist with countrywide regulation, on each institutional aspects, norms and felony substance. Conversely, the formation of countrywide regulation need to seek advice from the residing regulation in Indonesian society as a non-secular society. Trade has a completely crucial function in selling monetary development. To that end, the nation, or rather, the authorities need to defend the enterprise actors; specifically, exporters related to merchandise that require Halal certification or Halal label from MUI. The function of the authorities' right here is to create rules that offer the supposed safety thru alternate ministers. On the alternative hand, the Indonesian Ulema Council, that is legal through the authorities to difficulty a fatwa, is a network organization, now no longer a nation-owned institution. Consequently, the fatwa issued is not always a nation regulation that has sovereignty, binding, and ought to be obeyed through all citizens. It wishes safety associated with the export of processed uncooked substances of meat licensed under Halal through Majelis Ulama Indonesia. Lastly, to bolster the bargaining role regarding the legal foundation and legal status of official merchandise issued through Majelis Ulama Indonesia, the MUI wishes to be upgraded to nation institutions. This exercise will make certain that law and provisions for supervision of Halal merchandise are according to the legal guidelines of the nation and in addition to cause improving consumer pleasure within the marketplace outlets (Mannaa, 2020).

8.5. UNDERSTANDING MECHANISM TO PROMOTE HALAL FOOD INDUSTRIES

When auditing a place for halal certification especially in food rendering services there needs to be auditing by a team from a halal department. As the audit is about to be executed the owner is made aware of the audit date and their methodology. This information is supposed to ensure that the people required to be present during the audit are made aware so as to prevent any delays. A team is then allocated their different roles based on their competences on the type of certification the client needs. In these teams, one of the audit members is a qualified sharia expert and one shall be a qualified FSMS auditor.

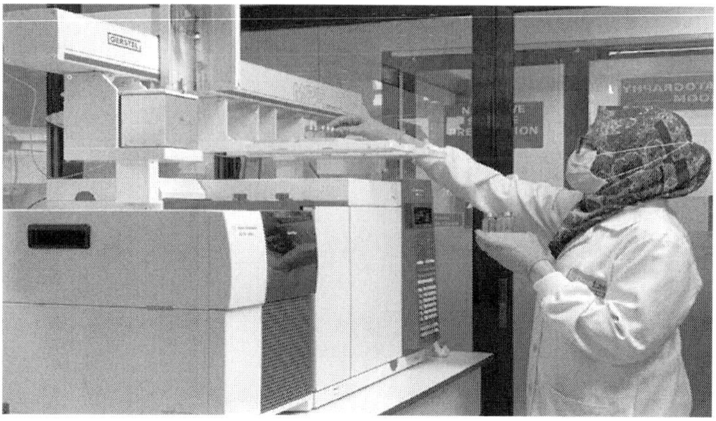

Figure 8.9. A halal certification lab, which is used for inspection and tests.

Source: DOST Region XI.

The team is led by the team leader who has the following roles.

- To represent the team in front of the client being audited. He/she conducting the opening and closing meeting, he/she shall also chair the meetings.
- To organize the team based on their roles and expertise as well as direct them during the audit process.
- To make a good plan for the audit by ensuring effective use of the resources they are allocated and also give the team adequate time and requirements of each individual to the team.
- To prevent and king of friction among members and also to resolve conflict that arises among the members.
- To prepare the audit report as soon as they visit the site and to complete it before presentation to the certification panel. The client has to fist apply for the certification by producing detailed information on the business. The first order of business is the initial audit where the audit team reviews the client's information and documentation. It is ten followed by the main audit where the team evaluates the implementation and include the how effective the client's halal management system, i.e., during the different stages of production preparation, processing, packaging, labeling, handling, distribution and how they serve the consumers. A report is then produced (Mathew, 2014). Sampling is sometimes

necessary and in some instances, the team can take sufficient amount of samples for inspection and tests in their laboratories. The inspection is carried out sometimes by laboratories outside and they have to be ISO/IEC certified or should be recognized by a halal competent authority. After that, there is surveillance audit and this is carried out for a period not less than 6 months or a period not exceeding 12 months. A recertification audit shall be planned from the last day after the stage 2 audit. After which there is remote auditing and lastly there is follow-up and short notice visits.

8.5.1. Understanding Mechanisms to Promote Halal Food Industry

In order to further mechanisms on how to promote the halal food industry we first need to understand the theory of planned behavior. The theory is an extension of the theory of reason and this helps in order to understand the people who enjoy halal food so as to understand their reasoning and with that, we can promote it to the other individuals who are yet to partake in halal food. This theory further includes the inclusion of perceived behavioral control. The theory of planned behavior consists of three components, which include; attitude towards a behavior, subjective norm and lastly perceived behavioral control, which then gives the link between belief and behavior. This will then give a clear picture that helps to relate what Muslims believe and the behavior towards halal food. This theory gives a clear picture on a person's behavioral intensions and their behavior. This then gives an explanation that when a person thinks that what they are doing is good and will affect others in a good way especially their family members or close friends will expect him to do it then he/she will do it. In essence such behavior will also depend on whether what that person is expected to do is difficult then this may make the person have second thoughts on whether to do it or not. This then shows that the theory of panned behavior in halal would then explain why an individual's behavior of a customer towards halal certified products.

When a product is, halal certified then it increases the confidence of a consumer. In Malaysia studies, show that perceived behavior control has been influential in making Muslims prefer restaurants that have been halal certified. This has made more and more restaurant owners to apply for halal certification to encourage and get new customers to visit their restaurants.

This then attracts Muslims and individuals that are health conscious as the Muslims want an area where food has been prepared based on the sharia principles (Lubis et al., 2016). When consumers were interviewed, they showed that confidence is key, as they believe that halal certified products have undergone safety protocols and hence before it reaches the consumer then it has been thoroughly vetted. This then shows that all products that are halal certified ted to promote customer satisfaction increased their confidence and boosted their trust. This certification increases competitiveness among industries and restaurants and his in turn increases their market share. When a consumer goes to the market or supermarkets the halal logo convinces the customer that the product has been halal approved and certified.

The halal certification then makes the non-Muslims to try and provide halal food and this is because; the use of the halal logo is seen as an interest to Muslim consumers and it helps them make an informed decision to buy the goods without fearing or doubting the halalness of the product, the certification also shows that the business owners can guarantee that the products found in their premises have fulfilled halal requirements and also are in accordance with the hygienic requirements and practices and hence the quality products they serve. A study has shown that the certification has been seen to be environmentally friendly and related to human resource in that there has to be personnel qualification to ensure that they understand what they are doing, employee motivation in that the employees are motivated to provide services and gods that are of good and respectable quality, multi-skill of employees in that the employees have to have different skills to carry out different tasks, efficiency, environmentally conscious as they aren't required to use any chemicals that are harmful in production of halal products and they save on costs lastly the certification helps to expand the customer base and can be used as a marketing tool. This will ensure the organization can get both Muslim and non-Muslims as halal products can be consumed by either.

In some instances, customers and/or consumers have been known to prefer to pay more for halal certified products. In some countries such as Belgium Muslims have been known to buy meat at a premium instead of purchasing the meat in supermarkets where they are not sure of the halal status of the meat. This then builds customer confidence in the purchase of halal food and brings about trust between the service provider and consumer.

Figure 8.10. Marketing of products to ensure they are halal certified to give consumers preference to choose.

Source: fooddivercity.today.

The marketing strategy also plays a vital role in that the halal certification logo is not only required but it can be insufficient. When the consumer sees the halal logo, it boosts their confidence but to some they have to check on the ingredients used. In Belgium of example the non-Muslims and some Muslims ended up referring to buy meat from supermarkets because the eat contains information on the hygiene and the control of the meat as compared to when they buy from an Islamic butcher where the information is not readily available. It has also been seen that consumers will see the halal logo will go further to go through the ingredients and this shows the halal logo will not determine whether the consumer will end up purchasing the product.

Education to the public is also very important so that they can understand the principles of halal and how they benefit the consumer. This shows the significance of the Muslims and also non-Muslims to understand why it is significant to consume halal food and products. This will give a clear explanation to the consumer on the procedures for halal food production and the benefits to the consumer, how credible the halal logo is hence they have to understand the procedures of pre and post certification and the role of halal agents in promoting halal certified products. An example is when non-Muslims perceive the Muslim slaughtering procedure as inhumane even though when in reality it is one of the best and efficient ways of slaughtering and it causes less pain as compared to captive bolt stunning. Muslims tend to practice Islam and are required to follow their rules as a way of life but to some they believe that religion does not factor in their purchasing power (Abderahman et al., 2021).

For instance, there are some highly committed Muslims who lack on halal awareness where they consume food so long as the food did not contain ingredients that are not haram. For some they have to check for the halal logo but to some they consider that if a food come from a Muslim majority nation then the food can be considered halal. A study in Malaysia has shown that some Muslims have less concern on the halal status of the product but they would just check on the price of the product and the environment it was made. People have to be educated on this information and this can be done through adverts so that the business owners can promote their halal products. With this it can stimulate awareness and perception. It also helps consumers to get facts on the brands instead of myths and rumors within individuals.

In order to further promote the halal industry then education and marketing are very vital. In essence the consumers and investors/entrepreneurs need to be educated on the principles of halal and enhance their understanding on halal production of goods and services from how materials are selected until the stage where the consumer gets the finished product. Another very important aspect to look into is to ensure that there is consistent dispersal of information on the latest issues on halal products and services.

In some instances, individual do not comply with the halal certification. With this, it leads to penalties.

The penalty for failing to apply for a halal certificate and permit can lead to a fine not exceeding US Dollars 5,800. The person can also be jail for a term not exceeding 2 years or sometimes the person can both the fine and a jail term. If they do not comply a further fine of not more than US Dollars 70 per day will be levied.

In some instances, some individuals display certificates that have expired. They have not renewed or re-applied for a new certificate. They can get a fine not exceeding US Dollars 2,900 or can be imprisoned for a term not exceeding one years or sometimes they can get both. This is a very common offence due to many individuals viewing the certification process as cumbersome and time consuming with many requirements.

Some individuals alter the certificates and permits. They may alter the date to extend the time or even change ownership without informing the relevant authority. This may lead to a fine not exceeding US Dollars 2,900 or a jail term not exceeding one year or sometimes both depending on the severity of the offence.

An enforcement officer can be sent to an establishment to enforce a directive and when they are obstructed, become non-compliant to the officer's demands or deny the officer entry it can lead to a fine not exceeding US Dollars 2,900 or a jail term not exceeding 1 year or sometimes both (Khan et al., 2018).

Some establishments use labels other than the certified halal label on their premises or on their products and the use of unofficial terms such as "makanan Islam" or "ditanggung halal" or any other term that tends to insinuate or tend to indicate that Muslims are permitted to dine or consume any food products and this can attract a fine of not more than US Dollars 5,800 or an imprisonment not exceeding 2 years or they can be given both.

8.6. MARKETING TO ETHNIC SEGMENTS: HALAL PRODUCTS PENN STATE EXTENSION

In the Muslim society the consumption of halal certified products, when and where they can find it. According to the Islamic way of life, which is based on their doctrines it is a requirement for every Muslim faithful, to ensure they pursue and observe the norms and any values required of them by the hadith and the holy Quran in everything that they are doing. In the recent past, there have been trials to try to convert non-Muslims to convert and assimilate them into the Islamic culture. According to most of the census carried out it can be noticed that majority of Muslim faithfully are found in countries where Islam is not practiced as the states religion and these countries include; Egypt, china, Bangladesh, Australia, India some of the European countries, Canada and even the United States. This then shows that the Muslims provide a considerable market share in the modern world. Although they provide a considerable market share the Muslim consumer has been neglected and has led to the rise of the halal food industry to develop at a very fast pace and this can be seen in countries such as Malaysia and Indonesia. In these countries, they have developed ways to improve the halal standards of food products such tracing systems and even halal science centers.

In recent years' industries found in and around Europe have started investing and developing in halal products. Some of the retailers found in

Europe have included fresh halal meat into their stocks and some industries have started exporting halal certified products to Muslim countries most of which are found in the Middle East and Africa. These exports are mostly channeled through Holland. They are channeled through the Netherlands because they were the first country in Europe to have a facility for storing halal products and with this; it has led to an increase in the halal supply chain. In the recent past there has been a scare for food insecurity and increase in food being unsafe and this has led to most of non-Muslims to start preferring halal certified foods because of their additional safety, safety practices when being handled hence become hygienic and assurance that one is buy good quality products. due to common knowledge that halal food products require strict adherence to specified ingredients and how they are handled and this leads to less probability that the food is not likely to be contaminated. In the past people believed that halal was only about how animals were slaughtered and how meat was handled but in the recent years they have come to understand that it also includes other types of halal foods, how people handle themselves in their day-to-day lives and also services that are provided to the Muslim faithful (Krishnan et al., 2017).

The population of people in the United States has been on a steady rise and this means with an increase in the number people then there will be diverse people in terms of their ethnicity, their culture and their religious beliefs. Based on these groups they tend to believe in certain aspects and values that they know they need to follow. This then makes them have a particular belief and behavior because of their culture or religion and this mostly is derived from the type of food they consume and the type of diet they take, e.g., some become vegans because of their religion rather than to have a healthy lifestyle. This makes people involved in the agricultural input sector to explore various options to be able to cater and maintain their businesses for future prosperity and maximize their profits. A group that is on the rise in the United States is Muslims who according to them believes should only eat halal foods.

Halal not only deals with food but also is very diverse as it deals with how a person carries themselves in their day-to-day activities. The are other products also that are involved and these include but not limited to cosmetic products, cleaning products and personal care products.

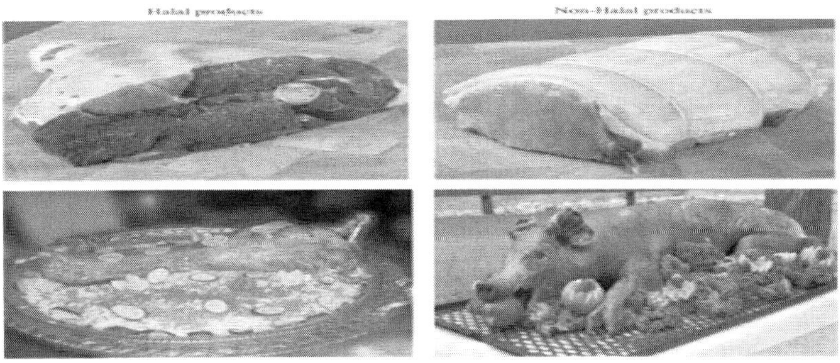

Figure 8.11. Dynamics of Muslim consumer preference.

Source: emerald insight.

It is estimated that almost 70% of Muslims adhere to halal principles and beliefs while the other 30% are not fully assimilated into the different cultures and norms including eating as a way or form of worship to Allah. Their similarities include how they slaughter animals in how they cut their throat and invoking the name of allay as they slit the throat. They also all believe that after the death of the animal they should not use the animals by product such as blood, gelatin or some finished dairy products that have been processed although they have an exception of milk products.

With an increase in population, it is known that on average a Muslim family is quite large averaging approximately 4.9 people per family. This then shows that in every family there is a wide range in terms of age. This then leads to an increase in consumption of halal food as this will be beneficial to the retailer and to the family as it will lead to production of more halal foods due to increase in demand or number of consumers. With this increase in number of consumers in the united states some of the industries are looking to expand into the middle east market a good example is Midamar corporation who are known to be worldwide producers of halal products and they offer consulting services for business that deal in food and are located in the united states but would wish to expand and enter the middle east market. This then shows that there is enormous market opportunity for those wishing to expand.

Muslims are expected to consume food that are halal certified and there are other examples of consumers who can be interested in these foods. A good example is where the use of animal by products such as blood cannot be used in halal foods this gives the vegetarians and vegans opportunity to avoid eating meat products and these groups represent a large and growing market and also halal foods are good for individuals who might be having any animal product allergies.

There are a few products that Muslims can consume that are already in the market for them to choose from which makes their choices very limited. This has then made producers to start making value added products for this markets and make their options more. Commonly known is the fact that many Muslims in the United States consume goat meat. This makes individuals who enter into this field early more likely to prosper rather than those waiting to watch the market.

With increase in population and eventual increase in market demand more and more Muslims will eventually purchase and end up loving the halal value added foods. This then makes educating the non-Muslims very important as it will give them a clear perspective and be informed on the goodness and value of halal foods. With the non-Muslim being educated and informed it will help demystify some myths some of them tend to believe even though they are baseless and fact less and with this, the name halal should be used to encourage and appeal to the non-Muslims (Karahalil, 2020).

With increase in demand for halal products more and more foreign importers, food service organizations and some of the consumers are request for the Islamic food and nutrition council of America to increase halal certified products in the market. This then leads to more marketing in the mainstream media and some can advertise through press releases, feature stories, cooking programs, some can advertise in journals and this will help increase the customer base. There is need for individuals or companies to do more research before they enter into halal certification and to increase their value addition, this will make their products more marketable and with this, their business will become profitable in the end.

Figure 8.12. Halal gelatine. It has been certified for vegan individuals.

Source: eHalal bot.

8.7. UNDERSTANDING HALAL CERTIFICATE AND HALAL PERMIT

There is a short history that is related to the Halal certification system. As a matter of fact, the short sweet History of the Muslims started in Malaysia in the 1980's and afterwards was able to expand to other countries especially when dealing with the product and the services that are provided by the Halal. Ideally, there are more than 400 countries that have had the capacity to implement the consumption of Halal food in their country ad an addition of the Halal certified organizations. With this case scenario, there have been a number of Halal certifying standards, which include those that have been implemented both locally in a particular country and those that have been implemented internationally through an agreement among the countries that are involved. In most instances, these standards are normally implemented by either a national standards development body or an organization that is duly given the responsibility to certify Halal products (Kamarulzaman et al., 2016).

Figure 8.13. Listing of halal certification agencies.

Source: my halal kitchen.

It should be noted that these products might range from edible ones to the ones that are not. With the case of the regional standards such as the Arab Gulf Cooperation Council's Halal standard and international Halal standards (IHI Alliance and SMIIC) are also normally tasked with the role of certifying or implementing standards. Ideally, the certification of the Halal food products need to be done by a third party. The purpose of this exercise is to ensure that there lacks biasness and to ensure that the standards that have been stipulated have been followed to the latter. Furthermore, the main reason as to why a third party is involved in the process is due to the fact that there needs to be credibility and can be assured in this process. One of the most reliable certification agency is the Islamic Food and Nutrition Council of America and the Muslim Consumer Group. These groups have gone a long way to show that the Islamic community s as honest as they appear to be because of how they conduct their businesses. In the process in which the halal operators visit such sites, there are a number of requirements that they are required to follow through including the fact that they are needed to submit an application online, via mail, or fax. After a cellphone discussion, an inspector will set up to go to the meals manufacturing facility to confirm that uncooked substances and manufacturing and sanitation practices are constant with Halal principles. For certification, the proprietor will signal an agreement mentioning the frequency of inspection, the goods being certified, and the expenses related to certification. The certification is commonly issued for a one-12 months' time, however can range relying upon the form of merchandise being certified. The agencies' touch records is indexed on the stop of this reality sheet (Junaidi, 2020).

The Muslim target market has specific religious' ideals that constrain their diets. By imparting ingredients, that match Muslims' prescribed diets, manufacturers can be capable of diversify their markets and boom their profitability. The most important task in Halal marketplace is aware of what Muslim keep in mind Halal. There is dissimilarity of Muslim customers throughout the extraordinary ethnicity. The degree of Halal meals notion amongst non-Arab Muslims is different from Arab Muslims. Non-Arab Muslims are extra cautious than Arab Muslims, while buying meals products. The most important task in Halal meals is decoding of what Muslims keep in mind, which is Halal, even this phenomenon has caused fraud and misunderstanding. The call for the Halal ingredients and offerings is growing each year. Despite the developing sales and significance of Halal grocery store, this section of marketplace has been ignored. Halal grocery store is not an unmarried marketplace however; it is far a fragmented marketplace in which each vicinity has its extraordinary characteristics. Muslims everywhere in the international are privy to significance of the Halal meals. This has led to enlargement of worldwide Halal meals industry. This approach globally shows that Halal wave is increasing, as Muslims are getting extra aware of Halal ingredients and offerings. The smooth manner for Muslims is buying services and products with Halal brand or certification, particularly in non-Muslims countries. Halal brand performs vital position in Muslims customers buying decision.

The system of Halal certification is important for the clients who choose to purchase and use Halal products. Here the definition of Halal is taken from the perspectives of eminent Islamic scholars. Different interpretations of Halal gadgets are being made, while many of the bodies are certifying those as Halal products. The supply of Halal Certification of services and products appears vital each for organization, and for the consumers. In order to apprehend the practices followed in a way means more than one of the bodies, that are certifying Halal, have attempted to become aware of numerous standards and sub standards on which Halal certification are being undertaken. The foremost contribution on certification of Halal meals has been made through means of JAKIM. This has been similarly prolonged to different countries. India being a main exporter of Buffen, its special groups attempts to observe the norms of the importer country. Thus, we have discovered the multiplicity of Halal Certifying Organization and this has additionally furnished principal threats than possibilities for Halal certification. However, in the attempted to make contrast amongst special Halal certification the bodies in India discovered that these certifications are targeted toward the slaughter of thc animal and feature comparable outlook. It was discovered that those Halal Certifying Organizations do now no longer have right norms for the tactics and upcoming era being followed within the meals industry. They want to expand higher norms for Halal bloodless chain and committed logistics to preserve the Halalness of the meals. The certification of the meals ingredients & components is principal opportunity. The codification of tactics is likewise necessary (Jia & Chaozhi, 2021).

In conclusion, Halal certification can be described as the certification of products or services as is stated by the Islamic law. In the process, it provides assurance to Muslim consumers especially when they are being informed on the Halal quality, the process of acquiring Halal certification and verification that is vital in their operation. Acquiring of permits or licenses is however required by various government institutions of different countries for carrying out of the business just like other businesses worldwide.

Chapter

9

Ethical, Organic, and Safety of Halal Food

CONTENTS

9.1. INTRODUCTION

Halal meat is a fundamental aspect of the Muslim belief and supporters contend that the acts of conventional Islamic slaughter is safe and respectful to the animals. However, some animal rights campaigners mention that halal causes unnecessary anguish and ought to be prohibited. Albeit the expression "halal" is used by non-Muslims only to allude to the slaughter and readiness of meat as per Islamic practices, but its significance in Islam is far more extensive. "Halal" alludes to any activity or conduct that is allowable in Islam, including what kinds of meat and techniques for preparation are adequate, while "haram" alludes to impermissible or unlawful activities (Ismail et al., 2018). With regards to dietary guidelines, pork and blood, just as meat from predatory birds and reptiles, are characterized as haram thus illegal to practicing Muslims. The Islamic practice for slaughtering an animal for meat is called zabiha. The slaughter-man uses a sharp knife to slit the animal\'s jugular, windpipe and the veins around its neck. The blood is then permitted to drain from the body. Just a single animal can be customarily butchered at a time, and other livestock should not observe its passing. The strict law likewise says how the creature should be treated during its life, with the creature not permitted to have been abused or brought about any agony. It should likewise be given adequate room to wander, fresh air, clean water, and food.

Figure 9.1. Today halal foods are available in the supermarket.

Source: https://www.npr.org/sections/codeswitch/2017/10/26/554298738/the-rise-of-halal-cuisine-in-an-age-of-islamophobia.

Some livestock butchered for halal meat in the UK are dazed electrically before their throats are cut, a process known as "pre-staggered slaughter." A few nations endorse low-voltage jolting to stagger poultry and electric tong shocking for sheep and goats. Nonetheless, it is illegal to use stunning strategies that can really execute the animal, for example, bolt firearms. Livestock not slaughtered using the customary Muslim standards are viewed as haram meat. In Muslim traditions, the interval between stunning the animal and cutting the throat is instant. There should be no delay between the dazing and resultant death stages. Animal welfare specialists and campaigners differ. They contend that executing animals without stunning them causes "needless anguish," while others call halal butchering "delayed torture," saying the animals "battle and wheeze for their last gasp, battling to stand while the blood flows from their necks."

In Europe, halal methods of slaughtering are currently prohibited in the southern Flanders region, where animals presently must be electrocuted before they can be slaughtered. The proscription is set be spread out to Wallonia in the south of Belgium, which means the only spot where it will be feasible to purchase halal or genuine meat will be Brussels, which is home to roughly 500,000 Muslims. The proscription has however been depicted as Islamophobic, with Muslim activists mentioning that "it assaults the center of their way of life and religious practice as equal residents with similar rights in the democratic society. The UK government has more than once resisted pressure from animal activists, for example, the RSPCA to ban halal slaughtering without pre-dazing, and gone against EU standards that expect meat to have marks affirming whether it came from animals that had been stunned before butchering on the grounds they disadvantaged Muslim groups. Nonetheless, it is still unclear how guidelines on halal meat will be influenced once UK leaves the EU (Indrasari et al., 2020).

9.2. THE HALAL MEAT MARKET

Figure 9.2. Halal food has spiritual importance among Muslims.

Source: https://www.thespruceeats.com/what-is-halal-food-2355726.

The interest for Halal meat is increasing and it is projected to keep on developing. Different factors add to the dramatic rise in popularity for Halal meat. The UK and France are the two EU nations where for about a decade there has been continuous rise in the interest for meats prepared by the Halal guidelines. The rising global Muslim population might be responsible for the increased demand of Halal meat market. Nonetheless, a few scientists have suggested that the development of the Halal meat market within the EU is credited to the expanded immigration of Muslims across Europe lately.

While this trend began decades earlier, the new displacement of Muslims from nations like Syria, Iraq, Afghanistan and Libya into the EU, because of radicalism and on-going conflicts in those nations, has reaffirmed immigration as perhaps the main variable affecting the rising development of the EU Halal meat market. Likewise, the proceeding expansion in the export of Halal-certified meat from the EU to Muslim nations, for instance, Indonesia, Malaysia, Turkey, Singapore, and the UAE is another significant factor impacting the development of the European Halal meat market (Henderson, 2016).

The Asia-Pacific territory represents the biggest market for the global Halal-meat market, whereas Singapore was identified as the absolute most significant community for the sale of Halal products, in comparison to other nations. It should be noted that the consumption of Halal meat isn't limited to Muslims only. In the UK and different parts of Europe, many non-Muslims still frequent Halal eateries and food stores that openly promote their meat as Halal. But there is minimal data available to show if the animals are actually pre-shocked. Key among these cafés and food chains include; Metro, Nandos, and Kentucky Fried Chicken (KFC).

A number of these establishments have exclusively "Halal" menu items, which are guaranteed Halal by various certification bodies that exist. It is along these lines not surprising that the mainstream retailers within the EU, such as Aldi, Albert Heijn, Carrefour, Sainsbury's, Waitrose and Tesco have all begun offering Halal meat items. These retailers stress that they don't sell unstunned meat under their own trademark, notwithstanding, unstunned meat may in any case be sold in some of the stores, as a rule under an external trademark. Notwithstanding the scramble for a portion of the Halal meat market by the leading retailers, the favored place to find Halal meat for most Muslims is the local Halal butchery.

Figure 9.3. The UK is a leading market for halal meat in Europe.

Source: https://www.theguardian.com/lifeandstyle/2013/sep/25/halal-food-why-hard-find-britain.

In an interview involving 300 UK Halal buyers, most of respondents (90%) revealed that they were unaware that a significant number of local store chains sold Halal meat. The discoveries additionally revealed that most of Halal consumers (96%) really prefer shopping at the neighborhood Muslim-butchery, since they confided in their consistence with Halal more than conventional store chains. While some non-Muslims keep on consuming Halal meat willingly (or unconsciously), others stay away from it since they consider such meats to be from livestock butchered in an cruel way, but a significant part of Halal products are paralyzed before slaughtering.

Truth be told, across the EU, the ratio of Halal meat stunned prior to butchering has been accounted for as 65% of livestock, half of all small ruminants and poultry. There is right now no lawful prerequisite for meat to be marked using the slaughtering technique or, all the more explicitly, regardless of whether the meat comes from livestock stunned pre-butcher, post-cut paralyzed or unstunned. Although some animal welfare advocates call for meat to be named as either stunned or not, to give clarity to customers, associations representing the veterinary field have necessitated a complete restriction on the butchering of animals without stunning across the European Union on animal welfare basis (Hanzaee & Ramezani, 2011).

9.3. HALAL MEAT IS BECOMING MORE COMMON

Figure 9.4. Muslim family saying a prayer before consuming halal food.

Source: https://theconversation.com/what-are-halal-foods-95696.

As per research, many non-Muslims are incidentally consuming meat from animals butchered while they are as yet conscious. The sharp rise in the quantity of sheep and poultry being slaughtered as per halal practice shows that it plausible that some unstunned meat is entering the "halal" marketplace as well, especially in fast foods such as pies. It's hard to have precise accountability on how livestock goes through its natural lifecycle up to the time of slaughter, since it passes through different hands. Different meats will go through various forms of processing, in a wide range of operations and diverse handling techniques.

The organization Eblex has assessed the worth of the UK halal meat industry to be around £2.6bn every year. It's most recent report into the halal meat market is England likewise recommends that while Muslims in the UK cover only 3% of the populace, they devour around 20% of all the mutton sold in the country. These are often added to foods such as hamburgers, the majority of which are halal. Notwithstanding, these records represent just a tiny part of the worldwide halal food market, estimated to be worth around $415bn per annum. Incredibly, three-quarters of the largest providers of global halal meat are non-Muslim nations, with Australia, Brazil, and India driving the way.

9.4. CONCERNS ON HALAL FOOD

Figure 9.5. Halal meat should be properly label for easy identification by consumers.

Source: https://www.dw.com/en/halal-meat-cannot-be-labeled-organic-ecj-rules/a-47700312.

With concerns around animal welfare rising, stores and restaurants facing criticism and fears on 'foreign ways,' the topic of halal meat in food is becoming a politically charged subject. Be that as it may, it's presently a billion dollar market and developing quick. For animal welfare organizations, such as RSPCA, the crux of the matter is stunning before butcher, legitimately required under EU guidelines for everybody except religious groups. Halal necessitates that an animal should be alive and sound, and executed with a fast slit to the jugular with a sharp blade, a strategy that permits the blood to drain from the body. But slaughtering without making the animal unconscious is coldblooded, contend some animal rights campaigners. Muslims hold a different opinion, claiming that the suffering is shortened and negligible for the animal (Han et al., 2021).

In truth, 88% of Europe's halal meat comes from animals that have been shocked before butchering, however the 12% that isn't causes some disquiet even among Muslims. While considered less painful, shocking can now and then kill the animal before butchering thus making it Haram. With different administrative bodies differing on what consists of halal and haram foods, consumers are left confounded: there have even been requests to have halal meat officially marked as "\stunned\" or "\non-stunned\." What everybody agrees to is that Muslims consume lots of meat. It's no wonder that individuals in the meat business are being mindful of their Muslim customers.

Maybe due to the concerns around halal, stores have been quite low key concerning their halal policies. Where previously, as one halal business insider kidded, they didn't have any desire to market halal products, now there is a growing acknowledgment that they can't disregard the Muslim group. As per the Muslim Council, halal food industry is worth several billions of dollars every year. A few stores also have meat counters run by certified halal specialists. The butcher's counter is often managed by certified meat providers, with Muslims and non-Muslims purchasing their mutton and chicken cuts there, under the label guaranteeing that the meat is prepared as per the standards of the Qur'an and Sunnah.

While most halal meat is pre-stunned, the primary point of difference between halal and non-halal slaughter is the recognition that it is a present from the creator. Even as factory farming strategies and mechanical slaughter persist, a question still lingers on whether "the stun/non-stun debate is simply an argument for the vets?" Others claim that the halal industry, has a tendency to worry too much on how animals die instead of on how they live. Halal certification audits pay attention on the details of whether or not there is alcohol inside the hand sanitiser at abattoirs, or use of the illegal "blessed blade," with a pre-slaughter prayer inscribed on it. But there are other broader issues at stake, springing from Islam's emphasis on sustainable farming and care to animals.

The Qur'an instructs Muslims to "eat of what is lawful and healthy on the earth," but too often, the emphasis remains on the lawful – halal – in place of tayyib, the nutritious and natural (Debney, 2016). Many halal meat producers too often mirror the pitfalls of the conventional food industry: convenience and cheapness frequently exceeding Islamic decrees on natural ways of farming and treating animals. Halal is much broader than simply how the animal is slaughtered or about meat. It's about taking food that blesses a man or woman in their bodily and spiritual wellness.

Figure 9.6. There is no way to determine whether meat from local butchers is halal or not.

Source: https://islamicanews.com/nobody-really-knows-trusts-local-halal-butcher/,

Because the halal enterprise varies in size from butcher's and kebab stores to big wholesalers, there is unavoidable tension between the need for convenience and requirement for spiritual nourishment. Different chains such as KFC and Nando's are currently developing halal shops, besides Pizza providers and supermarkets are also experiencing a growing demand for frozen halal foods. Products that permit for a convenient way of life are increasingly becoming popular. Inclusive of meals that you could just 'grab and go' like pre-packed halal meat, there has further been an increasing demand for kids products such as fritters, popcorn, nuggets and burgers. If halal actually means anything, it must be a whole lot holistic. It must distinguish itself. With the swelling of the Muslim middle-class population, a brand new breed of consumers now desire halal foods, and the urge to experience a wide range of luxurious foods. With the ability to now order halal food online, the demand is expected to grow even further.

With a more youthful Muslim generation demanding extra variety, restaurants are increasingly offering delicacies like southern fried chicken, in addition to halal steak. It is more youthful diners who generally tend to order the Mexican style burgers and rib-eyes. For some reason, they want halal steak to be added to their food choices. They also want their steaks nicely prepared, for the reason that Qur'an proscribes eating whatever carries blood. Before, Muslims lived in certain areas, but now they reside in the major cities, and triggering huge demand for halal meat (Damit et al., 2018).

The goal is to offer Muslims the best dishes they eye, such as fast food burgers, but have never had the opportunity to consume them due to halal restrictions. For Muslims, having to choose the safest meat to eat is not an easy task, it may appear a small matter for those who don't follow any strict religious dictates. But for Muslims who have no means of consuming what everybody else enjoys, or for new converts who must adjust their lifestyle according to the Quaran, the halal issue remains a thorny matter they must navigate. Meat producers are responding to this demand by providing traditional fast-food style meals, such as shepherd's pie, burgers and meat cuts in a halal friendly environment, and getting muslins to understand they're buying something that's halal, certified ethical and tastes great, just like the other standard fast-food meals.

Figure 9.7. The demand for halal meat is rising both among Muslims and non-Muslims.

Source: https://www.greenprophet.com/2011/11/zabiha-organic-halal/.

Getting meat to the marketplace isn't easy, since suppliers must be keen to uphold the "healthy and natural" aspect of Islamic halal foods, which begin even before the slaughtering of the animal, going back to the raising style and supply chain dynamics. Loads of time is spent focusing on halal, and 50% of the instructions – but the tayyib component is regularly ignored. To this end, a few suppliers have considered reducing industrial pollution in their meats by using packaging from sustainable forests, and keeping a keen eye on maintaining a halal food chain.

As halal food becomes more popular, there should be a need to protect Muslims in need of quality meat products– meat producers need a higher knowledge on how to process, package and label their products. If somebody comes along and says halal is barbaric and inhumane, and if Muslims do not have adequate information on what halal truly means, then the temptation is to hit back by saying the criticism originates from Islamophobia is quite high. Future projections for the halal market suggest that the business will do well heading into the future. In fact, a recent report from the market research company Dinar discovered that the global halal meat market was worth $1.62tn in 2012, and was set to expand to $2.47tn come 2018. This success shows that the halal market has great potential, but it needs rework to determine what the Muslim youth want, being the largest group that consumes halal meat.

9.5. HALAL AS A DIETARY ETHIC

In the family circle of Muslims in France, halal strengthens cultural ties and faith. Most children see and copy the culinary know-how of their parents in keeping up with the dietary practices permitted in the Quran. Halal seeks to reconcile the connection between ethnicity, national and spiritual welfare through quality and sanctioned food picks.

The phenomenon of immigration has motivated the development of halal foods in non-Muslim countries. In France, a new belief on the concept of 'halal' has transformed from one that was associated with Muslim immigrants, to now include every citizen. Earlier on, halal was a nerve-racking experience for non-muslims, but it has since grown to cover much more than a religious meat factor. The ethnic traditions of the countries of origin are also displayed on the table. For example, the Berber populations in Morocco who are majority Muslim have their unique way of preparing halal food, which motivates their traditional cuisine. Following their immigration to France in the Seventies, their socioeconomic status improved. This triggered a sharp increase in the consumption of halal meat, which until then was mainly reserved for special events, such as the Eid al-Adha festival (Cuesta-Valiño et al., 2020).

This newly-received privilege brought about a need to protect their now minority culture, in addition to showing their advanced social reputation to others who perceive Berbers and other Muslim immigrants to be of an inferior culture. They are contributing to the European culinary environment with their strict observance of halal requirements defined in the Quran.

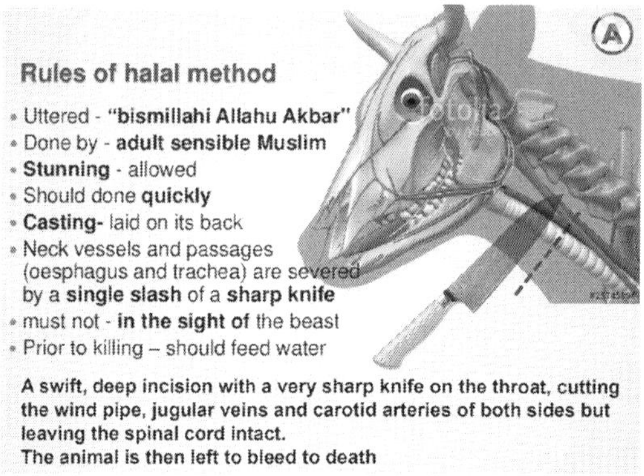

Figure 9.8. Slaughtering should be quick to reduce the animal's suffering.

Source: https://www.facebook.com/Humans.Uvas/photos/.

9.6. THE NEED FOR INTEGRATION AND BALANCED DIET

Figure 9.9. Halal abattoir where maximum hygiene is maintained.

Source: https://ati.da.gov.ph/ati-12/news/06272019–1122/regional-halal-focals-get-training-halal-abattoir-slaughtering-practices.

The trends in Europe keep changing with increasing waves of immigrants, for the maximum part born and raised in their host nation. They generally tend to opt for meals choices favoring social integration. They need to be accepted in everyday community and not considered as foreigners. Halal has therefore become the critical link between the need to contribute to European community, while still preserving the Muslim identity and way of life. This way, societal differences may be much less prominent since 'halal' foods fill up the gap between traditional Islamic culture and modern European society.

Halal certification requirements in the agri-food business have soared ever since the mid-2000s. Likewise, many more young Muslims are embracing open interpretations of the halal rule, unlike their parents, they now very particular on the labeling of halal meat in supermarkets. Their parents preferred buying halal meat from a trusted local butchery, but they have more options and variety to choose from thanks to the internet. The youth admire their cultural heritage, but now consider a broader interpretation of halal. But some Muslim parents complain that their children have lost sight of the healthy and sacred nature of meat, which they deem to be too fatty, and urge them to consider healthier, purer, and extra-balanced food choices and not just halal.

9.7. ETHICAL DIET

Figure 9.10. Electrical stunning reduces the pain in animals during slaughter.

Source: https://www.halal-slaughter-watch.org/return-to-consciousness-after-electrical-stunning/.

For some people, vegetarian and pescatarian diets provide a solution that is attuned with their need to respect the ecosystem, consume a balanced diet and maintain a feeling of sociocultural & religious belongingness. In many cases, more youthful individuals who abstain from consuming meat products define their desire as an ethical posture in reaction to the violent handling of animals. Since livestock slaughtering is a delicate religious topic among Muslims, they deserve the right to know how their meat was prepared and whether it matches their religious standards.

9.8. HALAL MEAT CERTIFICATION (HMC) IN EUROPE

The purpose of the endorsement of meat as Halal through halal certification bodies (HCBs) is to provide assurance to Halal clients that some key measures have been met during the slaughtering, processing, packing, and shipping of the meat. This is particularly crucial for the EU and different other industrialized nations, where some people may be with the requirements of Halal. However, there is an increased threat of contamination of Halal foods with non-Halal products during the processing stage, including throughout storage and delivery stages (Bergeaud-Blackler, 2015). The concept of Halal approval in the EU is still new. In the UK, the first authority to certify meat as Halal was the Halal Foods Authority, commonly known as HFA. Their primary objective was to "screen and authenticate" the Halal standards of bird meat, and clearly label pork since the Halal quality of around 85% of "meat" in the UK at the time could not be tested.

Opponents of Halal food certification have frequently questioned the motives behind these ventures. It has been argued that the exponential growth of Muslim populations across Europe in recent times may have triggered the growth in a variety of unregulated HCBs, all seeking to independently verify Halal standards, and facilitate changes in Halal products. In the United Kingdom, there are more than 10 HCBs who are all competing to apply various Halal standards in their quest to provide consumers authentic and Halal-certified meat. There have been complaints and counter-complaints as to whose Halal certification is genuine. Lack of government involvement and professional tracking of HCBs has meant that any person can establish an HCB, even with minimal technical understanding on how to prepare Halal meat. Needless to say, there is still widespread ignorance on what constitutes Halal meat. Reduced technical expertise has triggered reduced monitoring and analysis of the few Halal approved web sites, which has caused a situation where Halal and non-halal products are produced side by side with the possible effects of cross contamination.

Others certification bodies have been accused of endorsing slaughter technology that contravenes the basic principles of Halal. While some Muslims may prefer meat from livestock slaughtered without stunning, the stunning approach is in fact painless to the animal. They argue that having an unhurt animal at the time of slaughter is fundamental, however, activists also mention that systemic abuse and harassment of animals meant for the Halal food chain is something that must be looked at.

These practices may absolutely violate the animal welfare rights of Halal slaughter enshrined in the Quran and Hadith. It should be emphasized that such desecrations are also rampant in Muslim-majority countries, where rather painful and violent practices are used in pressuring and restraining animals before slaughter. These include the hoisting of conscious livestock (especially ruminants) via their hind legs prior to slaughter, cutting of tendons on the hind legs to immobilize conscious animals before slaughter, and the lifting of small ruminants via their wool or hind-limbs (Adekunle & Filson, 2020).

There's also a need for sufficient tracking and regulating of Halal meat in Muslim-majority nations, the mere fact that livestock isn't always bowled over before slaughter does no longer suffice the meat to meet all the Halal slaughter requirements. Some of the matters concerning Halal certification will be resolved using a unified global Halal model. This will make sure that all HCBs function under the same policies, and might be equivalent to the modern-day European Union 'organic' standard managed by different certification bodies all following similar overarching regulations. The 57 member state Organization of Islamic Cooperation (OIC), an inter-governmental organization is presently working towards the development of an international Halal standard. Until there's credibility or consensus on the standard meaning of Halal, enforcement agencies may struggle to protect Halal consumers. In addition, consumer law, presently does not provide adequate protection to assist Halal consumers, notwithstanding the Muslim government having made attempts to build the best standards to provide some confidence in Halal items.

Figure 9.11. A customer shopping for halal meat in the supermarket.

Source: https://halalfocus.net/eu-european-court-of-justice-says-halal-meat-not-allowed-to-carry-the-eu-organic-seal/.

The high rate of Halal accreditation to FBOs is yet another area which has attracted great interest. The yearly certification rate for an abattoir or meals-processing plant can range from a few hundred to thousands of pounds, depending on the HCB. The certification rate may be negligible to the primary players in the meat sector, however, for some food companies, this capacity cost may be good sized. In a bid to keep away from hefty fees, some FBOs deliberately mislabel non-Halal food as Halal, whereas others have gone the "self-certification" way, meaning where the FBO verifies its particular Halal repute and communicates this information to the Halal consumer. This practice is commonplace among Muslim-run food businesses. Even as a fewer meat companies have efficiently performed this duty, others are struggling to successfully put things into practice. "Self-certification" may be used when the ultimate buyers are nearby, that is because Halal nations require a Halal certificate to complement different Halal meat items, before they are given any clearance. The French Halal lamb supplier, Halaldom, can be described as a company that has successfully utilized the "self-certification" rule of Halal meat. In line with government, this has been possible due to a "robust communication approach with Muslim consumers" and their community commitment displayed by way of donating a large fraction of the profits acquired for every meat order across the distribution network.

Regardless of the (halal certification bodies) HCBs limitations mentioned above, many Halal customers consider them as the implementers of the Islamic nutritional law guidelines in developed countries. They're also considered by many FBOs as supporters of Halal trade. It is because certificates distributed by a few of these companies have come to be reputable and are approved by indigenous Halal customers and distributors of Halal meat to Muslim nations (Battour & Ismail, 2016). It's also worth noting that in spite of the existence of a considerable amount of HCBs throughout the 28 European member states, just a few of them can provide certificates for exporting to the global Halal marketplace. It is because certificates provided with aid of regional HCB can best be endorsed in the importation destination if governments in those nations approve them.

9.9. HALAL MEAT FRAUD AND SAFETY CONCERNS

Figure 9.12. The stunning of chicken before slaughter is a common practice.

Source: https://www.foodmanufacture.co.uk/Article/2015/06/11/More-humane-halal-slaughter-option.

The technique for the slaughter of animals for consumption by Muslims isn't strikingly different from conventional slaughter, apart from animals slaughtered after a shocking session to numb them from pain. Preparing Halal meat, however, entails the recitation of a quick prayer before or during slaughter for satisfying the spiritual requirements. One may thus expect that the meat safety need to not be impacted by the two procedures defined above, albeit halal-slaughter management may additionally affect food safety. When the Quran and different Islamic scriptures were discovered around 1400 years ago, there were no food safety guidelines, but, the model of Tayyib (wholesome/safe meals) later included Halal to cater for food safety, albeit this factor is seldom given the attention it merits within the Muslim community. It's been mentioned that the idea of Halal meat protection consistent with the HCB requirements is ambiguous.

This may be because of the reality that most HCBs have concentrated on the matter of slaughter, even while ignoring other essential elements including the Tayyib requirements. The failure of Muslim governments to include Tayyib into Halal meat production has exposed gaps in the Halal meat safety, it is recommended that a greater holistic methodolgy in deciphering the scriptures around the "Halal-Tayyib" concept of meat production to be instituted. Halal meat must always be prepared under strict standards in accordance to established slaughtering requirements. This will ultimately improve the quality of the Halal food (Bashir et al., 2019). On the contrary, the hygiene of the infrastructure of Muslim butcheries has often raised critical meat safety concerns. Many of these premises lack basic hygiene amenities, such as, facilities for hand washing or changing rooms.

It isn't always uncommon to find a Muslim butcher dealing with or cutting meat with no coat, hairnet or apron. Researchers have also mentioned that although Halal meat may provide spiritual purity, it does not necessarily guarantee safe meat. Some of places wherein Halal meat is sold are undeserving for human intake, due to poor hygiene standards. Some of the biggest seizures of risky Halal meat by food safety officials was in Glasgow, where about 1 tonne of hazardous meat, believed to be lamb was being supplied to 2 Halal butcheries in the Glasgow vicinity. The (2016) Evening Times newspaper reported that these butchers have been suppliers to some of the city's diverse food stores.

9.10. ADULTERATION AND MISLABELING OF MEAT

Following the discovery of horsemeat in processed pork products in early 2013, there has been extended speciation review of meat products starting from the production stage. There has also been the discovery of porcine DNA and even beef meat in various processed "Halal" products in the UK. This situation causes a great deal of agitation and distress among UK Muslims, because the eating of pork or its byproducts is forbidden in

Islam. Adulteration and mislabeling of meat and its derivatives is not an entirely new idea. In the European Union, stringent measures have been put in place to protect and sell halal meats which can be specialties, and have geographical tags with indicators that follow up on their delivery process to avoid any cross-contamination.

Modern food safety and labeling rules moreover seek to prevent the contamination and production of components that may pose a health hazard to consumers, apart from misrepresenting meat products in a way that misinforms consumers. Regardless of these preventative measures, some people continue using unapproved labeling techniques, therefore providing meals that are unfit for human consumption or not sufficiently defined. Suppliers often tend to overlook Halal foods requirements, often driven by greed, and a need to maximize profits (Al-Ansi & Han, 2019).

Most practicing Muslims will only consume Halal meat, as many consider the intake of these meats a type of worship. Because of the religious importance of Halal meat to Muslims, further to the economic proceeds related to buying and selling of such meats due to the growth in the worldwide Muslim populace. Additionally, there has been immense competition for a fraction of the Halal marketplace by mainstream meat operators in industrialized countries. In 2015, The Pew Research Center estimated that if the present trends persist, the international Muslim populace may swell by 73%, reaching 2.8 billion by 2050. In spite of the obvious financial benefits related to trading in Halal meat products, many Halal customers have expressed worry on the lack of awareness of the guidelines around the slaughtering of animals, including the successive processing and handling of those items for the Muslim market.

The situation is exaggerated by the fact that most Halal meat operators in the West are non-Muslims, with limited or no knowledge of the Islamic food laws. Also, the recent detection of fraudulent activities in the Halal industry has worsened matters. The detection of undeclared horsemeat (including horse DNA) in some foods led to extra stringent measures on processed components for undeclared substances, something that has resulted in a few prosecutions. The subsequent increase in product testing measures led to the discovery of porcine DNA in various "Halal" products, meant for the Muslim market. For instance, Muslims are forbidden from farm, raising or consuming pork or any of its derivatives.

Many fraudulent traders in the Halal business insist on intentionally mislabeling non-Halal meat as Halal, or the contamination of Halal meat with pork (and its derivatives) including other non-Halal ingredients. May be prompted by the need to maximize profits, or ineffective Halal Certification bodies (HCBs) which do not agree on any single Halal standard for approving Islamic meat. A few HCBs, for instance, approve meat-processing sites, which, apart from processing Halal products, may also process pork or different non-Halal items using the same processing equipment.

Despite the fact these websites allege to be keen in the processing of their items, other HCBs hold the opinion that the processing may nevertheless expose Halal products to contamination whether knowingly or not. Within the UK, porcupine DNA has been found in 'Halal' beef pastry coming from processing plants, where red meat and the "Halal" items in question were processed using the same systems. However, the disagreement on processing standards for Halal or red meat and its derivatives has been a wire in the works.

Some scholars have described halal fraud as a widespread practice, commonly pushed by greed. The fraudulent trading in meat that is said to be Halal may take different forms, ranging from the trade of illegally slaughtered animals typically associated with low animal welfare, to the selling of contaminated meat for human intake, which poses a danger to human health. The fraudulent trading in meats that are not only non-halal, but pose a public health risk is a major cause of concern for governments around the world (Al-Ansi & Han, 2019).

Food industry crime is described as dishonesty on the part of manufacturers or suppliers, there are different kinds of food crime and the risks that each may also pose. Food crime in the Halal business may fall under different categories, including Halal manufacturers who are not keen on examining their processing and packaging processes.

Organized illegal meat suppliers are also commonly involved in this crime, a situation which due to the possible scale, threatens food safety issues and jeopardizes the safety of consumers. The most common offences include; the sale of recycled chicken that is bleached to enhance its aesthetic effect, the importing of untested bush meat from West Africa wherein such items are taken as cuisine. Some of these items find their way into the underworld halal market, where they are delivered to local butcheries that pass them as halal yet they are not. Apart from the risks these products pose to the public, there are also animal welfare concerns, especially the slaughtering of endangered wildlife in Africa that is smuggled into Muslim regions as halal food. It has been suggested that the meats of endangered species, including giraffes, chimpanzees and gorilla have all been found in meat markets globally. Some items may also be included in the Halal food chain without proper documentation to ascertain their Halal standing.

9.11. ILLEGAL SLAUGHTER

Illegal slaughtering is the execution of animals for intake without the appropriate licensure, or where consent is provided for the slaughtering to be carried out away from the authorized premises, which may include the on-farm slaughtering of livestock for a few individuals use alone. Generally, on-farm slaughtered meat is impossible to be bought by the majority, it must always be used by a proprietor who generally are the farmer, and their immediate family. Apart from fulfilling the EU legislative requirements on animal protect as captured in EC1099/2009, animals meant for the Halal food chain must also be slaughtered according to the Islamic culture (Zulfakar et al., 2012). Any meat which falls short of these 2 necessities is considered unfit for Muslim consumption. The halal enforcement agencies highlight the below scenarios that must arouse suspicion concerning the safety of meat:

- Slaughtering of livestock at unlicensed centers.
- Unlabeled or poorly halal-marked meat.
- Meat imported through illegal channels.
- Meat advertised or sold through temporary carriers, such as vehicle boot sales.
- Meat that is slaughtered legally but may be unfit for consumption due to poor sanitary conditions.

Muslims are informed, in line with the Islamic texts (Quran and Hadith) to only take Halal meat, many Muslims therefore regard the consumption of Halal meat as a spiritual act, subsequently the significance of taking Halal meat for Muslims can't be underestimated. It's worth pointing out that some Muslims, and food businesses owned by Muslims have been implicated severally on not directly mentioning Halal meat on their products. This, alongside professionals within the Halal certification and regulation business is the reason why greed has been blamed as one of the main causes of poor halal standards.

9.11.1. Halal Meat Mislabeling

The accurate labeling, packaging and advertisement of meat should be a personal commitment for those involved in the selling of the meat. It is especially an offence to label any food product to mislead customers concerning the quality, identity, ingredients, amount, and means of production, durability and geographical basis of the product. Regardless the lack of clarity around the authentic definition of Halal, the widespread mislabeling of non-Halal food as Halal to betray customers into buying such foods has been rampant, and actually constitutes an offence.

The contention surrounding the definite meaning of Halal meat can be attributed to the sketchy interpretation of this term in Islamic scriptures, it has been left to Muslim scholars to interpret the term and animal slaughter practices. This lack of agreement between halal control bodies makes it tough for local enforcement authorities to identify fraudulent activities in the Halal marketplace. Similarly, some Muslims are hesitant to accept whichever farming, livestock slaughter or meat processing method that has not been approved by Islam, there are Muslims that are however more liberal in their halal rule but do not overtly violate the Islamic doctrines. As the concept of halal wasn't so complicated during the times of the Prophet, Halal meat was not mislabeled; nor fake assertions of meat species, or undeclared meat species (Wan Hassan & Awang, 2009). Birds in particular are problematic to determine whether they are halal or not, since there are a variety of edible bird species consumed by Muslims from different parts of the world. With regards to the labeling of chicken as Halal, various conclusions have been arrived at including:

- There is considerable mislabeling of Halal food.
- In some cases, over 50% of the chicken's weight consisted of water.
- The water and feed used on chicken contained proteins with porcine and bovine foundation.
- Additives applied to chicken have also not been mentioned on halal labels.

Not long ago, Aldi grocery store apologized to its British Muslim customers after products comprising of pig blood and skin were mislabeled as Halal, by way of their international suppliers. The retailers indicated that their products did not pose any food safety risks to customers. But they did not certify whether it was halal or not. In fact, the mislabeling and adulteration of Halal meat was not at all confined. In another case, "Halal" meat (items in Malaysia were found to contain Halal-prohibited proteins from rats, cats, donkeys, pigs, and dogs, including other haram species. It was determined that 78% of the food products had been mislabeled. In addition, buffalo DNA was detected in 40 out of 58 products labelled as pork.

9.12. CONTAMINATION OF HALAL MEAT

Figure 9.13. Halal meat can be contaminated during the processing and packaging stages.

Source: https://shiawaves.com/english/news/world/7991-belgium-bans-traditional-halal-and-kosher-slaughter-method-sparking-religious-backlash/.

Meat derived from carnivorous animals, birds of prey, pigs, and animals slaughtered contrary to Islamic approach are considered non-Halal. The cross-contamination of Halal meat with any of these items will render the Halal meat polluted and unfit for consumption. Beef seems to be the common product prone to contamination, which is because the Muslims living in the West prefer beef more than other types of meat. Most Halal meat processing facilities in these countries additionally deal with more than one meat product. This practice increases the risk of plant-contamination between the Halal products and red meat, particularly where there are poor segregation and plant cleaning strategies.

The detection of even very low levels of red meat and porcupine genetic substances in Halal products can render the products non-Halal. Due to this, various researchers have sought to apply special checking out methods to define the identity of meat protein found in Halal foods, with the intention of reassuring Halal buyers of the validity of Halal meat. The Malaysia regime recently entered into a Memorandum of Understanding (MoU) with the United Kingdom based exclusively on checking out meat processing facilities, and for the availability of Halal proficiency testing (Shafii & Khadijah, 2012). The project's intention was to expand protocols for the detection of beef and liquor in low amounts in Halal products. These protocols, therefore are constrained to species or alcohol detection, but no longer the wider ethical requirements within the Halal system.

In conclusion, the intake of Halal meat is a vital component of the dictates of the Islamic religion. Nevertheless, the need for a few Halal meat providers to maximize their earnings has caused multiple incidents concerning the mislabeling of meat that don't fulfill the Halal dietary legal guidelines as Halal. Incidents of this kind can cause discomfort to practicing Muslims. Conflicting views within the Muslim community regarding what is real Halal have ended in confusion amongst regulators, Halal consumers and other industry stakeholders. This has also made it tough for law enforcement businesses to become aware of and prosecute culprits of the Halal meat fraud. Nevertheless, in recent times, there have been various successful prosecutions of Halal product suppliers who deliberately offered non-Halal meat as Halal. The general health and safety factors of Halal meat have additionally been questioned, as a large percentage comes from smaller, probably much less managed and structured processors.

A few researchers have also mentioned that the embracing of a holistic "Halal-Tayyib" model of farming and meat production may alleviate various food safety risks related to post-slaughter management of Halal meat. Additional research is also required to comprehend the Islamic academic explanation of the Halal-Tayyib idea and the way this could be integrated into modern farm animals raising and food processing structures. Successful implementation of this model can improve animal welfare standards during Halal slaughter, in addition to casting off the food safety risks related to Halal food production. Basically, Halal Certification agencies must interact and play a crucial role in making sure there's successful execution of this idea.

Just like any other meat consumer, Muslims deserve the right to know what their product consists of, and how it has been prepared. To them, meat is not just a delicacy but also bears great cultural and religious significance. Despite this, some meat sellers are taking advantage of the rising popularity of halal products to illegally label their meat as halal when it's not, for the sole reason of maximizing their profits. This is a shameful practice that should be condemned, and authorities must step up their game in bringing such people to book.

Chapter 10

Issues in Halal Food

CONTENTS

10.1. INTRODUCTION

Halal enterprises, both in terms of goods and services, are exploding. The Halal industry has grown to be a profitable one, providing tremendous economic opportunities for industry participants and entrepreneurs. Despite its enormous potential, particularly its vast market embracing both domestic and international markets, the local industry's performance in serving the halal market has been hampered by a variety of problems. As a result of this limitation, customers have a misunderstanding about the availability of halal products on the market. As a result, the goal of this study is to examine customers' issues and concerns, particularly when it comes to consuming halal products (Shaari et al., 2019). Future recommendations for coping with customers' concerns about halal products are also considered and offered. The following are some of the issues: Halal's Global Issues and Challenges Halal Misconceptions, Consumer Perceptions, Halal Products, and Halal Industry Overview. The notion of halal is of paramount importance to Muslim consumption, which adheres to the regulated value system established by Islamic of Syariah Laws, which includes allowed and prohibited foods (Mohani, 2014). Halal is most commonly linked with food goods; however it encompasses much more (Mohamed Syazwan & Mohd Remie, 2012). Halal cuisine is acknowledged to be required in the diets of Muslims all over the world.

Figure 10.1. In order for a product to be halal for consumption, it must be halal along the entire food supply chain, which is not a simple task. Meat and meat-related substances have always attracted the most attention, starting with the basic materials. Contrary to popular belief, halal does not only refer to the absence of pork. Pork by-products are also included. Carnivorous animals, birds of prey, and terrestrial animals without external ears are among the creatures that are not halal. If halal animals and poultry are slaughtered improperly, or are slain in the name of anybody other than Allah, they will be considered haram, or non-halal.

Source: https://www.linkedin.com/pulse/issues-halal-food-ingredients-production-mufti-fahad-ahmed-qureshi.

Halal is an Arabic term that means lawful and permissible in English. Halal also refers to anything that is free of any ingredients that are prohibited for consumption by Muslims. The notion of halal must be understood in conjunction with the notion of Tayyib, which refers to wholesomeness or purity, as well as being safe and nutritious (Kamaruddin and Jusoff, 2009). When it comes to food, Muslims are required to eat just what is permissible and legal. The products used by Muslim consumers must be free of haram or illegal elements (Mohani, 2014; Hassan 2013).

The Halal sector is expanding and becoming a big business locally and internationally, thanks to the rapid pace of trade globalization. The expanding Muslim population around the world has resulted in a massive demand for halal products. Furthermore, Halal is fast becoming a globally recognized trademark that underpins the connected trade's quality guarantee and credibility (Mohamed Syazwan et al., 2013). Despite the halal industry's rapid growth, several Halal concerns are having a noticeable and significant impact on the market. Previous literary works (e.g., Othman et al., 2009; Mohamed Syazwan & Abu Bakar, 2014; Mohd Aliff et al., 2015) have extensively examined the obstacles and concerns that industrialists face when selling halal products to the market. Nonetheless, research publications on consumer concerns in relation to Halal eating are still scarce.

Consumers are a vital success component for most firms; in fact, this has become the subject of this study as it examines consumers' concerns with Halal concept items. As a result, this evaluation focuses on the consumer's perspective to analyze the concerns and obstacles, as well as the current state of halal products. The rest of the paper is laid out as follows. The introduction of the Halal industry is the first topic covered in this study. The report then goes into the problems that consumers face when it comes to halal products and consumption. In addition, future recommendations are debated and presented in relation to consumer issues relating to halal products.

There is incredible growth in halal businesses with goods and services. The Halal industry has become a lucrative industry which provides the players and entrepreneurs with exceptional business opportunities. Despite its high potential, in particular the huge local and international market, the local industry's various challenges limited its performance in serving the Halal market. This restriction leads to a misunderstanding of consumer availability of halal products on the market. This study aims therefore to look at the challenges and concerns of consumers, especially with regard to the consumption of halal products.

Figure 10.2. Wherever there are Muslim consumers whose tastes and inclinations are governed by halal food specifications, a halal food industry occurs. Halal food may appear to be similar to other foods, but its nature, manner of processing including the components, handling, and usage of numerous procedures from start to finish are always authorized and recommended by Islamic law.

Source: https://www.foodnavigator-asia.com/Article/2018/07/30/Fake-halal-food-in-Malaysia-Factories-accused-of-packing-products-originating-from-China-and-India.

The issues addressed in the evaluations include a halal logo issue, a misunderstanding of the product's provenance, a labeling issue, the uncertainty about ingredients used in the production of halal products, and a problem with Halal literacy among consumers. Finally, this paper offers some suggestions for addressing the aforementioned concerns and obstacles (Samori et al., 2016). The researchers outline various concerns and obstacles that consumers encounter when it comes to Halal consumption in light of this publication. The concerns and challenges are discussed below.

10.2. ISSUES WITH HALAL CERTIFICATION

Halal Auditors employ a number of methods of recruitment from the Federal and State governments. The shariah auditors of JAKIM (Jabatan Kemajuan Islam Malaysia) have shariah credentials, and the Ministry of Health has their technical auditors. On the other hand, JAIS directly recruits its own technical officers and shariah officers. The recruitment processes for Halal Auditors by federal and state governments differ. The situation becomes even more complicated by the introduction of additional schemes such as halal certification for the logistics and pharmaceutical industries. This problem does not arise in the food industry since most of its auditors come from a food science background.

The incapacity of Halal Auditors to tackle the challenges of the halal auditing procedure demonstrates their lack of expertise. The biggest problem that Halal Auditors face is the identification of new source materials (Lockley and Bardsley, 2000). When Halal Executives ask about the usage of new raw materials, they expect the answers to come from the Halal Auditors. However, rather than the other way around, the industry representative is frequently the one to describe the status of the raw material. Industry representatives may be able to falsify their explanations, leaving auditors unable to ascertain the truth.

JAKIM/JAIS must increase the competency of their Halal Auditors by giving clear instructions or checklists to help them through the application papers evaluation process. The Halal Executives noted that, in comparison to MUI's thorough recommendations, JAKIM only provides a brief description of how to execute the Halal Assurance System. The lack of supervision is evidenced by the lack of a sufficient checklist to check the important background of the raw materials. Because there are no clear guidelines on permissible raw materials in the crucial ingredient list, this problem affects not only Halal Executives but also Halal Auditors.

Figure 10.3. The regulation of what defines halal in the United States is fragmented and arbitrary. The Department of Agriculture is in charge of overseeing federally regulated plants as well as inspecting exporters to ensure that they fit the requirements of the importing country. Since 2000, eight states have passed halal consumer protection legislation that is similar to kosher consumer protection laws. However, the extent of these rules is frequently ambiguous and inadequately enforced.

Source: https://theconversation.com/amp/regulating-the-sacred-why-the-us-halal-food-industry-needs-better-oversight-34108.

JAKIM is also having trouble coordinating their knowledge as the halal authorities with the industries. One of its flaws is the manner of information dissemination adopted, which is through industrial associations. Because not all companies join their industry associations, those who are not members may not have access to the most up-to-date information.

Halal certification authorities need to provide more detailed and industry-friendly halal system guidance that can help companies create their halal assurance systems depending on aspects including firm size, staff count, product type, and export/import manufacturing. The Halal Professional Board course can be integrated into a Bachelor's degree program, particularly in fields such as food manufacturing, food services, logistics, and others where halal or related items are used.

Considering that halal management is required throughout fields in shariah, management, marketing, law, business, science, and technology, university students should be exposed to the program so that they have some fundamental knowledge of halal management. More research is needed to improve the halal certification authority's image as a reputable and trustworthy certifying agency in Malaysia.

10.3. HALAL ISSUES WITH THE LOGO

The Halal emblem is one of the most important aspects of halal food packaging. Consumers place a lot of trust in the Halal label on the product package since it conveys crucial information about the product's halal status (Hifza et al., 2010). Consumers value food credibility because it validates items that are considered to be Halal (Rezai et al., 2012) and casts doubt on the manufacturer's usage of the Halal logo (Shafie et al. 2006). For example, there have been reports of some food establishments putting various types of private Halal logos on their premises in order to deceive customers and entice them to visit them (Ilyia et al., 2011).

Interestingly, regardless of the fact that the Halal label on food packaging is approved by a prestigious institution such as the Department of Islamic Development Malaysia (JAKIM), some consumers have expressed doubts about its authenticity (Mohamed et al., 2008). As a result, customers, particularly Muslims, were dubious about the manufacturer's usage of the Halal mark (Grunert, 2005). Muslim consumers are confronted with serious halal issues; doubts about the legitimacy of products claiming to be Halal, as well as a lack of compliance in monitoring Halal food certification, have become key concerns for them.

10.4. PRODUCT MISINTERPRETATIONS

Another challenge that Halal goods purchasers may face is the provenance of the product. According to Bonne et al. (2007), Muslim customers are the most cautious when selecting and purchasing food products. They chose to buy and eat halal food from their own nation or from other nations with a large Muslim population. As a result, people are suspicious of food products imported from non-Muslim nations such as China, New Zealand, Europe, and even Thailand (Rezai et al., 2012).

This can lead to a consumer's misperception, with the consumer supposing that a country associated with the Islam faith is likely to provide the majority of Halal products. Although it is true that Islamic countries have a strong tendency to make Halal products, the quality of the product is dependent on the producer. Furthermore, much of the westerner's misunderstanding is strongly tied to the concept that all Arabs are Muslims, which might be perplexing to certain customers because proper Arab countries and Islam people can vary. According to the previous discussion, there is an urgent need for the scholar to continue to investigate the topic of the Halal product's country of origin. Furthermore, customers are concerned about the proliferation of Halal emblems from various nations and certification authorities (Mohamed Syazwan & Mohd Remie, 2012). Consumers may be confused and find it difficult to select an authentic halal product as a result of the problem.

10.5. AN ISSUE WITH TERMS ON PRODUCT PACKAGING AND MISUSE OF ISLAMIC IMAGES

Words and images used on product packaging were also deceiving consumers. To confuse consumers, there are items on the market that use Arabic language and exhibit pictures linked to Islam. Shari et al. revealed that some unethical businesses purposefully adopted Arabic-sounding or Islamic-signalled brand names, even going so far as to display selected Quranic passages to deceive customers into believing the product was Halal. Furthermore, some customers take the phrase Halal or the Halal label for granted, never scrutinizing its legitimacy. Furthermore, some unethical producers utilize Islamic images on product packaging to imply that the product is Halal.

Figure 10.4. Rather than perceiving the forbidden as a barrier to eating choices, one might embrace an entire globe of fascinating, delicious, and healthful options. Islam teaches us to respect our bodies because they have authority over us and will testify against us on the Day of Judgment for any injustices we may have perpetrated against them during our lives.

Source: https://seattleglobalist.com/2016/07/14/halal-eat-halal-even-not-muslim/53928.

There are even others that dare to use the term "sunnah" on product labels to entice consumers to accept the product (Muhamad Shukri). The implications of the labeling exploitation may cause consumer misunderstanding and put the company's survival in jeopardy. The packaging must include the name or brand of the product, the lowest possible content in metrics, the name and address of the company or distributor, a list of items, a product code indicating the manufacturing shipment, the production and expiration date, and also the Halal logo from recognized certification agencies in place to direct the consumer in purchasing a halal product. All of this information has to be true. In addition to foodstuffs, other non-edible products for Muslims are also subject to the Halal standard. In the recent report by Norzamira (2017), in three hardware shops in the state of Selangor, the Ministry of Domestic Trade, Co-operators and Consumerism of Malaysia confiscated paint brushes of different types, supposedly made from swine briskets. The incident attracted a lot of attention and gave rise to discussions among Muslim consumers, which also caused concern about halalism of non-food products on the market today.

As a result, many customers, especially Muslims, are suspect of the options on the market because they are not deprived of the product Halal status. Entrepreneurs dealing with food and non-food products have strong needs to clearly separate their products into their Halal status. In Malaysia, although the labeling of their product as Halal and otherwise is not mandatory for entrepreneurs (Hashanah & Hifz 2011), the labeling of a product is strongly recommended for consumers to inform about the product classification. Today's burgeoning advanced food sector offers a wide range of dietary ingredients derived from either plant or animal sources. Notably, Muslim customers' perceptions of the Halal product were most likely influenced by their familiarity with the ingredients. Almost all of the time, customers seem unable to ascertain which food products are Halal based on reading the tag on the packaging of products (Batu & Regenstein, 2014). This is because some manufacturers use scientific method for the element in their good or service, which is most likely inconceivable to the end user (Davies & Wright, 1994). As a result of their lack of familiarity with the content, some customers are distrustful about the material employed in the product. Only after a thorough investigation of the product by specified bodies can the ingredient be identified. Furthermore, today's global food business is being propelled forward by fast advances in food technology. One recent advancement in food technology that has piqued the interest of consumers is genetically modified (GM) food. Genetically Changed Foods are a type of food that has had a portion of its genome genetically modified (Zhang, Wohlhueter & Zhang, 2016). GMO foods, in layman's terms, are foods that have been genetically modified to resemble natural foods.

Figure 10.5. Following reports that uncertified meat, including potentially ill kangaroo and horse meat, was imported by a labor organization over decades and sold on the local market as halal beef, Malaysians have chastised the Islamic Department (Jakim) for being more concerned about policing halal-certified shops than reassuring people. These are some of the issues surrounding halal certification.

Source: https://www.straitstimes.com/asia/se-asia/halal-meat-scandal-malaysian-authorities-slammed-for-perceived-inaction.

The Malaysian Standard (MS1500:2009; 3.5.1.6) explicitly states: "Foods and drinks including products of genetically modified organisms (GMOs) or components manufactured by the use of genetic material from animals that are non-halal under Shariah law are not halal." Despite the administration's desire to assist GMO development, the public, particularly Muslim customers, have expressed concerns about the GMO's ethical and halal status (Mariam, 2016). Clearly, any meal claiming to be Halal must be free of any genetically engineered ingredients derived from non-Halal sources, according to the above-mentioned Halal criteria. When it comes to the topic of genetically modified foods, consumers are growing increasingly wary about ingesting Halal products that contain genetically modified substances, as it raises concerns about the food's contents (Mohd Aliff et al., 2015).

10.6. HALAL LITERACY

Another key issue that demands serious consideration is the consumer's Halal literacy. Consumers' familiarity, awareness and understanding with the food they consume, according to Connor (1988), is based on a number of elements, including personal sentiment, sociological, and other environmental influences. Despite the fact that the majority of consumers today are well educated and can quickly access any type of information, their degree of Halal literacy varies, as proven by a study conducted by Hashanah and Hifza (2011). Because they misinterpreted the genuine meaning of Halal, some consumers have expressed strong opposition. Some of them equate Halal with religious rituals, particularly slaughtering, and as a result, customers are wary of products claiming to be Halal due to a lack of awareness on the matter (Elasrag, 2016).

Halal in production of food has the universal concept to be hygienic, healthy and free of all sorts of pollution, not only from pork and alcohol (Kasmarini et al., 2015; Selvarajah et al., 2017). The principles of Halal are unmistakable and religious, but they contain healthy and hygienic food and make healthy people attract. To promote the Halal concept, and make it easily acceptable to all types of consumers, it cannot be regarded as offensive to any religious convictions because the Halal product, where it raises the topic of hygiene and safety for the product, should be understood as a good standard.

10.7. GLOBAL HALAL FOOD CHALLENGES

The halal sector is quickly becoming one of the most profitable and powerful segments of the global food industry. Over the last decade, the halal food sector has risen significantly, and it is now worth an estimated USD667 million. Halal food accounts for over a quarter of the worldwide food market. The future demand for halal food is substantial, with predicted growth in both population and income of halal consumers, as well as an estimated growth in food demand of more than 70% by 2050.

Based on four fundamental trends, many food economists believe the halal food business will become a major market force in the near future. To begin with, Islam is currently the world's fastest growing religion, fueling a global demand for halal items. The annual growth in halal food consumption is predicted to be 16%. Second, non-Muslim consumers are increasingly adopting halal food products for ethical and safety grounds (Rejeb et al., 2021). In the United Kingdom, for example, there are over 2 million Muslims but only 6 million halal meat customers. Non-Muslim Dutch customers have showed a strong interest in halal food in the Netherlands, with yearly demand estimated to be around USD3 billion. Halal items have become mainstream consumer items as a result of these two causes working together. Third, halal consumer power is growing as a market force in parallel with the Muslim population's growth and disposable income.

Lastly, Muslims are more aware of the importance and requirement of eating only halal food. The quick rise in annual sales of halal food throughout Russia, as well as the growing demand for halal products of 30% to 40% yearly, is a solid illustration of rising consumer awareness.

Halal cuisine was available in conventional corner shops and neighbourhood butchers until about a decade ago. The demand and supply chains for halal food products have shifted across the board in the halal sector. They're becoming more common in Western-style grocery stores, such as supermarkets and hypermarkets. In many Western countries, retailers and food producers are beginning to cater to Muslim customers by expanding their halal product offerings.

Figure 10.6. There is a need to raise Muslim consumer understanding of the intricacies of the substances in the meals they consume. While nutrition labels can clearly tell consumers about the ingredients in their food, they frequently raise more issues than they answer. Processed foods have long lists of components with a variety of origins and production processes that aren't always obvious. For the ordinary Halal customer, this raises uncertainty about whether the product is Halal and thus suitable for consumption.

Source: https://knowledge.ulprospector.com/9922/fb-keys-to-successful-halal-food-beverage-manufacturing-ingredient-and-processing-concerns/.

Halal food is becoming an increasingly important component of the Western diet, and it has grown into a multibillion-dollar worldwide sector with corporations like Tesco, Unilever, and Nestlé aggressively expanding their halal-certified product categories. With annual sales of more than USD5 billion, Nestle is currently the largest food maker in the halal market. Nestle's global sales of halal food account for around 35% of total sales.

From a marketing standpoint, Asia and the Middle East remain the usual significant target markets. However, because they are markets that play defining roles in other markets throughout the world, halal markets in the UK, Europe, and the United States will see their responsibilities in the development of the halal market greatly strengthened. It will usher halal into the mainstream of global culture. As the structure of the Muslim world change, and neoliberalism trends continue to transform consumers' tastes, habits, and spending habits around the world, it is highly likely that emerging halal markets will play an increasingly important role in established Middle Eastern and Asian markets, especially by affecting global corporate halal methods.

It is no surprise that the world's largest halal food producers and exporters are non-Muslim countries like China, Australia, Argentina, Brazil, and the United States. Due to the traditional structure of the business, corporations from these nations are expected to control 90% of the worldwide halal market. Muslims in Malaysia, for example, spent an average of 14% of their food budget on meat. In New Zealand, Australia, and India, 60% of the halal meat is imported. Saudi Arabia, Egypt, and Algeria, among other Muslim countries, import meat from non-Muslim countries to meet domestic demand.

Halal foodstuffs are not limited to fish and meat, including other foodstuffs such as candy, canned and froze foodstuffs, milk, bakery, organic and herbal products. With the evolving lifestyle and increased purchasing capacity of Muslims, demand for ready-to-eat food and packaged food still conforming to Islamic dietary laws is widespread. Another food sector growing is replacing products that traditionally include non-halal ingredients such as pork gelatine or alcohol. These products, including yogurt, cookies and chocolates, are now being amended to be sold as halal.

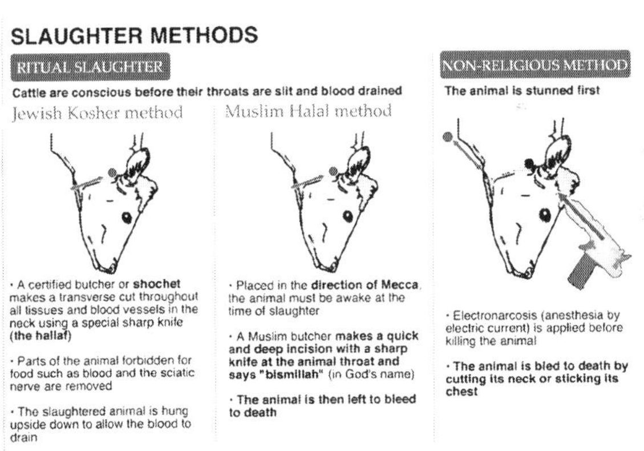

Figure 10.7. There are 1.6 billion Muslims worldwide who following conditions a halal food business worth more than $1 trillion. Because a vast number of Muslim-majority nations do not have adequate agriculture and animal resources to feed their rising populations, demand for halal products from countries like the United States is set to rise. By 2020, Saudi Arabia, Qatar, and the other Gulf Cooperation Council countries are expected to import US$53 billion worth of halal food.

Source: https://theconversation.com/amp/regulating-the-sacred-why-the-us-halal-food-industry-needs-better-oversight-34108.

Some of the issues include:

1. Halal standards are confusing because they are produced by a variety of private organization, government-linked organizations, and independent Halal certification bodies (HCBs); national standards bodies, regional bodies like GSO, ASEAN, and the EU; and international bodies like the SMIIC/OIC initiative. The problem for manufacturers is determining which standard will allow market access, and in many cases, exporters will need numerous certificates.
2. The Halal business has long struggled due to a lack of acceptable worldwide methods to accredit Halal Certification Organizations (HCBs). The majority of Halal food is produced in nations with a non-Muslim majority, and it is certified by independent HCBs with no government monitoring. While current accreditation initiatives such as those produced by SMIIC, GSO, and ESMA are all positive steps forward, better cooperation between certifying agencies is required to avoid excessive duplication or competition. Obtaining Shariah-compliant funding is difficult. Obtaining shariah-compliant funding can be difficult for businesses looking to develop or vertically integrate their supply chain (Rezaee, 2019).
3. If manufacturers fully conformed to the principles of Halal and Tayyib as stated in the precepts of Islam, Halal food has the potential to become the world standard for safe, healthful, and humane food. Globally, there is a growing desire for organic and natural foods, which is beginning to show itself among Muslim customers, particularly the younger millennial age. While the expense of producing farm-raised, organic-fed beef may be more than the cheaper options sought by many Muslims, despite these obstacles, this is a long-term aim that Muslim producers should strive for.

Non-OIC countries willing to expand their Halal skills have the chance to form collaborations with OIC countries with expertise in Halal food procedures. China, South Korea, and South Africa are already collaborating with Malaysia and the United Arab Emirates to improve their Halal capabilities. A chance to work on tracking technology. When we talk to specialists in this field, one of the biggest challenges they face is ensuring supply chain integrity. One option to address this is to develop technologies that can track raw meat and food ingredients back to their source. The Brazilian Beef Exporting Industries Association (ABIEC) created the e-seal, a gadget that monitors meat shipments as it passes through their terminals.

There is a growing demand for hormone-free meat. Whether hormone-treated beef is permissible is a point of contention among regulators. Experts disagree about how safe such meat is for human eating, citing concerns about cancer and other negative consequences. Following customer demand for hormone-free meat, the UAE grocery chain Spinneys has become the first to sell hormone-free beef. Create high-end organic product lines. Organic and natural foods are in higher demand around the world. This increased interest is also being noticed among Muslim customers, particularly among the younger millennial age. Build a solid brand. Even well-known firms have a lot of opportunity for development in terms of branding. The quality of the product, the marketing messages, the packaging, and overall communication may all be considerably improved. This presents an opportunity for both established firms and newcomers to identify themselves through effective branding.

Figure 10.8. Food has always been a topic of debate among academics. This is due to the fact that eating is a basic requirement for human survival. Food production has recently been improved thanks to advances in modern science and technology. In the creation of food products, a variety of ingredient sources have been utilized. These ingredients are either allowed (halal) or forbidden (haram). In addition, materials such as chemical additives and synthetic ingredients are mixed together. The procurement of source material, processing, packaging, shipping, and other issues are also discussed among the scholars.

Source: https://www.elfacosmeticos.com.br/8e7797lifestyle/travel/finding-halal-food-in-south-korea-is-a-tall-order.

Investment potential in the integration of the Halal food value chain is possible. In the Halal food sector, many businesses are small and fragmented. Funding vertical supply chain management, from slaughterhouses to wholesalers, is an investment opportunity that could yield profitable returns for investors while also fostering the development of strong enterprises in this sector.

10.8. ISSUES IN HALAL PHARMACEUTICAL AND COSMETIC PRODUCTS

The worldwide halal business is also seeing significant expansion in pharmaceutical and health-related products. In Muslim-majority nations, demand for halal pharmaceutical, generic medial, wellness, and healthcare products is expected to be around USD555 billion. The inclusion of non-compliant components in these products, such as animal derivatives and animal-based gelatins, is a major source of worry for Muslims. In 2009, the worldwide pharmaceutical market grew by 4% to a value of over USD820 billion, presenting significant potential opportunities for the halal pharmaceutical business to capitalize on.

The growth of the halal cosmetics sector is mirrored by a rise in consumer consciousness of the materials used and brand recognition, both of which are fueled by social media. The global halal cosmetics sector is valued at USD13 billion, with a 12-percent annual growth rate. The global halal cosmetics sector currently accounts for 11% of the total halal industry. Analysts predict that the lucrative halal food sector will be followed by the developing halal cosmetics and personal care market (Rahim & Abd Rahim, 2020).

The demographics of the young, religious and dynamic Muslims are the main driving force behind this massive demand for halal cosmetics and beauty products. Significant areas of manufacture such as halal ingredients and the use of acceptable substances are included in Halal cosmetics, all of which must be prepared, stored, packaged and distributed under Shari criteria. Modern consumers, ecologically aware and prepared to pay an insurance premium for organic, natural and earthy cosmetics, are gaining popularity.

In the Asia and the Middle East, the market for halal cosmetics is growing. Halal cosmetics generate a 12% annual rise in the total value of cosmetics sales of US$12 billion across the Middle East. The interests in halal cosmetics have risen in markets in Asia, particularly in Malaysia and Indonesia as well as in Europe. Halal cosmetics make up 10–20% of the local cosmetics market in Malaysia. However, non-Muslim companies dominate the global cosmetics industry, and to some extent it is monopolized. The problem of halal ingredients in cosmetics produced by companies has been seriously challenged.

Despite the fact that Muslims are normally permitted to use haram (forbidden) items in life-threatening situations, the demand for Muslim-compliant medications is increasing. The expanding global demand for halal pharmaceuticals corresponds to Muslims' increased interest in and concerns about the halal status of medications. Many of them are questioning the industry's claims about the origins of these goods' ingredients and whether they are compatible with an Islamic lifestyle. Not only should halal pharmaceutical products be free of haram ingredients, but they should also be tayyib, a term used to describe commodities and products that meet certain quality requirements. Tayyib, in essence, alludes to things that are clean, pure, and made according to established procedures and processes. As a result, a pharmaceutical product should not only be halal, but also clean in the eyes of Sharia law.

The halal pharmaceutical sector, on the other hand, is beset by a lack of global halal standards. Many cosmetics contain alcohol, which is regarded haram, as well as animal-sourced ingredients, which are regarded impure by Islam. Concerns about animal-derived chemicals in cosmetics, such as gelatine and collagen, are driving demand from both Muslim and non-Muslim consumers (Park & Lee, 2021). Consumers seeking honesty and authenticity in their cosmetics and personal care goods will appreciate the halal mark on cosmetics and beauty items. Despite the fact that the concept of halal cosmetics is relatively new to the Muslim world, there is a growing market, particularly among conscientious consumers that become more specific in their personal grooming purchases and consciously planning to spend cash on cosmetics and beauty products that meet their cultural and religious requisites.

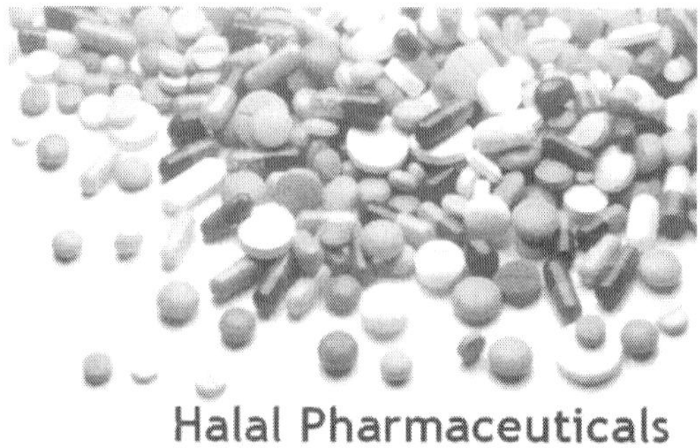

Figure 10.9. With Muslims accounting for over a quarter of the global population, the pharmaceuticals business has seen a rise in halal awareness. Many of us, even Muslims, rely on modern medicine to treat our illnesses. We rely significantly on the pharmaceutical sector, whether it's popping a fast painkiller to treat a headache or going to the doctor when our knee hurts. Without our knowledge, the medications we take may contain non-halal substances (or excipients) or be prepared in a way that is not consistent with Islamic beliefs.

Source: https://www.biospectrumasia.com/news/52/15307/halal-pharmaceuticals-market-2020-forecasts-muslim-consumer-market.html.

Some of the key challenges include:

1. Future rapid advances in synthetic biology are creating concern, such as future microorganisms and plants that have been genetically altered to the point of including major sections, and possibly full, edited/synthetic genomes (in other words man- made designer microorganisms and plants). This will have ramifications not only for antibiotics, but also for future food produced by such "synthetic" organisms. Despite the fact that this is something that will happen in the future, officials are already looking at ways to manage such occurrences.
2. Numerous Muslim inspectors are untrained in Good Manufacturing Practices (GMP) rules, which are critical for quality control. The implementation of Good Manufacturing Practices (GMP) rules for cosmetics and personal care products that correspond to a country's legislation has been established to improve product quality and traceability in order to safeguard human life and ensure that products are clean and healthy (tayyib). It's not just about detecting haram substances; it's also about avoiding

unethical masbooh ingredients (which should be avoided) due to the harmful effects of them being absorbed via the skin or taken internally with medicines. Many Muslim inspectors may be untrained in GMP rules, causing them to overlook potential contamination points. It is critical to ensure that Halal auditors and technical specialists receive this training in order for Halal certified personal care and pharmaceuticals to thrive (Omar & Jaafar, 2011).

3. One component of Halal standard requirements that varies between nations is the use of alcohol in different forms, both for the upkeep of equipment and in the products themselves. It remains to be seen whether the viewpoints can be standardized on this.
4. Because they are not tayyib, the use of substances in cosmetics that are hazardous to humans may be considered Haram in Halal certification. Some substances used in skin whitening lotions, such as hydroquinone and mercury, for example, fall under this group. Many countries have outlawed these substances, although they are still used in others. Because they are hazardous inside the body, they are likewise detrimental on the outside. They kill melanin cells, which can cause cancer among other problems.
5. Obtaining financing for research & innovation is a challenge. Horizon 2020 is the EU's largest ever research and innovation program, with over €80 billion in financing spread out over seven years (2014 to 2020). The primary issue with Horizon 2020 (and other federal and European financing programs) is that they are quite thematic—that is, the call subjects are not 'open.' The authorities select on and prioritize the themes a number of years ahead of time. When the subject of the calls are announced, the type of Halal study we intend to conduct is not required, thus we are unable to apply our Halal concepts directly to a topic "on the table." We need to have an impact on future calls by employing some strategies for getting the themes that are essential to Muslim and other religion communities on the table.

There are numerous chances in Muslim nations to inform both producers and consumers about the transdermal (skin penetrating) nature of certain cosmetics. In Western countries, safety regulations demand that any new forms of cosmetic components, such as nanoparticles, be thoroughly evaluated to ensure that they are safe in people. These safety concerns are pushed aside in Muslim countries in favor of Halal concerns. We prefer to think of porcine-derived compounds as Haram or Najis (ritually unclean) because they may be wiped off the skin. Human safety, on the other hand, should be factored into Halal cosmetics requirements.

Figure 10.10. Trade is crucial. Take a look at how much attention is devoted to global currency devaluation. The Ringgit is devaluing, the Chinese yuan is declining, and the Kazakh Tenge has become free-floating. The value of the currency in the nations where goods are produced and consumed has a considerable impact on the quest for a competitive edge in trade. Another unit of currency for halal business is the halal certification, which impacts the value of a halal product differently depending on where it was made (and certified) and where it would be eaten. The producer's certification value impacts the size of the market for their product.

Source: https://www.halaltimes.com/halal-certification-a-fast-growing-hard-currency-for-trade-in-halal-products/.

The European Medicines Agency (EMA) is now debating new technologies, such as nanoparticles used in creams, face powders, and other cosmetics, from a safety standpoint, yet Muslim nations are lagging significantly behind the West. Non-Muslim countries and non-Muslims are currently conducting and funding research on new technologies, materials, and their safety in humans. This is a fantastic chance for Muslim scientists and investors to take the lead in research in these disciplines and obtain knowledge in order to promote and evaluate the Halal status of this technology.

Possibility of selling Halal cosmetics to non-Muslims is high. The majority of Halal cosmetics emphasize natural ingredients, environmental friendliness, and fair trading. Some are also vegan, which means they could be sold to non-Muslims. PHB Ethical Beauty, based in the United Kingdom, and Ecotrail, the Indian company behind the Iba brand, both aim to appeal to a broader audience with products that are not only Halal certified, but also cruelty-free, free of harsh chemicals, and organic and free of animal-derived products in the case of Iba. Possibility of resolving the issue of Halal gelatin shortages by devising a realistic solution to use the relevant portions of sacrificed animals during Hajj (Nurrachmi, 2018). Vegetable-derived replacements may also be provided as halal options. The pharmaceutical sector, for example, has gotten obsessed on utilizing gelatin for capsule production since it is low-cost, inexpensive, and has been used for a long time. More natural alternatives, such as alginates and pectins, that can be reformulated to provide the same physical qualities, need to be educated into the market.

10.9. CONCLUSION

This essay summarized the consumer difficulties with reference to the Halal idea, based on literature and study by prior scholars. The issues surrounding Halal consumption are becoming more complicated as consumer expectations rise in tandem with increased awareness of food safety and quality concerns. Kleinnijenhuis and Van Hoof (2008) proposed that the government should use public information to gain a better understanding of the population. As a result, in order to minimize misinterpretation of issues relating to the Halal market, governments and the general public must collaborate with consumer interest groups such as the Malaysian Muslim Consumers Association (PPIM).

Figure 10.11. The halal concept is absolutely critical to consumption in Malaysia, which has a Muslim majority. Today's Muslim customers have access to a wide range of products and services. Furthermore, each product category offers a variety of brands, both locally known and internationally recognized.

Some local firms attempt to carve out niches for themselves by representing themselves as "Islamic" companies through imaginative packaging and labeling. This also serves as an indirect indication to their primary target market – Muslim consumers – that their products are halal. Similar efforts are being made in the banking and insurance sectors on the service side.

Source*:* https://seattleglobalist.com/2016/07/14/halal-eat-halal-even-not-muslim/53928.

Communication is critical in reaching out to customers in this situation. The consumer special interest group, which represents the end user, might act as a whistleblower, revealing the true market situation. The government should also be involved and actively engaged with the public because consumers are the best source of information when it comes to detecting transgression and deception in the Halal market. Collaboration between the government and consumer interest groups will help to disseminate information and strengthen the public-government relationship.

The Halal emblem allows manufacturers to identify that their product complies with Islamic standards. To achieve an effective monitoring and controlling effort to prevent irresponsible manufacturers from abusing the Halal emblem, all market participants must commit fully. It will gradually increase the consumer's trust in the Halal mark. As a result, in order to minimize consumer confusion, a well-regulated and robust coordination of world recognized certifications Halal system should be put in place.

Entrepreneurs are also urged to establish a good segregation system to distinguish Halal from non-halal products, in addition to utilizing the Halal logo to designate the status of the product. Another important tip is to label non-Halal products with an appropriate non-Halal label, as this will assist the consumer in making an informed buying decision. This effort denotes companies who are dependable and considerate of their customers' needs. Obtaining a Halal certification will give the manufacturers a considerable competitive advantage over their competitors (Nusran et al., 2018).

Notably, JAKIM, Malaysia, currently recognizes 67 recognized Halal bodies from 40 different countries (JAKIM, 2017). Each of the Halal certification authorities has also affixed their own Halal mark, which properly shows the product's Halal status. Having a variety of valid IDs helps to make Halal products available all over the world. As a result, a Halal authority in Malaysia is needed to explain the message of what the Halal label genuinely means and where it may be found. To better comprehend Halal in the context of food products, consumers are recommended to seek reliable and up-to-date information on the subject through a proper channel.

Figure 10.12. The certification procedure is a thorough one that includes an audit of the facility, a study of the stated ingredients, the size and complexity of the production location, and personnel training. Some businesses, on the other hand, try to get around these regulations in order to deceive the public and save money. In today's mass-production atmosphere, unethical behavior and profiteering are only encouraged. The blame game is one of the most significant issues that halal certification authorities face. Some companies even accuse the certifying authority of being "untrustworthy," despite the fact that the fraudulent acts are the consequence of their own mistakes.

Source: https://theconversation.com/amp/explainer-what-is-halal-and-how-does-certification-work-36300.

An open means of communication, such as social media, provides a wonderful chance for consumers to offer their opinions on food product safety and quality while also learning about the Halal issue in a more engaging way. Special interest organizations devoted to similar issues could also be a good source of knowledge. Despite the prevalence of social media in transmitting information, media social users should exercise caution when dealing with information transmitted through the media. At times, the information is dubious and may be deceptive. Consumers should double-check Halal information with a reputable source. Appropriate authorities are required to ensure that information about the halal issue is disseminated through a valid and authorized agency. The information should be presented in a straightforward and understandable manner to both Muslim and non-Muslim consumers.

Science and invention are permitted in Islam as long as they are carried out ethically and provide a beneficial effect for mankind. In terms of GMOs and Halal, GMO food is legal for Muslim consumers to consume as long as it does not include the transfer of genes from Haram origins. Furthermore, an authorized organization should be in charge of monitoring and regulating the proper production of halal and GMO-related products by the producer in order to prevent fraud and deception. It is strongly advised that manufacturers who utilize alternative or GMO ingredients in their manufacturing offer clear and consistent labeling on Halal products to minimize consumer confusion (Mohsin et al., 2016).

Despite the problems and concerns that consumers face, Halal products are still considered to be a superior option because they reflect product quality and assurance. Given the multiplicity of cultures, the Halal concerns that perplex the consumer must be dealt with caution, since this may cause public sensitivity. Prior to implementing any choice linked to the halal problem, thorough research should be conducted (Mostafa, 2020). This is critical in order to maintain the society's peace and tolerance. The Halal business has grown in lockstep with the Muslim population. In light of the Halal industry's potential in the local and worldwide economic environment, continued and robust efforts are required to assure the Halal industry's advancement.

Bibliography

1. Ab Talib, M. S., Sawari, S. S. M., Hamid, A. B. A., & Chin, T. A. (2016). Emerging Halal food market: an Institutional Theory of Halal certificate implementation. *Management Research Review*.
2. Abderahman, R., Karim, R., & Kevin, D. (2021). Halal food supply chains: A literature review of sustainable measures and future research directions. *Foods and Raw Materials*, *9*(1), 106–116.
3. Adekunle, B., & Filson, G. (2020). Understanding halal food market: Resolving asymmetric information. *Food Ethics*, *5*, 1–22.
4. Al-Ansi, A., & Han, H. (2019). Role of halal-friendly destination performances, value, satisfaction, and trust in generating destination image and loyalty. *Journal of Destination Marketing & Management*, *13*, 51–60.
5. Bashir, A. M., Bayat, A., Olutuase, S. O., & Abdul Latiff, Z. A. (2019). Factors affecting consumers' intention towards purchasing halal food in South Africa: a structural equation modelling. *Journal of Food Products Marketing*, *25*(1), 26–48.
6. Battour, M., & Ismail, M. N. (2016). Halal tourism: Concepts, practices, challenges and future. *Tourism Management Perspectives*, *19*, 150–154.
7. Bergeaud-Blackler, F. (2015). Islamizing Food: The Encounter of Market and Diasporic Dynamics. *Halal Matters: Islam, Politics and Markets in Global Perspective*, 91.

8. Cuesta-Valiño, P., Bolifa, F., & Núñez-Barriopedro, E. (2020). Sustainable, smart and Muslim-friendly tourist destinations. *Sustainability*, *12*(5), 1778.
9. Damit, D. H. D. A., Harun, A., Martin, D., Shamsudin, A. S. B., & Kassim, A. W. M. (2018). Non-muslim consumers attitude and repurchase behavior towards halal food: An application of buyer behavior model. *WSEAS Transactions on Business and Economics*, *15*, 413–422.
10. Debney, B. (2016). Halal hysteria. *Arena Magazine (Fitzroy, Vic)*, (140), 7–9.
11. Han, H., Lho, L. H., Raposo, A., Radic, A., & Ngah, A. H. (2021). Halal Food Performance and Its Influence on Patron Retention Process at Tourism Destination. *International Journal of Environmental Research and Public Health*, *18*(6), 3034.
12. Hanzaee, K. H., & Ramezani, M. R. (2011). Intention to halal products in the world markets. *Interdisciplinary Journal of Research in Business*, *1*(5), 1–7.
13. Henderson, J. C. (2016). Halal food, certification and halal tourism: Insights from Malaysia and Singapore. *Tourism Management Perspectives*, *19*, 160–164.
14. Indrasari, A., Giyanti, I., Sutopo, W., & Liquiddanu, E. (2020, April). Halal assurance system implementation and performance of food manufacturing SMEs: A causal approach. In *AIP Conference Proceedings* (Vol. 2217, No. 1, p. 030104). AIP Publishing LLC.
15. Ismail, I., Abdullah, N. A. N., Ahmad, Z., & Sidek, N. L. (2018). Halal principles and halal purchase intention among Muslim consumers. In *Proceedings of the 3rd International Halal Conference (INHAC 2016)* (pp. 131–138). Springer, Singapore.
16. Jia, X., & Chaozhi, Z. (2021). Turning impediment into attraction: A supplier perspective on Halal food in non-Islamic destinations. *Journal of Destination Marketing & Management*, *19*, 100517.
17. Junaidi, J. (2020). Halal-friendly tourism and factors influencing halal tourism. *Management Science Letters*, *10*(8), 1755–1762.
18. Kamarulzaman, Y., Veeck, A., Mumuni, A. G., Luqmani, M., & Quraeshi, Z. A. (2016). Religion, markets, and digital media: Seeking halal food in the US. *Journal of Macromarketing*, *36*(4), 400–411.

19. Karahalil, E. (2020). Principles of halal-compliant fermentations: Microbial alternatives for the halal food industry. *Trends in Food Science & Technology*, *98*, 1–9.
20. Krishnan, S., Omar, C. M. C., Zahran, I., Syazwan, N., & Alyaa, S. (2017). The awareness of Gen Z's toward halal food industry. *Management*, *7*(1), 44–47.
21. Khan, M. I., Haleem, A., & Khan, S. (2018, April). Defining halal supply chain management. In *Supply Chain Forum: An International Journal* (Vol. 19, No. 2, pp. 122–131). Taylor & Francis.
22. Lubis, H. N., Mohd-Naim, N. F., Alizul, N. N., & Ahmed, M. U. (2016). From market to food plate: Current trusted technology and innovations in halal food analysis. *Trends in Food Science & Technology*, *58*, 55–68.
23. Mathew, V. N. (2014). Acceptance on halal food among non-Muslim consumers. *Procedia-Social and Behavioral Sciences*, *121*, 262–271.
24. Mannaa, M. T. (2020). Halal food in the tourist destination and its importance for Muslim travellers. *Current Issues in Tourism*, *23*(17), 2195–2206.
25. Mostafa, M. M. (2018). Mining and mapping halal food consumers: A geo-located Twitter opinion polarity analysis. *Journal of Food Products Marketing*, *24*(7), 858–879.
26. Mostafa, M. M. (2020). Global halal food discourse on social media: a text mining approach. *The Journal of International Communication*, *26*(2), 211–237.
27. Mohsin, A., Ramli, N., & Alkhulayfi, B. A. (2016). Halal tourism: Emerging opportunities. *Tourism Management Perspectives*, *19*, 137–143.
28. Nusran, M., Razak, M., Numba, S., & Wekke, I. S. (2018, July). Halal awareness on the socialization of halal certification. In *IOP Conference Series: Earth and Environmental Science* (Vol. 175, No. 1, p. 012217). IOP Publishing.
29. Nurrachmi, R. (2018). The global development of halal food industry: a survey. *Tazkia Islamic Finance and Business Review*, *11*(1).
30. Omar, E. N., & Jaafar, H. S. (2011, September). Halal supply chain in the food industry-A conceptual model. In *2011 IEEE Symposium on Business, Engineering and Industrial Applications (ISBEIA)* (pp. 384–389). IEEE.

31. Park, H., & Lee, Y. (2021). Globalization of Halal Food. *Communicating Food in Korea*, 157.
32. Rahim, N., & Abd Rahim, S. I. (2020). 5 Bridging Halal Product Acceptance Models for Muslim and Non-Muslim Consumers. *Global Halal Perspectives: Past, Present and Future (UUM Press)*, 56.
33. Rezaee, G. R. (2019). Acceptance of Halal Food among Non-Muslim Consumers. *Biannual Halal Journal*, *2*, 5–21.
34. Rejeb, A., Rejeb, K., Zailani, S., Treiblmaier, H., & Hand, K. J. (2021). Integrating the Internet of Things in the Halal Food Supply Chain: A Systematic Literature Review and Research Agenda. *Internet of Things*, 100361.
35. Samori, Z., Salleh, N. Z. M., & Khalid, M. M. (2016). Current trends on Halal tourism: Cases on selected Asian countries. *Tourism Management Perspectives*, *19*, 131–136.
36. Shaari, H., Ahmad, N., Mohd Mokhtar, S. S., Yusoff, R. Z., Khamwon, A., & Putatchote, N. (2019). Consumer purchase intention on halal packaged food products: does halal logo and ingredients matter?. *Journal of Islamic, Social, Economics, and Development (JISED)*, *4*(23), 78–86.
37. Shafii, Z., & Khadijah, W. W. S. (2012). Halal traceability framework for halal food production. *World Applied Sciences Journal*, *17*(12), 1–5.
38. Wan Hassan, W. M., & Awang, K. W. (2009). Halal food in New Zealand restaurants: an exploratory study. *International Journal of Economics and Management*, *3*(2), 385–402.
39. Zulfakar, M. H., Jie, F., & Chan, C. (2012, June). Halal food supply chain integrity: from a literature review to a conceptual framework. In *10th ANZAM Operations, Supply Chain and Services Management Symposium* (Vol. 1, No. 61, p. 4).

INDEX

I